The *Baltimore* Affair

JOYCE S. GOLDBERG

The

«Baltimore»

Affair

UNIVERSITY OF NEBRASKA PRESS

LINCOLN · LONDON

Copyright 1986 by the University of Nebraska Press
All rights reserved
Manufactured in the United States of America

The paper in this book meets the minimum require-
ments of American National Standard for Information
Sciences–Permanence of Paper for Printed Library
Materials, ANSI Z39.48 1984.

A portion of chapter 7 has been previously published
in a different form as "The Heroic Image of a Pennsylvania Sailor," *Pennsylvania Magazine of History
and Biography* 104 (January, 1980): 74–85.
This book is based in part on "The *Baltimore* Affair:
United States Relations with Chile, 1891–1892,"
Ph.D. diss., Indiana University, 1981, copyright 1981
by Joyce S. Goldberg.

Library of Congress Cataloging-in-Publication Data
Goldberg, Joyce S., 1950–
The "Baltimore" affair.
Bibliography: p.
Includes index.
1. United States – Foreign relations – Chile.
2. Chile – Foreign relations – United States.
3. USS Baltimore (Ship)   4. United States –
Foreign relations –1865–1898.   5. Chile – Politics
and government – 1824–1920.   I. Title.
E183.8.C4G65 1986   327.73083   86-4342
ISBN 0-8032-2122-3 (alkaline paper)

For Mom and Dad

Contents

ILLUSTRATIONS

Preface

IN A RIOT outside the True Blue Saloon in Valparaiso, Chile, on the evening of October 16, 1891, a sailor from the U.S. ship *Baltimore* was killed, another was mortally wounded, others were seriously injured, and many were arrested. The result was a bitter controversy and a considerable diplomatic row that embroiled United States–Chilean relations for months thereafter. This regrettable incident may not have merited the attention that United States and Chilean officials devoted to it, but the diplomatic consequences were so extraordinary that the details of what may have been only a street brawl acquired meaning and momentum transcending the violence of the event.

Disagreements in the reconstruction of the disturbance were marked, and the contrast between what the U.S. government wanted to see in the affair and what the Chileans believed to have occurred led to an international dispute of great importance. Diplomatic bickering between nations of the Americas was not new or unusual, but the United States and Chile both were struggling to develop a dominant position in the Western Hemisphere in the latter part of the nineteenth century. Their understanding of themselves, the manner in which the rest of the world saw them, and their desire to alter or maintain the images other nations had of them all became inseparably intertwined with the details of a tumult involving sailors and civilians in a rowdy neighborhood of Chile's second largest city.

Concentration on the details of the riot—the sobriety of the sailors, the spontaneity of the brawl, the type of wounds received—can lead to the conclusion that the *Baltimore* affair was a mere tempest in a teapot. But such an emphasis overlooks the historical significance of this unfortunate imbroglio. First, the event closes an important gap in the history of United States–Chilean relations. Second, it offers a microscopic study of U.S. diplomatic reactions. Third, and most important, closer attention to how and why United States and Chilean officials acted to bring about a serious crisis in international relations highlights complex issues and raises disturbing questions that focus attention on the emergence of the United States as a world power. Although it is always easy and usually tempting to place primary responsibility for a diplomatic crisis on the stronger party, particularly in the case of U.S.–Latin American relations, where the United States has indeed acted in a condescending, patronizing manner, the events of 1891 and 1892 clearly indicate a remarkably increasing projection of U.S. national power.

Historians of late-nineteenth-century U.S. diplomacy generally divide into two groups. One set sees the decision for war in 1898 and the acquisition of noncontiguous territory as the culmination of a long and continuing trend in U.S. history. That trend extends, depending on the historian, from the very origins of the republic or at least from the end of the Civil War.[1] The continuity school of historical thought assumes that events necessarily followed logically from those that preceded them, and accordingly emphasizes whatever evidence can be mustered on behalf of that thesis. James A. Field, Jr., in an important essay entitled "American Imperialism: The Worst Chapter in Almost Any Book," has pointed out the dangers of what he calls the "backward approach to history," of "insisting on seeing the past through the prism of the present," and the pitfalls of stressing "presentism, moralism, and a proclivity to see false continuities." He warns against imposing too much rationality on events and ignoring chance, which also plays a significant role in the life of nations.[2]

A second set of U.S. diplomatic historians contends that the United States was transformed into a world power only at the end of the nineteenth century, and that it was a complex, largely unforeseen process that caused a world power to become an imperial power. The catalytic agent in that process was the Spanish-American War because only that conflict, involving territory removed from immediate U.S. strategic interests, could have produced the kind of empire that emerged. Perhaps the United States' ascent to world power could not have been avoided, these historians suggest, but the imperial power of the sort that developed after 1898 was highly unlikely to have emerged from anything that happened before the confrontation over Cuba.[3]

Was the *Baltimore* affair a way station on the road to the Spanish-American War, a preseason warmup for the emergence of an imperial United States, as some historians of the first school might imply? An affirmative answer strains the evidence. It is impossible to maintain that the tumult in Chile led inexorably to the events of 1898. The lack of such a strong connection, however, need not reduce the significance of the riot in Valparaiso.

Was the *Baltimore* affair totally unrelated to the events of 1898, as some historians of the second school might suggest? Was the event only an unfortunate and isolated attack on unsuspecting sailors in a rough port city? A study of the *Baltimore* affair—its causes, its place in U.S.-Chilean relations, and the manner in which it was handled and finally settled—contributes significantly to an understanding of the emerging themes of late-nineteenth-century U.S. foreign policy. Like the war with Spain, the imbroglio raises questions about the role and influence of national newspapers, their partisanship and methods of competing for circulation. The brawl in faraway Valparaiso also serves to underscore the importance of the new U.S. Navy as calculated by Captain Alfred Thayer Mahan and promoted by Secretary of the Navy Benjamin F. Tracy. In addition, the episode in Chile illuminates the contemporary state of Anglo-American relations: was the U.S. government twisting the lion's tail by sending as its representative to Chile Patrick Egan, a recently naturalized Irishman, who was under warrant for arrest by the British because of alleged crimes committed in the cause of Irish independence? Did desires of the United States to displace British economic domination in Latin America influence U.S. diplomatic positions in Chile?

Finally, the *Baltimore* affair raises familiar questions about the conduct of U.S. foreign policy at the turn of the century. It reveals maneuverings within the State Department, especially when President Benjamin Harrison and Secretary of State James G. Blaine, who was in ill health, disagreed on the arts of diplomacy. In the course of the controversy, President Harrison moved to determine policy almost single-handedly and took the United States to the brink of war in an era usually thought of as one of congressional ascendancy. The incident stirs anew the old historical debate: did an unfortunate event become an international crisis because of bungling and emotionalism, or was the U.S. diplomatic stance the consequence of deliberation and calculation?

The riot in Valparaiso may have been an accident, but the *Baltimore* affair offers a useful approach to the study of U.S. diplomacy in the late nineteenth century. It helps answer the important question of whether the 1890s "represent an abrupt departure from the past or the logical product of earlier developments and trends."[4] As historian Robert L. Beisner has suggested, the decisions of policymakers depend on the lenses through which they view the world, "lenses tinted by altering circumstances and shifting perspectives."[5] The *Baltimore* affair provides the opportunity to analyze the lenses through which Americans and their policymakers viewed U.S. relations with the outer world in the last decade of the nineteenth century.

I AM PLEASED to acknowledge at long last the assistance of some of those people who aided me in the research and writing of this manuscript. A Fulbright-Hays Award, for which I am grateful, made possible an unforgettable fifteen months in Chile, where I was welcomed with warmth and friendship beyond expectation. The debts I incurred there are many. The librarians of the Biblioteca Nacional (especially in the Seminario Enrique Matta Vial) and the archivists of the Archivos Nacionales and Ministerio de Relaciones Exteriores assisted in ways both imaginable and unimaginable, often helping me overcome problems of bureaucracy or space and financial deficiencies. They made my work easier, and to them and to the numerous librarians, archivists, and assistants all through the country's university libraries and military and judicial archives, I offer "un millón de gracias."

To my friends at the Fulbright Commission in Chile, especially Teresa Vial, I am enormously thankful for their time and cooperation in helping me cope with some of the problems of living in another culture. I am grateful also for their aid, comfort, and sympathy at depressing or frustrating moments. I offer thanks to those from the U.S. Embassy in Chile who helped when called upon, above all Brian Bell, Public Affairs Officer, and Peter N. Synodis, Cultural Affairs Officer, and their competent and helpful staffs. I am pleased to have this opportunity to recall their friendship and assistance. To my good friend Patricia Restini C., this "gringüita" is appreciative of help in locating the present-day site of the True Blue Saloon but more so for the love and shelter provided during frequent research trips to Valparaiso.

Valuable historical assistance in Chile came from don Ricardo Donoso, whose octogenarian energy and enthusiasm for my project were inspiring. The late don Eugenio Pereira Salas, who epitomized the academician as gentleman and scholar, was available for advice and encouragement. Don Joaquín Barceló, at that time director of the Fulbright Commission, provided special assistance by helping ease my sense of intellectual isolation. I remain indebted to don Cristián Guerrero, who was always willing to listen, reassure, and cheer whenever called upon and who remains friend and counsel despite the distance.

Enduring appreciation and affection remain for some special friends I made in Chile—Wesley and Diane McNair and their children, with whom I shared good times and bad, laughter and tears. In exchange for my knowledge of Spanish they offered me a sense of family life when I was so far from my own. I definitely got the better of the deal.

In the United States I had the able assistance of librarians and archivists at the Library of Congress, especially the Manuscripts Division; the National Archives and Records Service; and other libraries around the country—notably Indiana University, the University of Rochester, the University of North Carolina, the University of Michigan, and the Huntington Library.

Others corresponded with me both before and after I traveled to Chile, and I thank them for sharing ideas and offering advice. Professors Charles S. Campbell, Frederick M. Nunn, and Allan B. Spetter were among the most helpful. Professor Peter J. Sehlinger also provided invaluable service by allowing me to read a manuscript he was preparing, since published as *A Select Guide to Chilean Libraries and Archives*. I am indebted to him for furnishing special information about Chile, as well as for bringing European documents to my attention.

Many people took the time to read this manuscript, sometimes more than once, and offer perceptive, incisive comments that substantially improved it. They were Robert L. Beisner, Edward Buehrig, Bernard V. Burke, Robert H. Ferrell, Walter LaFeber, Walter Nugent, Frederick M. Nunn, Elaine and Irwin Suloway, David P. Werlich, and John E. Wilz. I am grateful for their efforts. Olga Esskandanian cheerfully typed the manuscript. I reserve most special "cariño" for the assistance and continuing support of Deborah L. Goldberg and Stephen E. Maizlish.

Finally, I would like to express special appreciation to Professor Robert H. Ferrell, who in 1968 showed interest in a young, somewhat naive, intellectually unsophisticated college freshman who disliked American history but who liked to read. In just twelve years he molded a historian—one who endeavors now to demonstrate her heartfelt gratitude by trying to emulate his patience, wisdom, kindness, and dedication to good writing with other young, somewhat naive, intellectually unsophisticated college students who are just beginning.

1. The Riot in Valparaiso

THE HISTORY of Valparaiso, where the trouble began, has been the history of the sea. A venerable old port built around and on top of steep hills reached by rickety lifts, Valparaiso has a grace and character unlike that of other ports. Its landscape resembles an untamed San Francisco. At one time it was a thriving commercial center, a hub of naval activity, important not only for Chilean history but for that of much of the rest of South America as well. In the nineteenth century, with Chilean independence and the decay of the Peruvian port of Callao, Valparaiso became the maritime capital of the Pacific and a focus for the naval defense of the continent. Then, after decades of prosperity, its importance declined, and the fortunes of other coastal cities arose.

The trouble in 1891 occurred in part because Valparaiso was one of the Western Hemisphere's principal ports, bound to attract the commerce of industrial powers like the United States. North Americans interested in trade were frequent visitors, able to savor the charm of a port heralded by artists, poets, writers, and tourists. Visitors found the city bustling, friendly, industrious, and prosperous. Valparaiso's climate, geography, and pecuniary possibilities attracted foreign ships, and so in the Chilean spring of October, 1891, the presence of a ship of the U.S. Pacific Squadron seemed innocuous.

The ship involved in the trouble, the USS *Baltimore,* was a considerable vessel for its time. Built at Philadelphia by William Cramp and Sons, one of the largest ship building works in the nation, at a cost of $1,325,000, the dynamite cruiser *Baltimore* rated 10,064 horsepower, displaced 4,600 tons, and could maintain a speed of almost twenty knots. It was heavily armed with four eight-inch, three-mark breech-loading guns and six six-inch, three-mark breech-loaders. Secretary of the Navy Benjamin F. Tracy was justifiably proud of the ship. "The *Baltimore* is undoubtedly the fastest ship of her displacement in the world," he declared. "She can whip any that can catch her and run away from any that can whip her."[1]

Appropriately, the captain of the new *Baltimore* was a native of Maryland, Winfield Scott Schley. His Naval Academy classmates had included Alfred Thayer Mahan, George Dewey, and William T. Sampson, all luminaries in the rise of U.S. naval power in the 1890s and at the turn of the century. A lean man of medium height, known as a raconteur, Schley was amiable, generous, unreserved, and enthusiastic. He was not inclined to be pensive; he was impulsive and eager for action. He was also an astute politician, careful to keep an eye out for newspaper reporters and solicitous of his superiors.[2]

The *Baltimore* was one of several U.S. ships sent to Chilean waters during the revolution that began in Chile in early January, 1891. It was a confused affair in which the U.S. minister, Patrick Egan, asked for naval forces to protect his country's interests. Responding to State Department concerns, Schley and the *Baltimore* departed from Villefranche, France, stopped in Montevideo, and arrived in Valparaiso on the morning of April 7, 1891. Captain Schley soon reported to Washington that his ship's presence gave great satisfaction and contributed to the security of U.S. citizens living in Chile during that nation's civil war.[3] It may be that what he said was true. Rear Admiral W. P. McCann of the USS *Pensacola,* commander of naval forces in the South Pacific, cabled Secretary Tracy that the "arrival of the *Baltimore* on this station has attracted a great deal of attention, and has also had a very good effect in increasing the respect of these people for our navy and showing them that the United States had the power to protect the interests of her citizens should it become necessary to do so."[4]

The *Baltimore* remained in Chilean waters after the civil war ended in late August, even though the collapse of government forces after the battle of Placilla on August 28 lessened the need for protection. On September 9, Rear Admiral George Brown of the USS *San Francisco* telegraphed Tracy that because absolute quiet prevailed in Chile there was little reason for the *Baltimore* to remain there. He repeated his opinion on September 20, emphasizing that the provisional government had restored peace. He saw no benefit in the *Baltimore*'s presence, for "perfect order" existed at both Santiago and Valparaiso, and naval forces could hardly improve the situation. Captain Schley concurred in a note to Tracy on September 23, adding that his ship needed repairs that could not be made locally. Other foreign ships were withdrawing and he could not justify a longer stay. He was not ordered to move, however, and his ship remained at Valparaiso.[5]

FRIDAY, OCTOBER 16, 1891, was a pleasant day in Valparaiso, with clear skies and gentle breezes from the south and west, and sometime between one and two in the afternoon 117 crewmen from the *Baltimore* were granted twenty-four hours of shore leave. Because of the civil war the crew had enjoyed liberty only once since their April arrival in Valparaiso, and the last time they had received liberty at all in Chile had been late July or early August when the ship had been north of Santiago, in Coquimbo. Unlike the *Baltimore*'s crew, the crews of foreign men-of-war—German, British, French, even the crew of the USS *San Francisco*—had received liberty in Valparaiso throughout the turmoil. On September 14 when the *Baltimore* returned from a short mission to Peru, the captain of the Valparaiso Port Authority and the senior Chilean naval officer in the port visited the *Baltimore* to extend the usual welcome, courtesies, and hospitalities. Schley later noted that he had questioned the police commissioner, Intendente Juan de Díos Arlegüi, about shore leave, and Arlegüi responded that he could see no reason for withholding a privilege enjoyed by other crews.[6] Still, on September 25 Schley cabled that he sensed "strong feeling and great hostility" against North Americans, that public opinion was unfriendly—even bitter—and that although all was quiet, he could not predict what might suddenly occur. To avoid conflict he granted no liberty. It was not until October that he thought he saw a change in attitude and reported, "Everything is quiet at Valparaiso, and the chances of everything being more settled improve daily."[7] He then deemed it safe for his men to go ashore.

After inspection by the officer of the deck to ensure that the

The USS *Baltimore*. From *Harper's Weekly,* January, 1892. Courtesy Indiana University Library.

sailors were not armed, the first three cutter loads of uniformed men landed and broke into small groups that went their separate ways.[8] The men sought to exchange currency, see barbers or doctors, find places to spend the night, find out about theatrical productions, buy tobacco, purchase clothing or books, play billiards and checkers, and roam the city. About 2:30 P.M. Captain Schley and Lieutenant Commander Uriel Sebree went ashore for an afternoon walk and estimated they saw between forty and seventy of the crew before returning aboard ship around half past five. "I was very much impressed," the captain later said, "by their orderliness, their cleanliness and their politeness to everyone whom they saw on the streets. It was a matter of such gratification, that the first lieutenant and myself, commented very frequently on the spectacle."[9] The men were in good condition, conducting themselves properly, sober and well behaved, saluting all officers of British, French, German, and Chilean vessels, Sebree noted.[10]

Around 3:30 P.M. Schley saw two of the crew of the *Baltimore*, Boatswain's Mate Charles W. Riggin and Seaman Apprentice John W. Talbot, driving west in a carriage in the direction of the main plaza. There they met two friends and continued driving to the western part of town, then left their friends to go into the Shakespeare Saloon. They did not stay long, for the proprietor informed them he was going to close. Apparently he told the two men that a crowd of recently discharged Chilean sailors and soldiers was going to attack them that afternoon. "He said there was going to be trouble," but Talbot and Riggin chose to pay no attention. "We laughed at it. We laughed at him," Talbot said later.[11] But because the owner anticipated trouble and indicated he would not tolerate any in his tavern, they left, turned a corner, went up the street to a dance hall called the Home of the Free, decided not to enter, and proceeded into the next bar, called the True Blue Saloon.

The decision to enter the True Blue Saloon would be a tragic one. The place itself was nothing extraordinary, and nearly a century after the *Baltimore* affair it appears that not much about the building's appearance has changed, although today it is a private residence and no longer a saloon. Situated close to a quiet intersection on a twisting, narrow cobblestone street, the True Blue Saloon is a two-story structure with a balcony and long, narrow barred windows. It is, coincidentally, painted blue.

On the afternoon of October 16, 1891, Talbot and Riggin found four friends in the True Blue and stayed about half an hour before deciding to return to the eastern part of town. Riggin left first, but Talbot stopped to speak with a woman who worked at the bar, and when he reached the door he saw Riggin talking to a Chilean sailor in the middle of the street. The Chilean seemed to be provoking a fight. Talbot ran across the street and asked Riggin what the trouble was, and Riggin replied "something about the Chilean trying to pick a row with him, or something like that." Talbot shoved the antagonists apart, telling the Chilean to "Go off" or "Here, you shove off."[12] The Chilean spat in Talbot's face, and Talbot knocked him down. The street immediately filled as sailors, longshoremen, boatmen, recently discharged soldiers, and townspeople streamed out of every door, heading for the two U.S. sailors.

Thereafter the action was quick and deadly. Talbot and Riggin ran down Calle Arsenal to the west, where they jumped on a passing streetcar, but the car stopped immediately, surrounded by a mob hurling cobblestones and bricks. The mob broke in the sides of the car, smashing windows and doors. The men tried to escape through the crowd, Riggin jumping out one side of the car and Talbot the other. As soon as they did they were surrounded. Talbot looked

Present-day view of the site of the True Blue Saloon (two-story building with balcony), Valparaiso, Chile. Photo by author.

around, saw Riggin fall, and tried to move toward him but felt a knife in his back. Realizing he would not get closer, he turned and managed to bolt through the crowd.

Chased by about a hundred people, he later estimated, Talbot ran for two blocks, turned a corner, and went east on the street closest to the pier. He turned once more and headed for a saloon, but again he was stabbed. He turned on the assailant, shoved him, and ran into the saloon; the owner and bartender seized him and threw him into the street. He broke into the saloon again, and for a second time the owner and bartender threw him out. The third time, he forced his way in, ran past the occupants into a small room in the back, and tried to bolt the door. Five or six people broke down the door and dragged him into the street, where they hurled cobblestones at him. He picked up one, made a fourth dash into the saloon, hit the owner on the head with the stone, hit the bartender with a chair, and went into a corner of the bar and sat down. When four or five members of the crowd entered with cobblestones in hand, Talbot charged them and they ran. When they returned, Talbot repeated the charge, and as they ran out the second time he shut and barred the door, went over to a corner, and sat down at a table, where he stayed for an hour while the mob tried to break the door by hammering from the street.

Then a young man came in the back way. He tried to approach Talbot and talk to him, but the sailor would not let him get close. Two women who were inside with Talbot began to attend to the sa-loonkeeper, who was lying unconscious under the bar. They tried to minister to Talbot also, for he was dizzy and weak from his bleeding wounds, but he would not let them near. One of the women went out and returned with a police officer, who came in and motioned for Talbot to give himself up. The officer drew a sword but put it back as the sailor made no effort to resist. "He took me out in the street, took my hat off and gave it to me . . . gave me an old white hat that belonged to the saloonkeeper. . . . The policeman was afraid that the crowd would attack us again . . . and take me away from him. . . . Without my cap they would not notice the uniform so quick."[13] They walked to the intendencia (police station) as a crowd gathered, people occasionally throwing cobblestones and bricks. Talbot was turned over to two mounted police armed with sabers, who put handcuffs—catgut nippers—on his wrists and started him off toward jail, abusing him as they went. When they arrived they took his name, searched him, and put him in a cell.

That was the experience of Talbot on the evening of the riot. His confusion that evening was pitiful as he ran this way and that, trying to get away from enemies with knives and stones, not knowing where to turn, finding a place of temporary safety, eventually landing in jail. When Talbot arrived there he found the cell already occupied by crew members from the *Baltimore,* who caused a great deal of commotion when they saw Talbot's condition. They yelled for the guards to take him to the hospital. In an office nearby another shipmate lay unconscious from a beating and wound in the side. He and Talbot and four or five other injured men ultimately were sent to the hospital, where their wounds were dressed and they encountered more of the *Baltimore*'s crew.

The best U.S. testimony of what happened to Talbot's companion, Seaman Riggin, came later from James A. Johnson, an armorer who had gone ashore with the others. He had exchanged money and, with a companion, gone to a dentist, a bookstore, and a barber, finally heading toward a boarding house and restaurant. While Johnson was waiting to eat, the boarding house proprietor began to shut the doors and close up the house, saying there was a fight, that a U.S. sailor was getting killed, and Johnson had better not go out. He was shown upstairs to a room in the back of the house overlooking Calle Arsenal and from this vantage point saw a streetcar stopped at the corner of Calle Marquez. "I seen one of our men laying face downwards in the middle of the street," Johnson recalled, "and two or three policemen standing around him, and a mob of citizens, and they were stabbing him while he was laying down."[14] Johnson made an attempt to jump from the window but finally persuaded the owner to open the boardinghouse doors. He had no side arm, so he seized an empty bottle and pushed his way through the crowd to reach the wounded sailor, whom he recognized as Riggin. "To all appearances he seemed to be dead."[15]

Johnson called out Riggin's name several times, opened the buttons on Riggin's cuffs, unbuttoned his undershirt at the neck to feel his pulse. It was beating feebly, so Johnson lifted Riggin's head off the ground and placed it on top of his own feet to cushion it, as well as to be free to defend himself. He asked someone to bring a glass of liquor but was unable to make Riggin swallow it. "After several minutes," Johnson reported, "he opened his eyes and said 'For Christ sake, Johnson, take me out of here before they kill me, or before I die.'"[16]

Johnson picked him up and, partly carrying him, partly dragging him on his left side, began to take him away from the mob. A policeman standing nearby and armed with a bayonet made no objection. But when Johnson was close to a drugstore he saw a squad of police about ten yards away and noted a crowd following. At a distance of a yard, or what Johnson later described as close enough to look down the barrel of a rifle, two leaders of the police squad fired. At the first shot Johnson felt a burning sensation on his left cheek. The second shot struck Riggin:

His head was resting on my left shoulder, and at the time the bullet struck him his head dropped over my arm as if his neck was broken. One bullet went through my neckerchief, and overshirt and undershirt. When my retreat was cut off, with the soldiers to the front and the mob to the back, I thought there was no use carrying a corpse around, and I would make my escape in the best way I could. A citizen in the crowd hollered out "drop him Johnson, or else they will drop you next."[17]

Johnson claimed he then escaped by rolling up the collar of his shirt and running through the crowd back to the boarding house, where he found some workman's clothes and was led to a safe place to spend the night. The following day he made it back to the *Baltimore.*

Other testimony about Riggin's fate, not as detailed, came from other members of the crew. Seaman Charles Langen, dressed in civilian clothes, had been speaking to Johnson in the boarding house when the two men learned of the fracas near the True Blue Saloon. Langen went outside in time to see Riggin and Talbot jump off the streetcar. He followed them as the crowd, carrying knives, sticks, and stones, pursued. Langen saw Riggin kicked and stoned, ran to his aid, eventually helped him go a few yards before Riggin was kicked again and stabbed. Langen was able to help Riggin get up, and both men ran on until "police came towards him with their swords in their hand, and they knocked him down."[18] The crowd surrounded Riggin, stabbing, hitting, kicking, while, so Langen testified, the police passively observed. Langen left and ran until he saw three other sailors from the *Baltimore* being attacked. One was struck in the back of the neck, knocking his head against a house, and fell senseless face down in a gutter, bleeding profusely. Langen said he returned to Riggin just in time to see the soldiers fire at Johnson.

The Chilean version of what came to be known as the *Baltimore* affair did not confirm the U.S. testimony.[19] Police commander José Honorio Zamudio later testified that street violence began in the early evening of October 16, in the form of a brawl in an unknown tavern in one of the worst sections of town, a row between an intoxicated Chilean sailor and three U.S. sailors who were "the worse for liquor." When the Chilean said something offensive to the two sailors, Riggin knocked him senseless and fled with his friends. Juana Urrutía and Margarita Novoa, who lived nearby, saw a U.S. sailor beating a Chilean, whom the U.S. sailors "left lying senseless on the ground." When the two women began screaming, "They have killed him!" the sailors ran toward Calle Arsenal and a crowd started in pursuit.[20]

The Chilean explanation was quite detailed. Police lieutenants Leandro Gómez and Vives Bravo, sent to suppress the riot, said that the disorder began as a knife fight between a left-handed Chilean sailor and a man from the *Baltimore*. A crowd formed as groups of sailors of both nationalities aided the combatants. Because most of the men came out of bars in the area and the fracas took place in the most dangerous section of town, all the participants were inebriated and under such conditions only the worst sort of melee could be expected. Disturbances spontaneously broke out in several areas of the port.

Francisco Albórnoz, the conductor of the streetcar onto which Riggin and Talbot jumped, afterward testified that three sailors belonging to the *Baltimore* boarded the car as it reached Calle Arsenal. As the car began to move away, the crowd surrounded it and pelted it with rocks. Albórnoz learned that the sailors were accused of wounding a Chilean sailor and the mob was seeking revenge. Seeing the risk to the car and himself, he ordered the sailors out. As he did, he received a blow on the head from a stone thrown by the mob.

Compelled to leave the car, Talbot escaped in the direction of Plaza Wheelwright, but Riggin, recognized as the man who had beaten the Chilean sailor, was knocked to the ground by a stone and stabbed in the hip by Federico Rodríguez—the latter claiming that Riggin had provoked him. Police Sergeant Miguel Vergara, who arrived about 6:15 P.M. with a few men under his command, saw Riggin on the ground and ordered policemen Encarnación Jeria and José del T. Castro to transport the sailor to the closest pharmacy. The police had advanced about forty paces when Sergeant Vergara, holding Riggin from behind, heard a pistol fired from the crowd at close range. The bullet struck Riggin in the throat, and although the two policemen attended to him immediately, he died. Vergara noted the impossibility of the shot coming from the squad of police because they were some meters away. Judging from the sound, he concluded that the shot had been fired at close range.

Vergara and his two men said that they arrived and saw Riggin lying wounded on the ground. Vergara ordered Jeria and Castro to assist the man:

They took him by the arms, and, thus supporting him, he walked with them to the German drug store in Echaurren Square, which was the nearest apothecary's shop to the scene of the occurrence. I held the wounded American by the waistband, supporting him at times by the back to push him ahead. On arriving at the corner of Valdivia street there was a large crowd of people, and it was here that the shot was fired at such close quarters that sparks struck the face of Policeman Castro and burnt Jeria's left hand, which he had laid on Riggin's shoulder. I looked in every direction, but I could not see who had wounded him, as it was already growing dark. The wounded man fell to the ground, and I gave orders to raise him up: but the policemen replied that they could not do so, as he was already dead.[21]

They did not see who had fired the shot, but Vergara was sure it could not have come from the armed picket of police because they had not passed a sharp bend in the street.

The two Chilean policemen admitted they saw a sailor approach and try to revive Riggin with brandy, and that Riggin did recover considerably. An English-speaking gentleman arrived and begged Seaman Johnson to leave the scene, saying his presence was enraging the drunken crowd. Johnson left, the policemen said, and they were ordered to help Riggin to his feet and assist him to the drugstore. When they had proceeded almost sixty meters and were near the drugstore, a shot killed Riggin. From the sound the policemen concluded it must have come from a revolver.

Captain Zamudio had little to add. "I was at a few meters' distance from the aforesaid Riggin, as I was just arriving on the scene of the occurrence in command of a picket of twenty or twenty-five policemen armed with comblain rifles, when I heard the shot which wounded the said man."[22] He attested that the shot could not have come from men in his charge, since they had not yet arrived at the place from which the shot proceeded. The report was not loud, which induced him to believe it was fired from a revolver. The captain said he approached the mob and demanded to know who had fired, but the crowd dispersed without responding. Zamudio further testified that he was "sure that if the person who had fired the shot had been a policeman he would have been denounced at once by the crowd, owing to the well-known antagonism which exists of old between the police and the lower orders."[23]

Another Chilean witness, Andrew Löfquits, said he went out into the street to see what the commotion was about. At that moment the armed police were running toward the scene. Löfquits followed the police, heard a shot, and someone shouted "Oh! Oh!" in pain. He saw the victim, a U.S. sailor, on the ground with blood pouring from his neck. Löfquits withdrew, met Johnson nearby, and advised him not to expose himself to the mob. Löfquits was sure Johnson was nowhere near Riggin when the shot was fired.

Doctors Daniel Carvallo and Antenor Calderón examined Riggin's body on October 17 and 18 and reported that "the wound which caused the death of Riggin was made by a revolver and not a rifle bullet." Military experts Vicente Zegers and José María Bari examined the holes in Johnson's neckerchief and stated that the "holes in the sailor's uniform may have been caused by a large-sized revolver."[24]

Some policemen who were part of the picket sent to suppress the disorder also reported what happened. They all said they were ordered to the scene on foot, armed with rifles, because the melee was reaching uncontrollable proportions. There they saw "some hundreds of civilians in a confused mass." They advanced almost twenty meters when they heard a firearm, and from the slight report they inferred it to be a revolver. They were ordered to hurry, and when they arrived they saw Riggin on the ground and the unarmed Sergeant Vergara and two policemen rendering assistance.[25]

The owner of a drugstore in Plaza Echaurren, Guillermo Riegel, and his assistant Gregorio Sotello, testified that Riggin was taken to their shop by three policemen, who told them they had been carrying him when someone in the crowd fired a revolver and hit him in the throat. When they examined Riggin's wound, they too were convinced the bullet had come from a revolver because of the small hole it made.

Mounted policemen Leandro Gómez, part of the picket sent to quell the riot, told how he and Captain Zamudio arrived just ahead of the rest and saw Vergara, Jeria, and Castro conducting Riggin to the drugstore. Then they heard the shot that felled Riggin. Gómez was sure it had not come from the police; they were armed only with rifles. Moreover, he and all the other Chilean witnesses asserted there was no more than one shot.

TROUBLE WAS EVERYWHERE that fateful afternoon. The violence of the scene was clearly evident in the brutal death of Riggin, not to mention the pursuit of Talbot and other members of the *Baltimore*'s crew. Furthermore, the U.S. account of the event, beyond the death of Riggin, suggested a larger, more significant dimension of the *Baltimore* affair: a planned assault upon the uniform of U.S. sailors. That kind of account was bound to arouse officials of the U.S. government, notably President Benjamin Harrison, as well as the U.S. public that read the facts in their newspapers. The details of the riot were garnished by extra incidents, fine points, exaggeration, poor memory, invention, and imagination, but the outline seemed to prove that what the U.S. government through its diplomatic service announced as an unprovoked attack was nothing less than that.

Consider the case of John H. Davidson, who had been at the True Blue Saloon with Riggin and Talbot. He too ran to give Riggin aid when he saw him lying in the middle of the street. His attempt was thwarted by three or four Chileans who jumped him. Davidson had to fight off the mob as he saw Talbot flee from a crowd in the distance. Observing a one-armed Chilean with a knife running after another comrade, Davidson threw a stone and knocked down the Chilean. When he asked two policemen for assistance, one of them beat him with a sword until he turned on the policeman, struck him in the face with a stone, and ran off. At last finding some shipmates, he returned to the wounded Riggin, but as he neared, the mob attacked him with sticks and stones, forcing him again to flee. He ran to the dock, where he was kicked into the water by the crowd and then struck on the head by a rock. He managed to climb ashore, made his way to the statue of Chilean naval hero Arturo Prat in front of the pier, found a stick, and fought his way through the mob and up the street. The crowd tried to push him into a cellar, but he broke free and ran until a French naval officer helped him into a French clothing store. From there he was turned over to Chilean officers, who carried him to the hospital prisoners' ward.

Carpenter's Mate John Hamilton had gone ashore with a group of companions, exchanged money, drunk a lemonade—he said— bought cigars, and played a dozen games of "Spanish Poles." When Davidson came along and explained what has happening to Riggin, Hamilton started down the street and ran into a crowd of about twenty Chileans, who began to heave rocks. Hamilton hit one of the attackers with a piece of lead pipe but then was struck in the back of the neck. He staggered, crashed against a wall, and fell unconscious on the sidewalk. The mob piled onto him and he awoke next morning in the prison ward of the hospital.

Admittedly there had been signs of impending trouble. Riggin and Talbot had ignored the warnings in the Shakespeare Saloon. Johnson said all the men had been warned a week before by a Valparaiso resident who came aboard the ship: "He said we had

The crew of the USS *Baltimore*. From *Harper's Weekly*, January 1892. Courtesy Indiana University Library.

better stay aboard, or else, if we get ashore, there will be trouble; they are going to lay for you when you come ashore."[26] As the liberty cutters were passing Chile's formidable new steel cruisers, the *Esmeralda* and *Huascar,* anchored in the harbor, Chilean sailors shook fists from the portholes and drew hands across their throats. Johnson again was warned at the boarding house.

Immediately on landing, Seaman John B. Larson and three shipmates met a man who told them to look out and advised them to be inside before dark because "they are laying for you."[27] The owner of the Royal Oak Saloon suggested it was not safe for U.S. sailors to be ashore, since Chileans did not much like anyone associated with the United States. The proprietor of the Horseshoe Saloon gave the same warning, and his wife showed even more concern. Davidson claimed that the bumboat man on the dock, "One-Eyed Tom," had told him on landing that the U.S. sailors ought to stay together because there would probably be trouble. Hamilton said they were warned by the man who changed their money that they had better keep indoors; a mob was going to try to kill them. Other Chileans told a few members of the *Baltimore*'s crew not to be out after dark on the streets. "They said that the mob there was going to go for us.

That was the expression there all of the time, that the mob there was going to go for us. . . . We knew very well from what we had heard on board ship, that they were going to tackle us there." A Scotsman living in Valparaiso warned, "Boys, don't be out after dark. Get a room, and be in before dark."[28] He said the local residents hated U.S. sailors, had made threats, and planned to harm the crew any way they could.

But surely the attacks were far out of proportion to any of the warnings, however explicit. Everywhere the populace seemed inflamed, ready to wreak a vengeance upon the U.S. sailors that exceeded anything they could have expected. At the same time that Talbot and Riggin were attacked outside the True Blue Saloon, crew members were molested in restaurants, hotels, and on the street. Coalheavers Lee A. Wallace and Jeremiah Anderson were attacked about three blocks from the True Blue by a gang of rock-throwing Chilean sailors and soldiers, who forced them to run into a ditch and across a bridge. The mob overtook them and, with knives drawn, demanded money. Wallace gave in but Anderson resisted, striking the ringleader, only to be beaten unconscious and stabbed in the back. The crowd dispersed when a Chilean officer came along, after which the two men were carried to the wharf. Seaman Frank Honnors and Coalheaver John Downey were arrested inside the Rainbow Saloon about 8:00 P.M., for no reason they could discover. The police charged at them with fixed bayonets. Seaman John Butler and two companions were informed by Davidson that Hamilton had been attacked. They tried to help him and then were attacked by a mob armed with knives and stones. Butler was knocked down and beaten with clubs as the police watched. When he regained consciousness, the police arrested him and beat him as he was taken to jail.

Firemen James Gillan and Alexander J. Stewart were attacked about the same time as Riggin and Talbot, closer to the pier, by a crowd estimated at five hundred, as they went to the aid of Seaman John J. Bechtele and Oiler John Carson. Stewart was not reticent about the dangers the sailors faced:

One of the mob came after me with a knife, and just as he came . . . I knocked him down with the bottle. I turned around and looked to

my left and seen James Gillan lying face down on the ground. . . .
My heart went into my mouth. I was afraid. I thought to myself,
"there is one of our men down." I beat a retreat from where I was, up
to where Gillan was. . . . I got up there, and the Chilean man-of-
warsman was coming out. He had a knife in his hand. He was
pulling it out of his pants waistband. I knew what his intention
was, and I knocked him down with the bottle.[29]

Stewart retreated when he saw a Chilean citizen raising a paving stone over him. He then charged the attacker with a bottle and the Chilean fled. Two others came after him with a knife, and Carson moved to his aid. Carson remembered he went for the Chilean with nothing but his open hand, caught one of the assailants in the side of the head and threw him down, but did not stop to pick up the knife because by that time he was being stoned. Escaping, Gillan and Stewart managed to get hats and coats to hide their uniforms. Gillan found a place to spend the night and avoided further injury. Carson could not find a room and walked the streets all night.

Coalheaver Owen Canning ran to the Hotel Victoria when the trouble began and got a coat and hat from the proprietor. Disguised as a civilian, he was unmolested and reached the area where most of the fighting was going on. Pretending to buy pills, he entered a drugstore and saw Riggin on the floor, presumably dead. Not far away he saw Coalheaver William Turnbull, lying on his side, with ten or fifteen stab wounds in the back. Seaman R. J. J. S. Hodge was harassed by a crowd yelling, "Kill the Yankees," struck on the leg with a stick, and hit in the back with a stone before he was arrested. John McBride was assaulted by two Chilean policemen, who pushed him up against a building and beat him with their swords. Trying to escape, he was followed by mounted police, who struck him on the head with a saber, knocked him down, and beat him until they reached the jail. Gunner's Mate Peter Johnson had a pistol pointed in his face, and an officer with sword in hand attacked Coalheaver Joseph Quigley and knocked him unconscious. Coalheaver George Panter was beaten unconscious by a mob that pursued him yelling, "Americano's money."

The violence seemed unending. Seaman Charles G. Williams and his comrades were stoned and clubbed by a mob of Chileans on leaving the Victoria Restaurant near the harbor. Williams was hit with a club and knocked senseless. When he awoke, two citizens led him to a mounted policeman carrying a sword, who placed catgut nippers around his wrists and set off at a gallop, Williams falling underneath the horse. His friend Seaman Herman Fredericks was taken to prison in the same way, as was Coalheaver William H. Christie, who was arrested and beaten as he tried to walk along the street toward the dock. Coalheaver John Rooney was walking alone toward his hotel when arrested. Handcuffs were put on his wrists and then he was struck with the butt of a gun. The same occurred to Seaman Warren Brown and his companion, Fireman John W. Freese, beaten with cutlasses after their hands were secured. Firemen Patrick O'Neil and Thomas Gallagher and Seaman Edward Duncan were escorted to jail under heavy restraints. Coalheaver Patrick McWilliams was arrested, struck with a cutlass when he tried to escape, and taken to jail with a lasso over his neck and handcuffs on his wrists. "They kept pulling on each arm, and dragging me along the street. . . . They were calling me 'Gringo Americano,' and one fellow bit me in the left arm."[30]

The Chilean version of what happened differs greatly from the U.S. testimony. The official Chilean account of the fate of Coalheaver Turnbull stated that after the Riggin incident the mob, intent on avenging what they presumed was Riggin's murder of a Chilean sailor, pursued other *Baltimore* sailors congregating in the area and among the victims was Turnbull. Crisólogo Aguilar saw policemen take Turnbull, with numerous knife wounds in his back, to the drugstore of Manuel A. Guzmán in Plaza Echaurren. Carlos Gómez confessed he had been in the area when he saw a group of about thirty U.S. sailors beating three Chilean sailors and that one of them, Carlos Aravena, was lying wounded on the ground. Gómez admitted stabbing one of the sailors in the arm as the sailor was hitting Aravena with a stone. He identified the sailor as Turnbull. Demetrio Leiva said that on hearing the disorder he went to his door and saw Chileans chasing a U.S. sailor. One of the pursuers was Carlos Gómez, whom he saw overtake the sailor and stab him three or more times. The sailor managed to flee but was overtaken again by Gómez, who stabbed him several more times in the back. Shortly afterward, Gómez saw the police arriving and fled. The wounded

U.S. sailor was Turnbull, who later died. Gómez maintained that he had acted solely in defense of Carlos Aravena. At the same time, Federico Yentzen and Eugenio Francks insisted that it was José Ahumada, not Gómez, who stabbed Turnbull, even though Ahumada claimed that at the time of the riot he was just leaving the house of his mother, Juana Valencia.[31]

Coalheaver Turnbull was returned to the *Baltimore* from the city hospital on October 22, in critical condition, with a fever of 103.5. He was given a hypodermic of morphine to ease his pain and put on a diet of milk punch and eggs. The following day no change in his condition was reported, except that the morphine had freed him of pain so he took some nourishment. The third day his fever began to rise.[32] During this time he made a statement to Assistant Surgeon E. R. Stitt. "I was not intoxicated," he dictated:

I was talking with a friend, an American, and we went into a bar-room, and they in the bar-room told me there was a crowd outside waiting for me and not to go out, so I waited for awhile until I thought they had gone away. Then I went out and as soon as I was outside was struck on the head with a stone. I turned around and tried to get back into the saloon, but they would not let me in. The mob was around me on all sides, and in a short time I was knocked unconscious, and I only came to in the hospital. I do not remember when I was stabbed.[33]

According to the *Baltimore*'s medical journal, "during the evening of October 24 it was impossible to reduce his temperature below 101—it at times going up as high as 108. Pulse remained at 200. Respiration 50 and shallow. Was vomiting blood stained liquid constantly and dark splotches made their appearance before his death which occurred at 12:45 A.M. this morning."[34] Surgeon Stitt reported the death in the ship's log as a result of stab wounds inflicted with bayonets and knives.

No matter how different the accounts of the origin and development of the riot—and surely the truth will never be known—at the end of this brawl in faraway Valparaiso in October, 1891, two U.S. sailors lay dead and forty-eight had been arrested, of whom seventeen were seriously wounded.

2. Old Wounds

AT THE OUTSET, few persons in Chile or the United States appeared shocked by what occurred on October 16 in Valparaiso. Perhaps outbreaks among sailors in rowdy ports were frequent or only to be expected. In both countries some people must simply have assumed a lack of sobriety and that a trivial or seedy dispute had precipitated a deadly conflict among the lower elements of the city. Moralists must have wished that such charged emotions could be released in other, more productive pursuits, but initially no one was overwrought about the incident.

Soon, however, Captain Schley and the members of the U.S. legation in Chile began to suggest that the brawl outside the True Blue Saloon was the consequence of important diplomatic problems. U.S.-Chilean relations had been less than perfect throughout the civil war in Chile that had broken out early in 1891 and lasted almost until September. And the Chilean victors, perhaps exaggerating their own national *amor propio*, accused the United States of gross and flagrant misbehavior: disregard for the rules of neutrality during the Chilean civil war. Chilean hostility soon centered on the U.S. minister, an Irish-American named Patrick Egan, a worthy politician from Nebraska who had been appointed to the Chilean capital for good domestic political behavior. Egan's position immediately became awkward, for he was the U.S. representative at hand, and Chileans could focus on him the animosity they had felt for some years toward the secretary of state of the United States, another and much more important domestic political figure, James G. Blaine.

THE REMOTE CAUSES of controversy between the United States and Chile may have had roots in the first contacts between the two nations early in the nineteenth century—after Chile gained independence in 1810. But important problems originated with the confused struggle of Chile against Peru and Bolivia in the War of the Pacific of 1879–81 and the United States' blundering intervention. More immediate origins of what soon became known as the *Baltimore* affair of 1891 were probably the result of the ineffective U.S. attempts to remain neutral during the Chilean civil war of the same year.

Despite occasional rifts, relations with Chile had been mostly cordial up to the second half of the nineteenth century, for the interests of the two countries were economically complementary. Chilean traders offered furs, fish, whales, coal, silver, and copper, while United States merchants in return sent a few manufactured goods. Trade with Chile increased steadily even before U.S. recognition in 1823. The number of U.S. ships entering Chilean ports increased from 26 between 1788 and 1796 to 226 between 1796 and 1809. That trade did not amount to much financially, but it signified the extension of U.S. commerce to the very ends of the Western Hemisphere. That was the only type of relation that initially interested either country.[1]

Relations continued without incident until the late 1840s when the U.S. desire for Texas and indeed much more territory in the South, Southwest, and West led to a pathetic conflict with the weak government in Mexico City. It may have been the war with Mexico that first made Chileans sensitive to the potential for U.S. belligerence. A traveler at the time noted, "Chile is the only country in which I have travelled in Asia, Africa or the two Americas where Americans are not loved."[2] Minister David A. Starkweather noted a certain Chilean bitterness in 1855: "The press here teems with lampoons against the United States. . . . The government can hardly restrain a show of hostility. Any politician who says a good word for the United States has his fate sealed with forthwith. There is widespread talk of expelling all Americans from Chile."[3] Although the U.S. war with Mexico did not produce anti-U.S. sentiments in areas much closer to Mexico, this pattern of emerging Chilean hostility is confirmed by another incident some years later. Any remaining cordiality was replaced by ill will when, on March

31, 1865, U.S. warships in Valparaiso failed to act against a Spanish bombardment of the port. Secretary of State William H. Seward was pointedly told: "Chili looked upon the United States as her best friend, and that friend has failed to assist her in her hour of trial."[4] Perhaps Chilean sensitivity to U.S. policy harks back to the initial economic contacts between these two distant areas of the hemisphere. From the U.S. perspective, there may have been little to gain from demonstrations of friendship for Chile, for the fact is that from 1815 on, the United States had attempted to break into Chilean commerce, only to find it controlled by the British.

Then came the War of the Pacific, which broke out in 1879 between Chile and the combined forces of Peru and Bolivia over concessions and taxes in border provinces, the guano- and nitrate-rich territory in the Atacama desert. To the astonishment of foreign observers Peru and Bolivia were roundly defeated—Bolivia cut off from the sea when the province of Antofagasta was seized, Peru losing the northern provinces of Tacna and Arica.[5]

U.S. diplomats made a considerable effort to mediate the war. There was special interest in the war by other nations as well, particularly by British and French investors who had lent enormous sums to help develop Peru's nitrate and guano industries, and diplomatic activity initially centered on what nation might mediate the conflict. Perhaps to indicate the importance of the Monroe Doctrine, perhaps to take an aggressive role as befitted a nation hemmed in by what it considered to be weak neighbors, perhaps to outmaneuver the possibility of joint European intervention, the United States preempted all other offers to mediate at the same time that Chile skillfully neutralized threats of foreign intervention and brought the War of the Pacific to a military end.

Unfortunately, U.S. involvement had served only to prolong the conflict. At first U.S. diplomatic efforts appeared promising. Delegates from the belligerent powers met aboard the U.S. warship *Lackawanna* in October, 1880. But the mediation collapsed because of Chile's uncompromising demands for extensive territorial acquisition and a cash indemnity of twenty million dollars. Encouraged by its military advantage, Chile continued the war, captured the Peruvian capital, and eventually helped establish a provisional government under the docile Francisco García Calderón. The *New York Daily Tribune* later claimed that Chile had gone into the *Lackawanna* conference "prepared to dictate and not to discuss terms of peace; and the arbitration of the United States upon any questions of difference . . . was not acceptable and would not be accepted."[6]

With the failure of the mediation of the United States and with victory by the Chileans, in 1881 James G. Blaine took over the management of U.S. foreign relations. Here was an exceptionally strong personality, even if aggressive, nervous, and sometimes narrow-minded. Of almost unequaled political acumen, the shrewd and talented Blaine was dignified, eloquent, resourceful, and charismatic. He had dominated post–Civil War politics with a magnetism and "Dantonesque audacity" that appealed to the United States in the late nineteenth century. His special touch was renowned, as Fenton R. McCreery (son of the U.S. consul in Valparaiso in 1891) wrote after an interview with Blaine:

His eyes sparkled like two diamonds. His glance seemed to look into your very soul. There was a pallor over his face. . . . There is no doubt about his personal magnetism for you feel immediately upon meeting him that he is interested in you and a friend. This wonderful ability impresses you at once. His manner invites cordiality and yet one knows that he is a reader as much as a leader of men. Determination, steadfastness of purpose, quick perception and a very wide experience are written on his face.[7]

On Blaine's death in 1893 the *Chicago Times*—a Democratic paper—would accurately write, "No American was more deeply beloved, more enthusiastically followed, more profoundly hated, more cordially condemned."[8]

Blaine was not happy with the South American situation when he took office as secretary of state in March, 1881, for he viewed the war, or at least so thought many people, as inspired by the British for the purpose of ending U.S. commercial interests in the region. "It is a perfect mistake to speak of this as a Chilean war on Peru," he asserted. "It is an English war on Peru, with Chili as the instrument."[9] Indeed it would not be inappropriate to suspect Blaine of desiring to bolster Peru against Chile—achieving greater U.S. security in South America by lessening British (and French, German, and Italian) influence, and in so doing, procuring a larger market for the United States.

Blaine quickly indicated his belief that responsibility for the war lay with dispossessed British nitrate producers in Tarapacá, who were unhappy about the Peruvian government's monopoly in the area. But there is no evidence that they instigated the war.[10] In any event, the secretary of state actually did little to counter the Chilean victory, although he openly and vigorously sought to convince Chile that a liberal peace settlement would be best.

In addition to Blaine's muddled interference, there was, in 1881, the confused activity of Stephen A. Hurlbut, the U.S. minister to Peru, who proved inept when it came to soothing the belligerents of the War of the Pacific, and Blaine has often been blamed for that minister's blundering diplomacy. Hurlbut told the Chilean commander in Peru, Admiral Patricio Lynch, that the United States would tolerate a Chilean territorial settlement only if Peru refused to pay an indemnity, and he further announced that his government opposed any dismemberment of Peru. He indiscreetly implied that the United States would not permit and would forcibly prevent territorial annexation, and he tried to scare the Chileans by persuading their longtime rival, Argentina, to send a minister to negotiate with Francisco García Calderón. In addition, he formed an agreement to give the United States a naval base in Peru, he promised that a U.S. railroad company would complete a line to the Peruvian sierra, and, finally, he moved Peruvian government documents to the U.S. legation. All that was done by Hurlbut on his own, without authorization from the State Department.[11] The result was to encourage Peru's defiance of Chilean peace terms—a vain effort to save the Peruvian nation from humiliation. His efforts reinforced Chile's conviction that the nation faced a danger of invasion from other South American nations or from the United States. Blaine eventually reprimanded Hurlbut and might have done so earlier, but President Garfield's assassination in 1881 disrupted everything in Washington.

Blaine, it seems, was capable of remarkable efforts at interference. After his successor had been named in November, 1881, but before Frederick T. Frelinghuysen took office, the retiring secretary of state sent a special mission to South America, which included his son Walker and was headed by the department's chief clerk, William H. Trescot. Blaine told the members of the commission to ascertain from Chile if García Calderón's recent arrest had been meant as an insult to the United States. If so, he said, he would sever diplomatic relations. The mission was to continue to insist on a Peruvian indemnity rather than territorial cession to Chile.

The Trescot mission came to nothing. Blaine's words were simply talk, although that was unknown to the Chileans, who overestimated the threat of a U.S. attack. Before Trescot's mission had had time to achieve its purpose, Frelinghuysen cabled Trescot and ordered him not to be offensive to the Chileans, and Trescot was, in fact, warmly received by the astute Chilean foreign minister, José Manuel Balmaceda, who had received a cable from Paris making clear Trescot's change in instructions.

There could be no simple solutions in Chile. Because of the disclosure of Washington's reversal of policy, Hurlbut's sudden death in Peru, and the disclosure of the diplomatic correspondence, Chile knew there was nothing to fear regarding U.S. interference in the negotiations with Peru. Peru was prostrate, the Chileans remained adamant in their demands, and Trescot left Chile.[12]

The ineffective diplomacy of Blaine was now etched in the minds of Chileans, who saw it as tactless and harmful. Chilean historians consistently describe Blaine's policy as contary to Chilean interests and his activities in the War of the Pacific as the principal reason that U.S.-Chilean relations suffered dramatically after the war.[13]

Chileans could not have been happy when some years later, in 1889, Blaine was again named secretary of state, this time in the administration of President Benjamin Harrison. The appointment was expected and politically unavoidable, for no other position would have satisfied those voters who recognized Blaine as responsible for Harrison's election and perhaps the most powerful Republican politician since Abraham Lincoln. Recognition of Blaine's power and influence came from all quarters. In February of 1889 newspaper magnate Joseph Pulitzer wrote to a prominent Republican politico:

I'm glad the Blaine question is settled, though of course the most interesting of it still remains—upon what terms it was settled. . . . as usual the newspapers have completely ignored the most interesting question, to wit: whether Mr. Blaine was duly gagged to a second Harrison term before entering the cabinet, or whether he succeeded in receiving an invitation free from any commitment. Harrison's reluctance was strange; and it looked almost as if he wanted to . . . [disregard] the real interests of the party. . . . Blaine's Administration will be an interesting problem. After all, I know no-one in American History who has had such extraordinary hold upon the people and has been so near the very threshold of presidency with so little responsibility for actual Government. We all know of course that Blaine has been the real choice of your party for the Presidency since 1876. . . . Will power make him conservative . . . or will he really be able to carry out some brilliant audacious idea? I confess I am a little curious, as, though from the opposition benches, I cannot help admiring your friend as the most picturesque political figure in the country to-day.[14]

Unhappily, by the time of his second term as secretary of state, Blaine was a broken or at least a different man, disappointed in his ambition for higher office, ill, and depressed by family difficulties. He also proved unable to dominate Harrison as he had dominated Garfield when he first was secretary of state. Known as the Plumed Knight by friends and Jingo Jim by enemies, perhaps he sensed that his energies and ambitions were failing. Certainly his relation with the new president proved less than ideal. Blaine's second term in the State Department would rightly be described as "more protective than provocative, more defensive than defiant, more conciliatory than coercive."[15]

Blaine was undoubtedly an Anglophobe, and many of his attitudes and hemispheric policies show an open antagonism to British influence.[16] If he had recognized British politics behind the Chilean military adventure of 1879, he was certain to find further evidence a few years later when remarkable British economic expansion actually occurred not only in Chile but in Argentina, Brazil, Uruguay, Venezuela, and Mexico.

James G. Blaine, Secretary of State. From *Life and Work of James G. Blaine* (Manufacturer's Book Co., Philadelphia, 1893).

By 1889 the War of the Pacific was over and Chile had replaced Peru as the most vigorous and powerful commercial nation in South America, with the highest per capita income in all Latin America. Under British influence the Chileans were prospering; their foreign commerce averaged about $125 million yearly. Between 1844 and 1898 the total value of Chilean imports from Britain exceeded the total value of imports from France, Germany, and the United

States combined. In 1825, 90 British ships were reported at Valparaiso compared with 70 U.S. vessels. In 1840, 166 British vessels arrived at Valparaiso, compared with 56 from the United States. The British Empire purchased over half of Chile's exports in 1860, while Chile acquired one-third of its imports from Britain. By 1875 the respective percentages were almost 60 percent and 40 percent. In 1889, Britain purchased $48 million of the total produce worth $66 million exported by Chile and furnished $28 million of the total produce worth $65 million that Chile imported.[17]

As Blaine had warned, Chile's acquisition of the rich nitrate provinces in the Atacama Desert opened new areas for British investment to the exclusion of U.S. interests. After the war, export duties on nitrates extracted from the acquired territories provided much of the Chilean government's revenue for over forty years— about $25 million annually. Just before the conflict, British capital had controlled about 13 percent of the nitrate industry in Tarapacá. By the end of the war the figure had risen to 34 percent. By 1890 the British contolled 70 percent of the nitrate industry—the source of about three-quarters of Chile's exports. Between 1888 and 1889, eighteen new British nitrate enterprises were begun. Enjoying a unique reputation among Latin American nations for political stability and natural resources in demand, Chile was a favorite among British investors. Not surprisingly, U.S. trade with Chile throughout this era scarcely existed. As late as 1900, it barely reached $5 million, and it was conducted almost exclusively by three large firms.[18]

Commercial connections were not the only ties binding Chile and Britain. From the time of Chilean independence, the British had developed strong naval connections with the South American nation with the longest coastline. The British commander of the Chilean navy during Chile's formative years, Lord Thomas Nelson Cochrane, is even today honored as one of Chile's founding fathers. The navy came to be modeled on the British system and Chilean midshipmen were often apprenticed on British warships.

As commercial and military ties grew, so did the British community in Chile. In 1875 almost five thousand British were residents, and the number continued to climb, although the number of U.S.

residents remained fewer than one thousand throughout the century. In Valparaiso, where most of the British had settled, English apparently was spoken almost as commonly as Spanish by all educated classes. The image of an Anglophile Chile was perhaps best presented by the author W. E. Curtis, who in 1890 was working for the International American Conference of the State Department. In a letter to a friend he wrote, "Valaparaiso is almost an English Colony; most of the merchants are Englishmen and English is spoken as much as Spanish on the streets and in the stores. There are English papers printed there, and in fact, it is the only city in South America where a man who does not understand any Spanish can get along as well as at home."[19] There could be no doubt that in politics, commerce, naval training, and cultural influence Chile, by 1889, was turned toward Europe, especially Britain, and not toward its neighbor to the north. It had never been difficult to arouse Blaine's suspicion of Britain, but now realistic considerations of Chile gave him new reason to be apprehensive.

In his second administration of the Department of State, beginning in March, 1889, Blaine endeavored to convince Latin America to turn away from Europe. What he hoped to do was begin the process of usurping British control in Latin America. He distrusted the British, but what he desired in actuality was to emulate their success. He was both hostile towards and admiring of their dominance. The popular nineteenth-century slogan "America for Americans" came to mean the elimination of British influence in the markets of Latin America. Frustrated by British success, Anglophobes had only to look to Chile to see how British influence represented the principal obstacle to U.S. notions of hemispheric economic domination. Blaine surely sensed that the United States was evolving into one of the world's great powers, but he was also aware that the process would be gradual.[20]

The awakening national consciousness required that the country be taken seriously. The United States needed to demonstrate its independence—it needed to break out from under the humiliation of British commercial supremacy in its own hemisphere. "British subjects to-day hold a chattle mortgage over Chile," the *New York Daily Tribune* wrote early in 1891, one "so large as to give their

Government a tangible excuse for undertaking to exert a controlling political influence whenever it is thought that British interests would thereby be served."[21] Most likely, Blaine planned his political moves with that challenge in mind.

Meanwhile, in 1886 José Manuel Balmaceda had become president of Chile, and Blaine in 1889 may have desired to take advantage of the new Chilean president's known hostility to British dominance, which he interpreted as a challenge to his own. Blaine was aware of the United States' evolving sense of power and equally aware of the political capital his Anglophobia had in the Irish population of the Northeast. Was it, then, a coincidence that Blaine was able to persuade Harrison to appoint Patrick Egan U.S. minister to Chile?

The new minister played yet another role in late-nineteenth-century relations between the United States and Chile. Born in Ireland, forced to flee to the United States in 1883 because of his anti-British activities, Egan became a U.S. citizen in 1888 but never slackened in defense of the cause of Ireland. He was a powerful force at the Irish convention of April, 1883, in Philadelphia, when the Land League was dissolved and the Irish National League of America organized. At the league's convention of 1884 he was elected president and held that office for two years. From the beginning, he was an active member of the Republican party and a close friend of Blaine, whom he supported for president in the campaign of 1884. He was delegate-at-large to the Republican national convention in 1888, where apparently he declined the convention chairmanship and again supported Blaine for president until it became clear that Benjamin Harrison had a better chance of being elected.[22] Known as a "Blaine Irishman" with a "joyous Gaelic love for a fight,"[23] he worked to swing a large Irish vote to Harrison.

Egan had so clearly attached his political ambitions to those of Blaine that after the election of 1888 it seemed natural that the secretary of state would try to do something for Egan. Harrison probably would not have been elected had Blaine opposed him, and Blaine and Egan had worked diligently to get Irish support for Harrison. Egan's appointment could have been simply a display of gratitude to Irish voters—paying off political debts. But Blaine may also

Patrick Egan, U.S. Minister to Chile. From *Life and Work of James G. Blaine* (Manufacturer's Book Co., Philadelphia, 1893).

have had in mind a commercial war on the British in South America. If Chile was the most vigorous and powerful of the South American nations, if its financial success was due primarily to the nitrate industry, if Britain virtually monopolized Chilean commerce and particularly nitrates, there may have been more to the Irishman's appointment than simple political obligation. Politicians and the press recognized that and debated the appropriateness of Egan's appointment.

Some defended the selection of Egan. The political aspect of his appointment did not make Egan incompetent, explained Fenton R. McCreery, whom Blaine had appointed secretary to the legation at Santiago: "The Minister came to the United States from Ireland in 1882. He is a prominent Fenian charged with many crimes by his enemies. He is a very smooth polished gentleman with a slight Dublin accent and is in favor with all but the English. His eyes are sharp and his glance penetrating, he speaks deliberately and slowly and has nothing of the typical Irishman about him."[24] The controversy over Egan's appointment was also noted by the Chilean minister to the United States, E. E. Varas. He wrote the Chilean Ministry of Foreign Relations to explain that the democratic press in the United States saw the appointment as the satisfaction of political debts contracted by the Harrison administration to Irish voters who supported him in the election.[25]

IN JANUARY, 1891, the Chilean congress in collaboration with the navy under the direction of Admiral Jorge Montt revolted against the elected president, José Manuel Balmaceda, because of personality conflicts, currency inflation, bureaucratic corruption, anticlericalism, proposals for social and fiscal reform, attempts to control British investment in the nitrate industry, and what appears to have been a move to destroy the constitutional system of checks and balances between the executive and the legislature. Balmaceda was a tall, lean, imposing man in his fifties with penetrating and piercing eyes and a dark, bushy mustache. He was a gifted speaker who had gained wide administrative experience as congressman, cabinet minister, and diplomat. A romantic, a man of patriotic zeal, he attained the presidency of Chile just as that country was reaching the peak of its international reputation as the one Spanish-American nation that did not fit into traditional Latin stereotypes. Chile's decisive victory in the War of the Pacific did much to confirm the notion of Chile's uniqueness, but Balmaceda also contributed to Chile's growth and prosperity. He was a competent and enterprising ruler, a man of unusual foresight.[26]

When he took office as president in 1886, Balmaceda took on the obligation and mission to continue the nation's progress. His object was to use the extremely lucrative proceeds from the export duty on nitrates to invest in programs of public works.[27] Although the idea was not originally Balmaceda's, he contributed much to the plan's success. Within Chile, however, the program was not unquestioningly accepted, and Balmaceda came under attack from critics who believed that Chile needed primarily to retire its paper currency and reduce the national debt. Most of the new jobs created by the program were also at the disposal of the government, giving rise to charges of corruption. But in the beginning Balmaceda remained unharmed by his critics, who represented minority opinions in congress.

Unhappily Balmaceda's self-confidence soon evolved into vanity and arrogance, and he proved exceedingly stubborn about doing anything that appeared to decrease the enormous power of the presidency that he claimed the Chilean constitution of 1833 granted him. From 1886 to 1888 there was little opposition to Balmaceda, since he tried to conciliate the liberal and conservative groups in congress. In 1888, when he formed a cabinet entirely from liberals, he appeared to abandon his conciliatory policy. Congress became increasingly critical of his enormous expenditures for social programs and also of his autocratic nature. Balmaceda seemed to believe that if he could not have his way by persuasion he would have it by force.

The Chilean president was aware of the growing power of British capital in Chile and of British control over the principal source of finance for his internal program. He publicly suggested that it would be beneficial for Chilean initiative and capital to begin to play a larger part in national economic development. He was probably aware that if the nitrate market became saturated, British companies might agree to limit the supply of nitrates until it could be balanced with demand. The effect of such an agreement on government revenues would be disastrous.[28]

A crisis arose in Chile when the congress closed its session of 1890 without agreeing on an appropriations bill for 1891. On January 1, 1891, Balmaceda published a manifesto in the *Diario Oficial* declaring that because congress had not passed his budget, he decreed that the financial bills for 1890 would remain in operation in 1891—even without the constitutionally required legislative approval. He would rely on forthcoming congressional elections to produce a sympathetic majority in congress.[29]

One week later Chile was thrown into civil war. The president of the Chamber of Deputies and the vice president of the Senate sent a note to Admiral Jorge Montt, pleading for naval assistance against the usurper. On January 7 most of the Chilean fleet left Valparaiso and set up a revolutionary government in the north.

The civil war quickly drifted into stalemate. Balmaceda was able to maintain the support of the army, but the insurgents captured the nitrate province in the north. The president thus lacked a source of revenue to buy arms and ships to carry the war to the north. The rebels lacked sufficient arms to challenge Balmaceda's stronghold in the south.

There should have been little doubt about U.S. State Department policy during the Chilean civil war. On January 16 at the Chilean legation in Washington, Balmaceda's representative, Prudencio Lazcano, informed Blaine of the revolt and that the Balmaceda government had declared the rebellious fleet outlaw and was not responsible for its acts regarding foreigners. Blaine insisted the United States had the right to consider each case individually as it arose.[30] On January 17 Egan telegraphed Blaine that the fleet was about to blockade Valparaiso, Iquique, and other ports, and although he was making strong protests, he felt need of a squadron to protect U.S. interests. Blaine responded by directing the secretary of the navy to send U.S. war vessels to Chilean waters—thus the presence of the *Baltimore*.[31]

Perhaps Blaine was encouraged to move quickly by a telegram he had received from the U.S. consul in Talcahuano. Because of arbitrary arrest, detention, seizure, censorship, and violence—some occurrences involving foreigners—the consul insisted that U.S. interests were at the mercy of "those who seem to ignore that neutrals or anyone else have rights to be respected." He concluded he would feel insecure until safety was assured by the presence of U.S. vessels: "We have no guarantee of any kind and I should feel as safe amongst the Hottentots, as here. We need at once American vessels for our protection as that is the only kind of argument that can reach the comprehension of those in power at present."[32]

The U.S. Navy sought to observe strict neutrality in Chilean waters. Secretary of the Navy Tracy ordered Rear Admiral McCann to proceed from Montevideo to Valparaiso to take command of the South Pacific Squadron "for the purpose of protecting American interests."[33] But his telegram of March 4 was more explicit: "Observe strict neutrality. Take no part in troubles further than to protect American interests. Take whatever measure necessary to prevent injury by insurgent vessels to lives or property of American citizens."[34] McCann had no need to be reminded of U.S. neutrality. He had already written on February 22 to caution officers and enlisted men of the U.S. naval force on the west coast of South America to "abstain from discussing or criticising the present unfortunate state of affairs in Chile, and in no way to express any sentiments or opinions either favorable or unfavorable to either side." It was their duty to maintain strict neutrality, he stated, and to "refrain from any expressions that can possibly be construed as an offense by either party."[35]

Egan too knew his responsibility. He counseled neutrality on at least two occasions to U.S. residents in Chile, explaining, "[The] only practical advice I can offer you is to abstain scrupulously from all participation directly or indirectly in the political struggle now so unhappily taking place in the country and to rely upon the duly constituted local authorities for protection."[36]

What then was the conduct of the Harrison administration that so poisoned relations between the United States and the revolutionaries in Chile? Ever a diplomatic problem, neutrality had never been concisely defined. For the United States at the time, it meant recognizing the *de jure* government as long as it continued *de facto*—in this case the United States sustained communication with the Balmaceda regime while refusing recognition to the insurgent forces. In May, 1891, the president of the revolutionary junta wrote Blaine that a representative of the Chilean congress with authority to represent the rebels in the United States had been sent in the capacity of confidential agent. Upon receipt, a note was scratched at the top of the cable, stating: "By the President's direction this is to be filed without official notice being taken of it."[37] The Congressionalists could not legitimately demand recognition. They would, however, feel resentment at its denial.

Meanwhile it became known that Egan thought Balmaceda would win the civil war, and indeed personally he may have preferred such an outcome. In dispatches to the State Department he constantly noted the friendship the Balmaceda government had shown the U.S. legation. He wrote the U.S. minister in Argentina, John R. G. Pitkin, on January 12, 1891, "Revolutionary leaders calculated upon a responsive movement on the part of the Army which has not taken place and which so far as I can gauge the future is not now likely to occur." One month later he again wrote Pitkin: "No serious change in the situation here. When the revolution commenced on 7th January the Government had but 3500 soldiers in the entire country. It has now on a war footing an army of 25,000 men and it seems to feel entirely secure on land. The fleet so far controls no territory and unless they can conquer some it is difficult to see how the revolutionists can hope even to maintain themselves for any length of time."[38]

In April, Egan advised the U.S. consul at Iquique that government forces had made the best use of time to recruit, train, and organize the army, which seemed more able to make a desperate fight.[39] To Secretary Blaine he remarked in April, "I look for a long, a bitter, and a sanguinary struggle, with the chances of ultimate victory very largely on the side of the government." Egan wrote Blaine to estimate the strength of the revolutionary military forces and concluded that although the "leaders of the opposition seem to feel much confidence in the ultimate success of their cause, but on the whole their prospects, viewed from a disinterested standpoint, do not look very promising." Later he cabled a long report to deny "gross inventions and exaggerations" published in the United States about "imaginary cruelties and atrocities on the part of both of the parties to the civil war." In his report, however, his evidence referred only to the Balmacedists' action of unconditionally releasing eighty-seven political prisoners and to excellent conditions in government prisons for the remaining fourteen or fifteen political prisoners—an entire wing of the prison to themselves with ventilated and clean cells, free intercommunication, permission to receive friends, furniture, and luxuries or to be accompanied by servants. Here were prisons "supplied with food at the expense of a committee of friends from a French restaurant, the most excellent in the city."[40]

Egan was not the only contemporary observer to exhibit sympathy for the government forces or to express the likelihood of their victory. The U.S. consul at Valparaiso, in government hands, wrote Egan, "Whatever the outcome of the present troubles may be I shall always remember that the authorities here have treated me with uniform kindness and courtesy, and that so far they have refused me no favors I have asked."[41] Admiral McCann wrote, "President Balmaceda is master of the situation. . . . it is evident to my mind that the land and naval forces of the Congressional Party are wholly inadequate to a successful prosecution or ending of the civil war in Chile." A while later he noted, "My impression has been for some time that the success of the revolutionary party is about hopeless."[42] Egan's emotional partiality was apparently never very secret, as an incident his secretary witnessed indicated:

The whole country is in favor of the Revolution and so when one of the passengers [on a train] at cigarette time after breakfast declared for the Government a lively argument ensued. The opposition man declared that every decent Chilian and every foreigner who has interest in Chile favors the side of Congress. The Balmaceda man replied that he had on his side the American Minister to which the oppositionist retorted that he did not care a d—— if he did, that Mr. Egan was such a scoundrel that he could not return to his own country—and so went the argument almost to blows.[43]

There are, perhaps, other, less tangible reasons why the United States might have favored Balmaceda. A general disdain for revolutions, especially Latin American revolutions (fitting the general notion that Latins were less civilized than their Anglo neighbors to the north), was possibly a motive for upholding the status quo in Chile. Another reason might be the memories of the U.S. Civil War, little more than twenty-five years in the past. That tragedy, the single, most important turning point in the domestic history of the United States, had been the central political experience for most U.S. citizens in the 1890s, especially prominent Republican leaders. Perhaps they projected the U.S. experience to Chile. Perhaps the U.S. Republican leadership saw Chilean Congressionalists as southern, states'-rights aristocrats, favored, like the Confederacy, by the British. Perhaps U.S. observers presumed Balmaceda to be a Lincolnesque autocrat upholding the Chilean union. Those speculations raise interesting and important questions about U.S. support for the Balmaceda regime, but no concrete evidence has been discovered to resolve the mystery.

From later publication of cables and reports, many Chileans would conclude that the Harrison administration and the U.S. public were deliberately misinformed about the relative strength of the combatants, as well as about the nature of the struggle and its probable outcome. Egan was entirely too confident of Balmaceda's final success. The price for his error would be high. As the British minister to Chile, John G. Kennedy, rightly observed:

It is clear that Egan and his Admirals thoroughly believed in the triumph of Balmaceda and they publicly and officially expressed that belief. Now the feeling against Egan and his Admirals is bitter and strong. Both Egan and Admiral Brown have written explanatory letters to the newspapers—but the facts are too strong for them.[44]

It was fervently claimed by the Democratic opposition in the United States that Egan was guilty of impropriety when he forwarded to Washington Balmaceda's request to purchase two war ships. The message to the State Department, however, was simply a transmission of a request by the *de jure* government and contained no recommendation. Acting Secretary of State William F. Wharton (Blaine was ill from May to October, 1891) cabled that the navy had no ships for sale.[45] Less tangible evidence of Egan's prejudice was the complaint that two of the minister's fourteen children had married into families sympathetic to the cause of Balmaceda.[46] Egan and his sons were also charged with benefiting from economic transactions in railroad construction supported by Balmaceda, which was certainly a possibility even if Egan's son Francis vigorously denied it.[47]

Although British policy, like U.S. policy, was technically one of neutrality, the sympathies of the British residents in Chile, the British Squadron in Chilean waters, and most British businesses there were clearly with the rebels. On March 17, 1891, Egan reported to Blaine that the revolution had the "undivided sympathy and in many cases the active support of the English residents in Chile." He had information from a commander of government forces in the north that managers and superintendents of the British-owned nitrate centers in Tarapacá had promised employees two dollars a day to fight with the revolutionary forces and threatened blacklisting if they did not. Egan even alleged that "many English houses have subscribed liberally to the revolutionary fund" and that the British nitrate king Colonel John Thomas North had contributed one hundred thousand dollars to the insurgent cause.[48] That made Minister Kennedy uncomfortable. There is no doubt, he wrote the Foreign Office, "Naval officers and the British community of Valparaiso and all along the Coast rendered material assistance to the opposition and committed many breaches of neutrality."[49]

There is little evidence that British sympathy or even material assistance played a substantial part in the eventual outcome of the civil war, but it certainly earned the wrath of the Balmaceda forces.[50] On June 11, 1891, Lieutenant Charles H. Harlow wrote President Harrison:

The constant aid and assistance given to the Rebels by the English officials and the officers of English steamers makes Balmaceda and his high officials furious. They are powerless to prevent it, but they know very well that the English officials and the officers of English steamers plying up and down the coast are the constant and regular means of confidential communication between the Rebels and their sympathizers in Valparaiso and Santiago. . . . The constant aid and assistance given by the English to the Rebels will be atoned for after the war. . . . no set of men ever hated another set so bitterly. . . . Put it down as certain that Balmaceda is going to win, and when he does win the United States can have whatever it wants in Chili.[51]

Whether the anti-Balmaceda position of the British community caused Egan to demonstrate sympathy for the Chilean president or whether Egan's personal sympathy for Balmaceda helped the British decide to work with the revolutionaries is a difficult question. Balmaceda's pre–civil war hints at possible anti-British policies created conditions for the expansion of U.S. economic influence. That Egan was told to encourage such a development is believable. That Egan worked toward such ends is probable.[52] There is no evidence, however, that Anglo-American rivalry for commercial supremacy in Chile and South America or Egan's pro-Blaine, anti-British position made the minister disobey or bend the letter of his instructions to be neutral. Although lack of evidence leads to ambiguity in determining Egan's motives, surely his virulent Anglophobia blinded him to the realities of the Chilean civil war. He needed little more than those feelings once he saw the rebel-British partnership shaping up.

The British did not see the situation that way. Kennedy wrote the Foreign Office, "It would indeed seem clear that the United States Government convinced of the triumph of Sr. Balmaceda had taken every possible opportunity to ingratiate themselves with His Excellency, by rendering direct services to the Dictatorship against the cause of Congress." The British minister surmised the reason for the alleged prejudice, "The triumph of President Balmaceda would have involved the triumph of the ideas of Mr. Blaine, with a great diminution of the influence and commercial prosperity of Great Britain, France, and Germany." The minister cabled indications of the Congressionalists' growing hostility to Egan. He wrote the Foreign Office: "There is at present a strong feeling of resentment against Mr. Egan entertained both by the Opposition party in the North, and by their sympathizers here. . . . It is now believed that Mr. Egan did not act in good faith as regards the Opposition."[53] The British press did not miss the implication of the antagonism. The *London Times* reported very bitter feelings of hostility against the United States by the revolutionaries, which unless appeased, could undermine U.S. commerce in Chile: "The feeling against Mr. Egan is very violent."[54]

Egan could not escape criticism, for his good relations with the Balmaceda regime contributed to the notion that he had been partial. Dr. John Trumbull, a resident of Valparaiso, a scion of the Connecticut Trumbulls, by birth a Chilean, later published a vicious and hyperbolic condemnation that summarized most of the opposition to the minister. Egan's activities, he insisted, could be considered "intentioned evil, and studied purpose to arouse un-justifiable prejudice, warp the judgement of, and breed ill feeling in the State Department." Egan's silence about atrocities by the Bal-maceda regime and concealment of facts about the military situation indicated the extent to which the minister had prostituted his authority:

On what basis other than lack of moral standards can one explain that Mr. Egan should in his letters and telegrams assure the U.S. Government that "perfect order is maintained throughout the country"? When he wrote that, he asserted as patent a falsehood as was ever made, and he cannot find shelter behind the pleas of igno-rance. No! He was favorable to Balmaceda, his assistance had been secured and therefore he stopped at nothing. . . . Mr. Egan would have it believed prisoners were treated "with every consideration," and actually feasted by a French caterer. He makes out there were no "cruelties and atrocities"—that they are "imaginary." . . . Mr. Egan paints a picture without any outrage, without any flogging, without any murder, without any hounding persecution of defence-less women, without any orders such as were given by the tyrant's closest friends to have a prominent Opposition leader's property destroyed, his houses burned, and even an order sent that his daughters should be given over to the soldiery to gratify their lust.—Such were the friends whom Mr. Egan paints in glowing and admiring colors, and whom he deceitfully induced your Govern-ment to support.

Trumbull expounds on Egan's so-called hypocrisy: the U.S. govern-ment had been hoodwinked, falsely informed, deceived, weakened by its unworthy representative. Egan's information was untrust-worthy, unfit for descendants of the Puritan tradition of honor, up-rightness, and fair play. He concludes, "Is it not time that diplo-matic and consular appointments cease to be used in payment of political service? Better pay for such out of the national treasury, rather than allow your good name to be thus smirched again!"[55] Trumbull's hysteria should not be taken at face value, but it does summarize extreme Chilean sentiments toward the U.S. minister.

Not only Chileans criticized Egan. Well into the civil war, *The*

Nation, a notoriously anti-Blaine publication, wrote that what was needed in Chile was a first-rate diplomat, someone well known and trustworthy, who could accurately guide the administration and public. It seemed unreasonable—even grotesque—that the U.S. representative in Chile was a recently naturalized Irish rebel and British political refugee. After the civil war *The Nation* still railed. It was disrespectful and insulting to the South American republic to send a foreign adventurer to Chile as minister, a man who was a fugitive from justice in his native land.[56] Other anti-Egan U.S. sentiment, less polemical, simply contended that a trained diplomat in Chile might have made for better relations.[57]

Whether Egan was a patriot and hero or rascal and opportunist depended on one's view of the Chilean civil war. His opponents, whether in Chile or the United States, were convinced that Secretary of State Blaine's anti-British feelings were behind Egan's perceptions and U.S. policy during the civil war. Egan's appointment may have been unwise, since Blaine surely could have sent someone else to promote the same anti-British policy. But Egan, however indiscreet his personal prejudices, was certainly not incompetent. He was criticized primarily because he was minister from a nation whose government had decided not to maintain formal relations with both parties to a domestic quarrel and had erred in picking, as the probable winner, the loser.

3. Warnings

FEW OF THE COMPLICATED EVENTS of the Chilean civil war serve as evidence of Minister Egan's lack of neutrality for the simple reason that he had little to do with any of them. Still, they generated tremendous hostility and resentment toward the minister and toward his country.

The first problem appeared when the insurgents, not accorded belligerent rights, sent a confidential agent to the United States to purchase war supplies. The Congressionalists hoped they could defeat the Balmaceda forces before the government could obtain ships to rout the rebels. Richard Trumbull, a Chilean cousin of the famous Trumbulls, arrived in New York in March of 1891 and contracted with the steamship company W. R. Grace to provide about two million cartridges, together with 250 cases of Remington and Lee magazine rifles. The rebels thereupon shipped those items to San Diego, where they planned to transfer them to a Chilean steamer, the *Itata*, which would deliver the arms to the junta in Iquique. The steamer had been seized by the insurgents at the outbreak of the revolution from the Compañía Sud-Americana de Vapores. In the spring of 1891 the *Itata* was heading for San Francisco with passengers and merchandise.

The effort by the insurgents to use the *Itata* to send supplies almost begged for trouble. The suggestion that the *Itata* might violate U.S. neutrality laws was promptly brought to the attention of U.S. diplomats by Balmaceda's minister in Washington, Prudencio Lazcano, who informed Blaine on March 10, 1891, that the Chilean government had prohibited "importation into the entire territory of the Republic . . . arms and munitions of war of all kinds." Reaffirming Balmaceda's friendship with the United States, Lazcano hoped the State Department would prevent "illicit commerce." Pointedly he articulated his hope "that the friendly ties which unite the Government of this country with my own will be sufficient ground for your favorable reception of the request which I take the liberty of making." Three days later Blaine replied that the neutrality laws of the United States did not forbid manufacture of arms and ammunition or their sale and that he had no authority to act.[1]

Lazcano was not easily rebuffed. He secured the counsel of John W. Foster, then a well-known Washington lawyer, former U.S. envoy to Mexico and Russia, soon to be secretary of state (1892–93), and a politician of importance in the state of Indiana, and thus reinforced the effort to convince the Harrison administration that the *Itata* intended to commit acts that violated U.S. neutrality laws. Foster aroused enough suspicion that on May 5 state department officials ordered the customs house at San Diego to watch not only the *Itata* but to detain another vessel, the schooner *Robert and Minnie,* then involved in coastal trade. For that assistance Lazcano wrote Blaine that he was "deeply grateful for the friendly action taken by the United States Government." "I do not entertain the slightest doubt," he shrewdly intimated,

that the Government which unequivocally established the principles of the duties of neutrals in the treaty of Washington of 1871 will, without hesitating for a moment, exercise the power which it has to protect a neighboring and friendly nation from the outrages and injuries that would result from a violation of the laws of neutrality against which it then so forcibly and successfully protested.[2]

The British, having once been embarrassed by the issue of neutrality years before during the American Civil War (and perhaps vividly recalling the result of that embarrassment, an enormous $15,500,000 decision against them by the Geneva arbitral tribunal of 1872), were naturally interested in the problem of the *Itata*. The *Chilian Times,* an organ of the British community in Valparaiso, reported on July 18, 1891, that the *Itata* had aroused concern in England even among those who had no interest in the Chilean civil war: "What excited our people's curiosity was, with the recollection of the *Alabama* award, still vivid in mind, what would the United States do?"[3]

What would the U.S. government a generation later do in a similar situation where its "due diligence" as a neutral might be questioned? Fearing that the *Itata* would violate neutrality laws, a U.S. marshal in San Francisco on May 5, 1891, placed the captain and ship under arrest and put a deputy on board to detain the vessel.

The Chilean revolutionaries promptly took matters into their own hands. The *Itata* quietly steamed out of the bay, eventually released the forlorn deputy, and rendezvoused with the *Robert and Minnie* off San Clemente Island. Fearing that the Chilean government would hold the U.S. government liable for lack of due diligence, as the Geneva judges had held Britain years before, and now also moved by what it considered the Chilean rebels' affront to U.S. dignity, federal authorities in Washington issued orders to stop delivery of whatever might be the *Itata's* cargo. Some days later, when the *Robert and Minnie* was seized and found empty, it was understood that the schooner had either unloaded its cargo somewhere where the *Itata* might pick it up or had transferred the shipment directly to the ship on its way to Iquique. On May 13 the State Department issued an order to capture the *Itata* as a fugitive from custody, but the USS *Charleston* and USS *Omaha*, sent to chase the *Itata* and return it to San Diego "by force if necessary," embarrassingly arrived in Iquique without even having sighted the *Itata*.[4]

The *Itata* incident hardly worked out to the advantage of the United States. When the *Itata* finally slipped into Iquique on June 3, insurgent authorities expressed regret that the ship had fled San Francisco and decided that to avoid antagonizing the United States they would surrender the ship and seek recourse in U.S. courts. Earlier, on May 14, the Congressional secretary of foreign relations, Isidoro Errázuriz, had written Admiral George Brown that the Congressional party deplored the conduct of the *Itata* and was not disposed to support any infraction of U.S. laws, and that as an evidence of friendship, the junta would place the ship at the disposition of the United States.[5] But U.S. insistence on the return of the arms and ammunition taken aboard the *Itata* provoked bitter feeling against the United States, since the Congressionalists could later claim that the loss of the cargo delayed their victory and caused unnecessary casualties. Errázuriz sent another message to Blaine in June, which, like previous correspondence from the rebels, was not officially received. He insisted that the surrender of the cargo had hurt "the spirit which guided us in this affair."[6] Rear Admiral McCann noted in a cable to Tracy that detention gratified the Balmaceda regime "while the insurgents, on the other hand, are equally indignant."[7]

The *Itata* incident indeed produced a complex situation. In addition to resentment over the detention of the ship, the accompanying legal procedure suggested to the rebels that an exceedingly narrow interpretation of "due diligence" was only a cover for U.S. support of Balmaceda. When much of the evidence of the prosecution eventually proved false, and the U.S. Federal Court for the Southern District of California handed down a decision favorable to the Congressional forces, hostility increased. The Congressional party, by that time the government of Chile, fervently claimed the United States had not been fair. In the hearing held in September, the revolutionaries argued that the *Itata* was not a privateer or warship and that when it left the United States it had not been served with any papers. They argued that the U.S. government was obliged to prevent the fitting out and arming of warships in U.S. ports but not the sale and shipment of cargoes. Complicated questions of international law were involved, but the court agreed with the rebel lawyers. Judge E. M. Ross dismissed the charges and declared the ship wrongly detained. On appeal that decision was sustained, again by a decision that the *Itata* acted only as a transporter and not as a warship.[8]

Hostility compounded. Francisco Valdés Vergara wrote his brother Ismael, secretary of the insurgent army, "There is no longer any doubt that Balmaceda has obtained from Blaine that the American Squadron will actively intervene to deal with the Chilean fleet as a pirate. This seems an enormity, but unfortunately it is true and the country is just as lost if it tolerates the affront in silence." A month later he wrote again, "Facts have demonstrated that my information about the attitude of the Yankees in the Itata affair was well founded. . . . I continue believing that Blaine has the intention of turning over the steamer . . . so that they can make it come to the service of Balmaceda."[9] John Trumbull's bombastic indictment was representative of the Chilean government's view:

The chase of the Itata *was ludicrous and painfully belittling to a great nation. A Congressional transport had gone into San Diego . . . to receive and transport arms, not to be fitted out as an armed vessel. . . the* Itata's *arrest, was made by an officer who at first could show no papers of arrest . . . and was merely a detective in Balmaceda's employ. . . . The* Charleston, *with flourish of trumpets, was sent out to give chase, and the* Itata *ultimately taken back when, simply to avoid difficulties . . . the vessel was handed over with arms which had not been taken aboard in San Diego. . . . The U.S. Government took her from Chilean waters, which was of itself a breach of international law . . . it was unbecoming of the United States, and a flagrant interference in Balmaceda's behalf. Why the U.S. Government was so strenuous to thwart the Congressional plans can only, it seems to me, to be due to misconceptions and unjust prejudices under which it labored through having Messrs. Egan and McCreery in Chili.*[10]

Valparaiso's *La Patria* on September 14 announced that Washington had "abused of its military superiority to treat us with less respect than that employed with the Barbary pirates . . . and all this done to help Balmaceda."[11] In mid-June, Rear Admiral McCann wrote Tracy, "Surrender of the steamer *Itata* and arms had deeply wounded the feelings of the Insurgent leaders, and had excited an unfriendly if not hostile spirit towards Americans, who they conceived were sympathizing with the Balmaceda government."[12] George C. Remey, commander of the *Charleston,* later said that the "insurgents felt very bitter towards us. . . . We were of course very unpopular with the Insurgents on account of our action."[13] In mid-June, McCann wrote from Peru that the incident "very naturally had excited an unfriendly feeling against our Government and people on the part of the insurgents and their sympathizers, as they regarded that act as humiliating."[14]

Nor was the *Itata* incident the only reason for Chilean bad feeling. The so-called cable incident of July, 1891, was considered proof that the United States had assisted Balmaceda. The New York–based Central and South American Telegraph Company, with a concession from the Balmaceda government, had laid a submarine cable from just outside Lima, Peru, to Iquique, Chile, and from Iquique to Valparaiso. It planned to connect via Santiago with the line of another company at the Argentine frontier. The first line was completed in February, 1891, before the Congressionalists had taken control of Iquique. When they captured and occupied the North, the insurgents severed the line from Iquique to Valparaiso and prohibited use of the Lima-Iquique connection. The company remained neutral during the first part of the civil war, but Balmaceda pressed the company to use force to reopen the connection, and the company chafed under the loss of revenue from the inoperative cables. When the British companies that operated between Europe and Argentina began bargaining for rights to lay a competing line from Buenos Aires, the Central and South American Telegraph Company began to consider drastic action.

Thereafter the situation of the company became complicated. Several times the company petitioned the junta to permit the opening at least of the southern line of the cable or to allow connection of the northern and southern portions somewhere outside Iquique but still within Congressional control. By July the company, now financially desperate, had not received any permissions. At that point a company representative in Peru sent notice to McCann that sometime the following week they proposed to send the cable steamer *Relay* to cut the cable outside Iquique and rejoin it in international waters to establish communication between Valparaiso and Lima. On July 20 the cable was cut and then reconnected outside the three-mile limit of Chilean territory, protected by the presence of Captain Schley and the *Baltimore*.[15]

The insurgents made no attempt to interfere, but the action engendered hostility toward the United States, since the insurgents were convinced that the object of cutting and reconnecting the cable was to assist Balmaceda to suppress the insurrection—perhaps by facilitating the purchase of arms and munitions, perhaps by permitting his spies to transmit news of Congressional military movements. The new Chilean government later compensated the cable company for expenses, but resentment against the United States continued. Calling the suggestion to splice and rejoin the cable the idea of the "wily minister," Trumbull condemned the action and claimed, "It gave Balmaceda another prop, while it weakened the Opposition, and so caused enmity in the people of Chili."[16]

Still another event that resulted in antagonism toward the United States occurred in August of 1891, when the revolutionaries initiated an expedition against Valparaiso and Santiago by landing their forces at Quinteros Bay. On August 19, the commander of the *San Francisco*, Admiral Brown, telegraphed Secretary Tracy that although reports were so conflicting it was difficult to ascertain the situation, "it is thought that the insurgents are, at this time, on their way south by sea, and that a landing will be made at either Quinteros or Concón to the north, or at San Antonio to the south."[17] On August 20 Brown decided to verify the rumors, and after witnessing the landing at Quinteros Bay he returned to Valparaiso and cabled a dispatch to Washington to report the landing of eight thousand men and the concentration of government forces to oppose any advance. Brown's actions, well publicized by the Balmaceda regime, promoted the notion among Chileans that he had not only acted in a manner showing partiality but engaged in espionage and transmitted information on the enemy landing directly to Balmaceda or purposely cabled his report through government-held Valparaiso so that the operator could communicate the information to the authorities. The embittered rebels naturally thought the knowledge afforded Balmaceda opportunity to send out more forces and inflict greater casualties against the revolutionaries in the battles of Placilla and Concón that followed eight days later.

Brown properly denied the accusations, declaring that on the morning of August 20 all Valparaiso knew that the rebels were planning to land and fight at Quinteros Bay—in fact, he had learned of the landing from Balmaceda's administrators in Valparaiso. Seeking only to gather information, "having learned from experience to distrust the correctness of all such information given me as official," he took the *San Francisco* to observe.[18] He sent an officer ashore to telegraph the Navy Department but insisted the telegram was in cipher so its content would be unknown to anyone who saw it before it reached Washington, and he admonished his crew not to speak of the landing.

Despite Brown's endeavor to answer his accusers, the Congressionalists interpreted his action in the worst possible light, and ill will only increased with Brown's attempt to vindicate himself.[19] Anti-American sentiment rose when it was learned that it was one of Brown's lieutenants who had leaked the news of the landing by cabling the information in English to a newspaper in the United States.[20] In John Trumbull's view the consequences were enormous. Without Brown's information there would not have been six thousand men to oppose the insurgents and "victory would not have been so dearly bought." There would have been no need for a second engagement, resulting in, so he said, 1,460 deaths and 2,500 injuries. Trumbull summarized the Chilean view that ties between Balmaceda and the United States were growing closer: "Chilians generally recognized and felt all this. Do you wonder that they should have had bitter feelings towards the only navy whose acts in every instance assisted him who, though Mr. Egan's friend, was everywhere detested because he was clearly a proud, vain, unscrupulous and cruel tyrant?"[21]

Brown denied the charges and on September 8 sent a long cable to Egan in regard to the "slanderous articles." Under ordinary circumstances he would consider it beneath his dignity as an officer of the U.S. Navy to take any notice of the charges, but he had decided it imperative to give a full account of events. He had gone ashore, he said, out of uniform, for a customary walk about 9:30 A.M. and thereupon met a Balmaceda official who spoke English. Inquiring about news of the day, Brown was informed, "Yes, the opposition have made a landing at Quinteros." Seeking to verify the statement, he went to the office of the intendente, who gave a more detailed description of the landing. A telegram from Quinteros Bay had already reached him by 7:00 A.M., giving the names of the men-of-war and listing five transports and three or four small steamers in the expedition. "This was not held as a secret," he insisted, "for everyone on the streets of Valparaiso knew of it . . . and Admiral Viel told me that the advance of the opposition would be contested by a large force of Government troops and that battle would be fought near Quinteros."

Brown claimed to have informed the senior British and German officers of his intent to go to Quinteros. He had reached the bay about 2:30 P.M. and, seeing no evidence of battle, returned to port around dusk. He sent an officer ashore with a cable, in code, for the secretary of the navy. The officer returned to say that everyone was talking of the landing and the impending fight. "In fact," Brown insisted, "He obtained more information than I had. All I knew was that a landing had been made and that no fighting had taken place within sight of the ships. No information was given by me of what I had observed, and the crew . . . were cautioned not to answer any questions."[22]

By that time, however, there was virtually nothing Brown could do to dispel the ill will generated toward the United States. The record of U.S. involvement in the Chilean civil war could hardly be set straight.

WITH REBEL VICTORIES at Placilla and Concón on August 28, 1891, the government forces of Balmaceda collapsed, the president resigned, the city passed to General Manuel Baquedano, and many soldiers changed uniform and took up arms against former comrades or else fled. As the regime disintegrated, prominent military officers and important statesmen went into hiding. Some sought refuge aboard foreign ships anchored off Valparaiso, others within foreign legations at Santiago. With the exception of the British legation, all of them opened their doors to the refugees, aware that capture would probably mean death. The Spanish legation received about eighty persons, the Brazilian more than eight, the French about five, the Uruguayan and German and other legations an unknown number.[23]

The right of diplomatic legations to grant asylum to political exiles now became troublesome for the United States and added to the hostilities generated by the *Itata* incident, the cable incident, and the Quinteros Bay episode. And again the focus of ill will was the U.S. minister. The night of the Battle of Placilla and all the next day, "prominent Government supporters, including ministers of state, senators, deputies, judges, and others, sought asylum."[24] Following allegations of favoritism toward Balmaceda, the asylum issue created serious new difficulties.

One might well comprehend the sentiment incited by rumors

that Balmaceda had taken refuge in the U.S. legation and was being protected by minister Egan, or that he had absconded either aboard the *San Francisco* or the *Baltimore*. Despite assurances to the contrary, the possibility of Balmaceda's escape with U.S. connivance "caused much excitement and strong feeling."[25] Balmaceda's wife, three daughters, and two sons were within the legation only for a single day. But even when it became known that Balmaceda had fled to the Argentine legation (where he remained until he committed suicide on September 19) and the United States was absolved from responsibility for his escape, resentment against Egan and the United States continued. Other government supporters did flee aboard the *Baltimore,* which on September 4 sailed for Peru with nineteen or twenty refugees "whose lives were not safe in Chile" and who had no other means of reaching neutral territory.[26]

Meanwhile about eighty people sought asylum in the U.S. legation, but the number rapidly decreased, until by September 25 only about nineteen remained. Egan never did make clear what happened to those people who left nor the manner by which they escaped. Most of those who remained in October were ministers of the former government who feared capture. When officials of the provisional government told Egan they expected the refugees to be turned over to them, Egan contended that doing so would mean the sacrifice of lives. Consequently he agreed to terminate asylum only if safe conducts were granted so that the refugees might reach foreign sanctuaries.

The Chileans rejected Egan's demand for safe conducts, and because they feared the refugees might escape, they sent guards to surround the U.S. legation and arrest suspected enemies entering and leaving. Egan was enraged when he learned that two of his servants had been harassed and arrested. "It is my duty to say to Your Excellency," he wrote on September 23, "that a course of action is being pursued towards this Legation which is not acceptable." On September 25 he again protested Chilean conduct, "As representative of the United States I cannot allow, without serious protest, that the House of this Legation should appear as in a state of seige and that from day to day it shall be subjected to petty annoyances in order to inflict vexations upon those who come into or go out from it."[27]

It was Egan's insistence on safe conduct guarantees for the refugees and his support from Washington rather than any harassment from the new Chilean regime that prolonged the dispute. By late September Egan reported that twenty people had been arrested entering the legation. Acting Secretary Wharton instructed Egan, "by direction of the President to insist firmly that the respect and inviolability, due to the minister of the United States and to the legation buildings, including free access, shall be given and observed fully and promptly by the Chilean authorities."[28]

Egan's communication of that instruction to the Chilean Ministry of Foreign Relations halted the arrests for a while, but the new Chilean government continued to harass the legation in other ways. Claiming Egan was abusing the right of asylum, the government charged that the Chileans within, with Egan's consent, were plotting subversive activities and revolutionary acts and using the legation as a center for the transmission of propaganda. Egan denied the charges, as he had all others, insisting that there "must be some error in believing that there could have been in this Legation any attempt at conspiracy."[29]

In the United States the attorney general and other officials debated the issue of asylum, which had its awkwardness—it was not a clearly defined issue and the precedents were various and confusing. The United States had never consistently asserted the right to grant asylum and sometimes even denied it. President Harrison thought that in this instance, since Egan earlier had offered asylum to the insurgents during the civil war, he could support the same right at this time. In the earlier instance Balmaceda had been annoyed by Egan's granting asylum to the rebels and had threatened that if they did not leave the legation he might send forces to search it. Egan had berated the government he apparently favored in extremely harsh terms: "If the Government desired to raise the question of asylum I would be prepared to discuss it on the proper basis and in the most friendly spirit; but that, with regard to the threat to search the legation, it should be distinctly understood that this legation could only be searched by force and that I would myself shoot the first man that should attempt to enter the legation for that purpose."[30]

But the next day he had received assurance that there would be no search. Egan was quick to point out that weeks later he was indicating his impartiality by offering asylum to the other side. The State Department concluded that the right to grant asylum was tacitly if not expressly "a human expedient." Perhaps Captain Robley D. Evans of the *Yorktown* best explained that human or moral question:

I am told to-day that he [General Velasquez, secretary of war under Balmaceda] was shot to death on board that vessel [the Magallanes*] at midnight last night and the authorities do not deny it, but say that if he has not been killed he will be, and that his friends will never know how or when. Now this is a fine prospect for the gentlemen who are refugeed in the legation at Santiago! If they are given up, every one will undoubtedly be killed, and the nations of the earth will justly hold us responsible. While I do not believe in the right of asylum, and would not permit our legations to be used for that purpose, still, having once received these men, we must stand by them even if it leads to war.*[31]

President Harrison believed that the "trouble with these people and their kindred seems to be that they do not know how to use victory with dignity and moderation; and sometime it may be necessary to instruct them."[32] Given the U.S. belief in "malice toward none," observers in the United States were outraged at the vengeance of the Congressionalists. Evidence is lacking, but it is not unrealistic to speculate that U.S. observers were unable to comprehend the extent of Chilean bitterness, not just for Balmaceda's so-called dictatorial powers, but for wartime atrocities committed by the Balmacedists, the most distinguished of which was the "Lo Cañas Massacre," in which hundreds of sons of prominent Chilean rebel families were executed.

By early October, 1891, the refugees within the U.S. legation had dwindled to fifteen, which lent some credence to the Chilean assertion that Egan was spiriting them to safety. Perhaps for that reason, "acts of disrespect" and "manifestations of a most unfriendly spirit" toward the legation resumed, even though the Chileans repeatedly assured Egan there was no intention of insult. The new government showed no desire to compromise, and Egan refused to negotiate on the issue of safe conducts out of the country.

At that juncture Egan extended his argument. He began to argue that the right of asylum encompassed that of safe conduct—that the legation would be transformed into a prison unless safe conduct was attached to asylum. He may have construed the issue beyond international law, but the Harrison administration supported him.

In October when the provisional government moved from an insistence that all enemies be subject to trial and punishment to a position that decreed that only those specifically named would be prosecuted, Egan thought he had found a means for compromise. The Chileans agreed to the extraterritoriality of the U.S. legation and even grudgingly to the right to asylum, but safe conducts, they insisted, were only out of "courtesy, convenience, and will." Egan shrewdly responded that the United States would "interpret as an act of but slight courtesy and consideration" the refusal of the Chilean government to grant safe conducts.[33] Tension escalated when Egan reported in December that detectives and police had renewed harassment of the legation. Egan was understandably furious when he learned that one of his sons had been momentarily under arrest until he could establish his identity.

It was not until January 12, 1892, that the U.S. minister was able to obtain permission for the remaining refugees to leave the country. He never gained the desired safe conducts, but he did get oral assurance that the refugees would not be harmed. Why the Chileans conceded that much is difficult to say. Probably by that time difficulties over the riot in Valparaiso had convinced them they had better mollify the United States. On January 13, 1892, the remaining exiles sailed for Peru on the *Yorktown*.

The result of the controversy was the further discrediting of Egan and increased indignation against the United States. Of course those who received the aid and comfort of the U.S. legation wrote differently. "I owe to the representative of the United States in Santiago, Mr. Patrick Egan and to his distinguished family, in close to the five months that I was in that legation, all the thanks that a gentleman and a man of honor can offer," wrote the famous Chilean politican Juan E. Mackenna.[34] Julio Bañados Espinosa, exminister and Balmaceda's chief defender, wrote:

The life which I preserve for my children and for my country I owe to the chief of the North American squadron. Through you, as representative of that Republic, the most free, the most humanitarian, the greatest on earth, I give thanks from the bottom of my grateful heart. During life I shall bear testimony that I owe my salvation to the Navy of the United States, a navy which reflects in its brilliant swoops the glories of heroism and the virtue of generosity which characterize valor and nobility.[35]

John Trumbull and most Chileans could see only evil in Egan's action. He was responsible, Trumbull said, for increasing the difficulties of those reestablishing law and order. He had offered asylum in the U.S. legation to "men who had been most active and unscrupulous during the eight months reign of tyranny, cruelty and unspeakable outrage." The U.S. legation had been watched, not as an insult to the minister, "whose methods they actually feared," but to prevent the escape of criminals, since escape could only have been made "with the connivance and cooperation of the Minister himself."[36]

The new Chilean government received rapid recognition from the United States, on Egan's recommendation, and President Harrison exchanged cordial notes with the provisional president, Jorge Montt, and the new minister to the United States, Pedro Montt. Justly or unjustly, the climate of opinion in Chile in September and October of 1891 remained one of hostility to the United States and especially to Patrick Egan. Consul Merriam wrote Wharton on August 31 that the "feeling of animosity against Americans is very decided . . . in social gatherings and in groups of Chileans on the street corners, when I have passed, I have heard chants ' . . . abajo los Yankees.' . . . I can only say that I have noticed a very marked coldness on the part of some of the members of the Junta."[37] Egan, too, noted their wrath in a letter to Secretary Blaine on September 17, "The hostile element . . . has let no opportunity pass of misrepresenting and villifying everything pertaining to the United States."[38]

Sadly, Captain Schley had not sensed the depth of anti-American feelings when he granted shore leave to his men on October 16.

Jorge Montt, President of Chile. From *Harper's Weekly*, January, 1892.
Courtesy Indiana University Library.

4. *Wrangling*

DIPLOMACY IS SOMETIMES as tenuous as marriage, for the relationship can be sustained only if those involved wish to make it work. If one or both do not, then no amount of mediation, counseling, reconciliation, or negotiation can bring success. The diplomacy of the *Baltimore* affair demonstrated that perhaps neither the governments of the United States nor Chile really desired friendly relations. Barely two months after a brutal civil war, with Chile in a confused and distressed condition, the provisional government had not yet had time to determine what kind of relation it could sustain with the nation that it believed had supported the defeated regime. Diplomatic correspondence of the early period does not justify the belief that the Chilean government sought to embarrass or antagonize the U.S. government or that the United States sought to undermine the new administration. Egan reported that his relations with members of the new administration were cordial. The United States, however, failed to recognize the intensity of Chile's internal strife and allow for diplomatic repercussions. As the months wore on both republics proved stubborn, cemented to their own righteousness, determined not to be humbled.

EARLY IN THE EVENING of October 16, the day of the riot in Valparaiso, the captain of a U.S. merchant ship boarded the *Baltimore* with a young Chilean and reported the attack on the liberty party to Captain Schley, expressing his view that the police had contributed to the violence. The merchant captain described the assault as the "most shameful, brutal and inhuman" ever witnessed on "sober, unarmed and peaceful men." Schley later recalled that the captain was so indignant he urged Schley to open fire on the city. Schley claimed to have pointed out that doing so would be as inhumane as the action the captain found so despicable and instead related his faith in a French proverb, "Sleep brings counsel."[1] He did nothing until the following day.

Schley was busy for the next three days. On the morning of the seventeenth he sent Lieutenant McCrea and Dr. Stitt ashore, and they learned that Boatswain's Mate Riggin was dead, at least six other men seriously wounded, and thirty-one sailors imprisoned.[2] It is easy to imagine Schley's inability to understand the provocation, especially since late in the preceding afternoon he claimed to have seen the men orderly and sober. He ordered three officers to form a court of inquiry to determine the facts, then notified the Navy Department.[3] Minister Egan, informed by Schley, cabled the same information to the State Department. Egan cabled again on October 19 to relay Schley's impression that the attack was unprovoked and premeditated, citing as evidence a recent attack on German sailors supposedly made when Chileans mistook the Germans for U.S. sailors.[4] Lieutenant Sears made preparations for the funeral of Riggin and arranged release of the imprisoned men, while the *Baltimore's* doctors, Stitt and White, attended the wounded on shore.[5]

Schley had formed an opinion about the brawl even before the court of inquiry submitted its report on October 19, although it is impossible to say if he wrote his summary of the report before or after he received its conclusions. He had intimated something of his opinion in his note to Egan, and his formal summary coincides with those initial views.

Schley sent a summary to Egan on October 22 and his own and the board's findings to Tracy the following day. In his personal account he reported Riggin's death and the six serious injuries and traced the affair to a quarrel between Riggin and a Chilean sailor in a saloon. When the Chilean spat in Riggin's face and Riggin knocked the sailor down, Schley wrote, "There appears to have been a crowd on the outside ready and waiting, as numbers of men immediately rushed into the saloon and began the assault." Riggin and Johnson were "deliberately fired upon" by a squad of police as Johnson tried to carry Riggin to a drugstore. Although witnesses confirmed that a few Chilean officers sometimes "intervened most courageously to protect our men against the mob," as Schley re-

Officers of the USS *Baltimore*. From *Harper's Weekly,* January, 1892. Courtesy Indiana University Library.

ported, many of the crew's injuries were recognizable as bayonet wounds, and Schley inferred police participation. He attested to the "sobriety, orderliness, good behavior, and politeness" of his men, labeling the attempt to create the impression that they were drunk "malicious and untrue." He claimed the Sisters of Charity at the hospital where the wounded were taken "declared without reservation that the men were sober when they reached that institution." He would later slip in a remark, however, that even if his men were drunk, that "could not have justified their murder anywhere in Christendom."[6]

The assault, Schley concluded, was instigated by recently discharged Chilean sailors and longshoremen, and attacks on men who were in different parts of town "strongly implied premeditation." In time of peace, he said, "in a port of a nation with whom we are on terms of amity and friendliness, this brutal assault and butchery of my men is an indignity . . . and in transmitting the report to you I feel certain that it will receive . . . that attention and that serious consideration which it merits." Just what he contemplated is unknown, but he hastened to add, as if to reinforce his verdict of Chilean guilt, that because the intendente and judge of crimes had been "most humane" in discharging the imprisoned sailors as "individually guiltless," this fact confirmed his own judgment about innocence. The return of the released sailors' personal effects refuted the charge the men had been armed. He sent an expanded report to Tracy on October 23, charging the police with brutality.[7]

The board's report of October 19 described the "sober and orderly manner" of the liberty party while on shore, emphasizing that the men saluted all officers, especially Chilean. Trouble began when a mob of Chilean civilians, soldiers, and sailors began throwing stones and shouting "Yanks" at the *Baltimore*'s crew near the True Blue Saloon. The mob increased as U.S. sailors were stoned, beaten, stabbed—not only at that location but at several others. "The trouble was not the fault of our men, but was caused by the bitter feeling of the mob against our men and the desire to rob them," the report concluded. The police did not aid the sailors, and the men complained of brutal treatment—assaulted with butts of muskets, kicked, taken to the police station with catgut handcuffs around wrists or lassos around necks. The board listed the wounds suffered by twenty crewmen of the *Baltimore* and found that the men were all stabbed in the back. The tone of both Schley's summary and his officers' report left no doubt that whatever the immediate cause of the disturbance, the U.S. position would be that the sailors were forced to defend themselves as the mob attacked.[8]

Initially the U.S. public and the Harrison administration showed only the slightest concern. The *New York Times* decided that the riot was a result of anti-American feelings, although a week after the assault it prophesied, "It is improbable that any serious results will follow the incident. . . . it has been held that such occurrences are hardly ground for diplomatic rupture." When President Harrison conferred with Blaine and Tracy on the matter, the *New York Daily Tribune,* probably the most powerful newspaper of the administration in the nation, described it as a "long and earnest conference." The newspaper at first speculated that the White House considered the state of affairs as "grave and serious in the extreme," and vigorous measures might be necessary to obtain redress "for an outrage which has few parallels in the modern history of civilized nations." But despite the *Tribune*'s assertion that the assaults were "acts of assassination . . . upon a few sober, peaceable, unarmed and defenceless men," there is no indication that the administration considered the matter "atrocious and deadly." Three days later the *Tribune* had revised its tone, probably in response to administrative calm: "We do not believe that the most progressive and enlightened State in South America will refuse to make proper reparation for the affront. . . . No war with Chili is probable."[9]

The remaining days of October elicited little communication from the State and Navy departments. Egan apparently sent the *Baltimore*'s report to the president along with his conclusion that the assault was brutal and unprovoked.[10] Tracy asked Schley if he had notified Chilean authorities before granting liberty, and Schley responded he had not because it was not required. Tracy asked if the crew was attacked in different parts of the city at different times or if all men were injured in a single attack, and Schley answered that his men were attacked in various parts of the city simultaneously. Tracy later asked for information on the manner in which the sailors were arrested and taken to prison, and Schley replied, also at that time relating the death of Coalheaver William Turnbull.[11]

Secretary Blaine was recovering from an illness (later described as Bright's Disease) at his house in Maine when the *Baltimore* affair occurred and did not return to Washington until the end of October. Unfortunately his absence allowed Acting Secretary William Wharton to set the initial course. Wharton read the cables and unquestioningly accepted Schley's and the board's reports. He angrily cabled Egan on October 23, "This cruel work, so injurious to the United States, took place on the 16th instant, and yet no expression of regret or of a purpose to make searching inquiry, with a view to the institution of proper proceedings for the punishment of the guilty parties, has been, so far as I am advised, offered to this government." He instructed Egan to bring Schley's report to the attention of Chilean authorities and inquire if they possessed any explanation for a "pitiless" event that had deeply pained the people of the United States. He pointedly intimated that he considered it an expression of unfriendliness toward the United States that could imperil amicable relations. If the facts were as Captain Schley reported, he had no doubt that Chile would offer prompt and full reparation.[12]

From the beginning both Schley and Egan were in touch with Chilean officials. While the *Baltimore*'s officers looked into the riot, Schley sent a cautious message to the intendente of Valparaiso, Juan de Díos Arlegüi. Arlegüi replied that the riot had been brought immediately to the attention of Chile's department of justice, which would investigate.[13] The Chileans, however, communicated little during the remainder of October. Government bureaucracy was still in a confused state because of the civil war, with new administrators appointed to new offices every day. The Chileans were in the midst of a national election, held October 18, and Egan and the U.S. press gave considerable attention to the new Chilean political program.[14]

Gradually the wheels of inquiry began to turn. Four days after the riot Arlegüi notified Schley that the judge of crimes was Enrique Foster Recábarren (whose father was a U.S. citizen and then in Washington as an aide to the Chilean minister).[15] Foster Recábarren reported the proceedings relative to the "unfortunate occurrences" of the riot as "going rapidly to their conclusion" and he would announce the results as soon as possible but could not give details without violating the secrecy of the procedure.[16] The intendente wrote Schley on October 22 that he had been informed by the judge of crimes that all charges against the imprisoned crew had been withdrawn in relation to the "lamentable disorders," and thus he was returning all money and personal articles found in possession of the arrested sailors.[17] Foster Recábarren assured Schley the investigation would soon be finished.

Egan sent a note on October 26 to Manuel Antonio Matta, the minister of foreign relations, concerning the "most painful occurrence," reminding him that Schley had sent a copy of his officers' inquiry to the Chilean ministry and summarizing the U.S. report: the sailors were unarmed, orderly, gave no provocation; the attack was apparently premeditated, the assailants "animated in their bloody work by hostility to those men as sailors of the United States"; the police did not protect the sailors but joined the attack, "as in the case of the killing of Riggin," and dragged off to prison other sailors "under circumstances of the utmost barbarity." Egan pointed out that no expression of regret had been tendered and asked if Chile had any information or explanation for what Wharton had impatiently claimed was an exhibition of unfriendliness.[18]

About that point relations between Chile and the United States worsened significantly. Matta's response was not at all soothing. He acknowledged the deplorable event of the sixteenth but insisted that the minister "emits appreciations, formulates demands, and advances threats that, without being cast back with acrimony, are not acceptable, nor could they be accepted by this department, either in the present case or in any other of the like character." He did not doubt the sincerity or expertness of the *Baltimore*'s board of inquiry, but Matta bluntly stated that his duty would be to abide only by Chilean authorities, "which are the only ones which have full right and will have sufficient power to judge and punish the guilty." Until the secret Chilean investigation, or *sumario,* concluded, he assured the U.S. minister that his own silence was not an expression of unfriendliness.[19] Egan on October 31 received a further communication from Matta but noted in a telegram summarizing it for the department, "Like the minister's other note, this note expresses no regret."[20]

It is difficult to know how irritated Matta had been by the acting secretary's petulance as expressed in Egan's note of the twenty-sixth. Probably he had a right to be upset; the transmission was hardly tactful or judicious. Merely ten days had passed since the *Baltimore* tumult, and clearly Chilean authorities were not ignoring the event as Wharton and Egan implied. But it is unfortunate that at that juncture Matta chose to respond with similar irritation. The U.S. desire for an official statement of regret was neither humiliating nor insulting. Unhappily, the *New York Daily Tribune,* probably reflecting administration views, interpreted the language of the Matta reply as a "refusal to accept responsibility for the affair" and made much of the defiant and insulting tone.[21]

Chilean diplomacy may have been dependent entirely on Matta's decisions, but it is interesting to consider the reaction of the astute Chilean minister to the United States, Pedro Montt. A "small, shrewd looking Spaniard with a dark complexion," Montt was apparently well regarded in the United States. Fenton R. McCreery, secretary at the U.S. legation in Santiago, met with him on several occasions and was much impressed.

Dined with Sr. Pedro Montt, the Chilean Minister at his Lega-tion. . . . Montt is very affable—he is not a brilliant man but a hard student—a plodder. He is struggling with English at present. He has gained a great reputation among reporters for reserve in these times when Chili has become so interesting to the American public by his remark: "I do not talk with my mouth." Pedro Montt is looked upon as one of the ablest lawyers in Chili and is a member of the Chilian House of Deputies.[22]

Montt held several conferences with Blaine when the secretary finally returned to office on October 26. Montt assured Blaine that Chilean authorities would investigate the affair and apply penalties to those Chileans found guilty, "Contrary charges that have been published can only be erroneous." He boldly insisted "there was no bad disposition in Chile toward North American citizens." Writing to Matta afterward, Montt said that his conferences produced the impression that the "spirit which animated Mr. Blaine was one of peace and very distinct from that which had been inspired by the instructions sent to Mr. Egan before Blaine's return to the Minis-try." Montt noted that Blaine promised to take no steps before the *sumario* concluded and had complained, "In Chile I am misun-derstood. I do not want difficulties or questions, only peace and good friendship." Montt concluded that Blaine sought patience and har-mony and that his policy would reverse the antagonism inspired by Wharton's instructions to Egan. On November 9 he wrote to the Ministry of Foreign Relations to report that the excitement pro-duced by the *Baltimore* affair had diminished significantly, citing as evidence the tranquil tone of the U.S. press.[23] True enough, the Democratic press also seemed aware of what Montt interpreted as Blaine's policy reversal. The *New York Times* even suggested Blaine might be attempting to embarrass Harrison since the two were "animated by mutual jealousy, and each watching for an oppor-tunity to put a check upon the other."[24]

THE CHILEAN INVESTIGATION soon exacerbated matters. Schley learned on October 20 that the intendente would not give him details of the *sumario*.[25] On October 31 he reported that the imprisoned sailors of the *Baltimore* had been examined secretly, "although an officer of the ship was sent to court to request that he be allowed to be present at the examination."[26] Schley discovered that Chilean judicial proceedings were always secret up to a point. He also learned that before being discharged the sailors were required to sign a paper, written in Spanish. When one of the sailors asked a court official to translate the paper, his request was denied and he was informed that "it was nothing but mere form." Tracy instructed Schley not to allow any of his men to appear at a secret investigation and to testify only if accompanied by an officer who could speak Spanish. He then added another stipulation: not only must the crew's testimony be taken in English, but each must be able to read over his statement and sign copies, one to be kept by Schley, one sent to the State Department. The Chileans refused, and Schley attempted to explain that the Chilean *sumario* was akin to a grand jury inquiry.[27]

It seemed as if the *sumario* deliberately had been designed to annoy U.S. officials. The insistence on an officer to act as counsel, open testimony, and copies of the declarations would be contrary to the secrecy that Chilean law required. Still, Schley pressed the Chileans on the issue throughout the month of November.

And there were other problems. On November 5 the Chilean judge of crimes subpoenaed Talbot, Panter, Hamilton, Davidson, and Turnbull. Schley determined that his men were not in suitable enough physical condition to appear before the *sumario* and took the opportunity of embarrassing the Chilean authorities by reminding them of Turnbull's death. As for the others, the *Baltimore*'s surgeon was "of the opinion that their appearance at the court for the present would be inadvisable, as they are still too weak and nervously shattered to undergo the ordeal of such excitement." It was not until November 17 that the captain informed the intendente that his men would appear, and it was not until November 20 that the men began testifying. Not surprisingly, the crew members recovered their strength at nearly the same time that

Schley cleared up the conditions under which the men would testify.[28]

Another delay in the *sumario* developed when on October 29 the judge requested that Schley provide whatever data about the riot he might have collected. Schley implied that all such information had been passed on to the U.S. minister and then sent Egan a list of six witnesses to the assault. Egan feared that Schley's terse note to the intendente had been confusing and asked Schley to suggest that Chilean authorities contact him. The Chileans, frustrated, became convinced that the U.S. minister was holding up the investigation. On December 3, in Washington, Pedro Montt left Blaine a copy of a note he had received from Matta. Written on December 1, the message indicated that the *sumario* had not yet finished because Egan's testimony had still not been furnished although asked for twenty days before. Montt would register the same complaint again on December 11.[29]

The negotiations began to heat up. Schley wrote the intendente that because of lack of protection he was unable to allow even his officers to go ashore in market boats. Arlegüi ordered the Valparaiso police commander to post an officer with appropriate force at the entrance to the port. He suggested, however, that since Schley and his countrymen obviously held so little regard for the Chilean police force, such problems of protection would be left to Schley's discretion and prudence.[30]

At long last the Chilean investigation began to move, and despite his insistence on secrecy, Matta sent Egan a summary of the progress of the *sumario* on October 30. He had received two reports, he said, one from the chief of police, Colonel Ezequiel Lazo, and one from the intendente, denying as unfounded and "inexact" Egan's charges against the police: "They did no more than comply with their duty without mistreating any of the foreign sailors." It is likely that those two reports as well as other summaries of the investigation that leaked out all through November formed the basis of the subsequent diplomatic confrontation. It would arise in part from differing interpretations of the riot and from Egan's anger at being told that the proceedings were secret while the Chilean press published letters about the *sumario* from the judge to the intendente.[31]

Winfield Scott Schley, Captain of the USS *Baltimore*. From *Harper's Weekly*, January, 1892. Courtesy Indiana University Library.

The question that provoked the most controversy dealt with the sobriety of the sailors. While it was impossible to resolve, it became critical to everything involved. Since the *sumario* had the sailors' admission that they were frequent visitors to saloons, the Chileans concluded they were drunk. Schley insisted the sailors were sober. Even assuming that seamen who had not enjoyed liberty for almost three months might seek such recreation, recognizing the part of Valparaiso they frequented, realizing the sailors were hardly tee-totalers, their presence in that neighborhood was no proof the riot was merely a drunken sailors' brawl. But perhaps the question of the sailors' sobriety was, in a word, academic. Captain Robley D. Evans, commander of the *Yorktown,* whose ship joined the *Baltimore* in Chilean waters soon after the riot, added to the uncertainty of the issue by relating an early encounter with Schley:

He [Schley] was in the midst of a correspondence with the Intendente, conducted in the most perfect Castilian, to show, or prove, that his men were all perfectly sober when they were assaulted on shore. I did not agree with him in this, for in the first place I doubted the fact, and in the second it was not an issue worth discussing. His men were probably drunk on shore, properly drunk; they went ashore, many of them, for the purpose of getting drunk, which they did on Chilean rum paid for with good United States money. When in this condition they were more entitled to protection than if they had been sober. . . . Instead of protecting them, the Chileans foully murdered these men, and we believed with the connivance and assistance of armed policemen. That was the issue— not the question of whether they were drunk or sober.[32]

During the *sumario* one of the *Baltimore*'s crew, Coalheaver Patrick McWilliams, unfortunately did appear before the Chilean court so intoxicated it was necessary to eject him. Tracy learned about this contretemps from a British newspaper and asked Schley about it. The captain answered that while Lieutenant McCrea, in charge of the testifying men, was assisting in authenticating testimony, he gave permission for some men to eat supper, and when McWilliams returned to sign his statement he was "intoxicated and discourteous to the judge, for which offense he has been tried by summary courtmarshal [*sic*] and punished."[33] Foster Recábarren noted in a letter to the intendente the "inevitable excesses that people of the sea always exhibit when they go ashore, even when it is to comply before the justice of a friendly, hospitable nation, and even when they are under the immediate supervision of the cultured and honorable officer who conducts them." This incident, he hoped, "will make the commander of the *Baltimore* aware, better than accusations, of the true origin . . . of the disorder of October 16."[34]

The indefatigable Schley went on collecting information and on

November 25 sent a written report. He reviewed the attempts to hasten the *sumario*, request representation at the examination of the *Baltimore* sailors, secure release of the imprisoned seamen, and sort out the issues determining the guilt of the individuals. He lamented the death of Turnbull. He was almost certain that if Turnbull had been brought to the *Baltimore* in the morning following the assault, where he would have had more skillful treatment by the ship's surgeons, "his life might have been saved, but detained as he was for several days in the prison ward of the San Juan de Díos Hospital, where his wounds were hardly attended, and surely not properly, this poor fellow had a losing battle to fight when he was finally handed over to us." Schley's supplementary report is mostly a narrative, but his concluding remarks regretted that none of the Chilean newspapers expressed a demand for a full investigation. He claimed the Chileans "sought to count it as an offense of the *Baltimore's* crew, and they have industriously spread the idea that the brutal butchery of two of my men and the grave wounding of five others was a trifling affair."[35]

Schley was right on one account. In the aftermath of a civil war in which a conservative figure was ten thousand dead, the deaths of two U.S. sailors did not seem important. The *Chilian Times* of November 7 attributed what was by now called the *Baltimore* imbroglio to fabrication by a few individuals and counseled "coolheaded patience . . . to release the strain on the relations between the huge and powerful Republic of North America and the small but vigorous Republic of South America." Because both the United States and Chile were civilized powers, inquiry into the deaths was justified; so too would be a reasonable indemnity if the attack was due to negligence or an "unprovoked outburst of popular animosity," but because Blaine had embarrassed the United States in the *Itata* incident, surely he would not again use behavior that would "cause him to stand self-exposed as a blustering and consequently vulgar bull," especially after he had just abandoned the role of "upholder of a merciless tyrant, and a stumbling block in the way of a united people struggling for constitutional liberty."[36]

Behind the scenes Chilean officials were beginning to worry, and on November 3 the judge of crimes wrote the minister of justice to explain the difficulties in completing the *sumario*. He hoped the minister would defend Chilean justice, even if the United States did not. More important was a note he sent to Matta, expressing surprise that a common crime was being "carried into the craggy domain of diplomacy."[37]

The asylum issue flared, for Egan intimated that spies of the Chilean secret police stationed near the U.S. legation were molesting and insulting its inhabitants. Viewed through the narrow U.S. prism of diplomacy, Chilean behavior did not measure up.

U.S. OBSERVERS became convinced of their righteousness when the case of Patrick Shields became public in November. Not only did that case complicate the involvement of diplomacy in matters of Chilean justice, but it provided evidence that U.S. citizens were unsafe in the hands of Chilean authorities.

A native of Ireland, Shields was a thirty-year-old fireman aboard the U.S. merchant steamer *Keweenaw,* which in October was in Chilean waters, proceeding from Brooklyn. On Saturday, October 24, Shields was granted liberty by the captain and chief engineer and went ashore about 6:30 P.M. He visited an English restaurant, where he claimed he drank two bottles of beer with his shipmate Andrew McKinstry. The two sailors went to a barber shop, and later about 11:00 P.M., Shields, walking around the main plaza alone, was arrested by a policeman who said, "You are drunk," and took him to prison, over his protests that he was sober. Shields remained in jail overnight.[38]

During the night Shields had his hat stolen by inmates. He appealed to a guard who could speak English, indicating who had taken his hat. The guard only laughed, and Shields testified later that repeated requests to see the U.S. consul or the captain of his ship were denied. When he was released around 9:00 A.M. Sunday, without any hearing, he went to buy another hat, was arrested by a policeman about a half mile from the police station, and again locked up overnight. That was not the end of Shields's troubles. The following two days he was made to sweep the streets from sunrise to sunset and was clubbed and kicked if he stopped. At the end of the second day he was released and tried to get down to the pier, but because he had no money he went up a hill and slept that night on the ground, having been told by a Chilean that "an American citizen's life was not safe in Valparaiso."[39] Wednesday morning he again attempted to get down to a cutter to board his ship, but before reaching the pier he was arrested and taken to jail and there made to work in the horse shed cleaning the stables; grinding corn; carrying water, hay, and oats; and sweeping. Around noon he escaped and ran about a quarter mile before he was captured. He was beaten on the neck, arms, and back with a stick—until the stick broke, he said. He was struck with a broom. He returned to the horse shed for two more days, beaten if he slackened his pace. He claimed to have vomited "about a quart of blood and bled from the nose and ears in consequence of the beating."[40]

On Sunday, November 2, he was released, and this time went straight to the U.S. consulate. Finding it closed, unable to pay for a cutter to take him to his ship, unable to discover the private residence of the consul, he slept on a hill until the following morning, when about 8:00 A.M. he went to the consulate for medical attention. After testifying about his treatment, he was taken aboard the *Keweenaw,* whose captain had reported him as a deserter.[41]

On November 7, Egan communicated to Washington officials the treatment of Shields. Consul William McCreery of Valparaiso had already informed the intendente and asked for an investigation.[42] Arlegüi told McCreery that the judge of crimes had begun an examination and assured the consul that "full and impartial justice will be done." Again the judge rejected a plea for an open investigation, claiming compliance would violate Chilean laws, also intimating that McCreery was tendering "dishonorable suspicion that the court of crimes of Valparaiso might conduct the investigation, not with the purpose of impartiality and rectitude . . . but in a sense contrary to the rights of the complaining seaman."[43] McCreery also sent a report made by Passed Assistant Surgeon White of the *Baltimore,* who examined Shields and found his injuries serious: severe contusion of the back of the head, small cut over the right eye, body severely bruised, back and front, from the nape of the neck to the end of the spine, "unfit for duty for several weeks."[44]

Upon inquiry to the chief of police of Valparaiso, McCreery

learned that Shields's name was not in the arrest books at the police station. Chilean law provided that all persons arrested be brought before the judge of crimes within twenty-four hours from the time of arrest. Authorities explained that names of those arrested for drunkenness and not accused of additional offenses were not entered.[45]

The Chileans then took Shields's testimony aboard the *Keweenaw*. A crew member, Charles A. Wheeler, told McCreery that two men boarded and asked to see Shields, who declined to give testimony outside the presence of the U.S. consul, and who, after replying to a few preliminary questions and reading what the Chileans wrote he had said, declined to sign an affidavit, believing it incorrect. His declaration was given on November 18 to Vice Consul August Moller, Jr. Along with that statement, the engineer in charge of the *Keweenaw,* Charles R. Malcolm, testified that up to the day of his liberty Shields was a "strong, able-bodied man and a most excellent fireman," but since his return to the ship, "he has not been able to perform any manual labor in consequence of the injuries he claims to have received at the hands of the police of Valparaiso, and I am firmly of the opinion that he will never again be able to perform the duties of fireman."[46]

Andrew McKinstrey, fireman and liberty companion of Shields, testified he was also arrested and taken to prison, where he was put in the same cell as Shields, who had been arrested the previous day. They both worked in the horse shed and as corn grinders. While sweeping the streets together, McKinstrey escaped, slept on a hill at the back of the city, and next day reported at the consulate. He claimed to have mentioned that Shields was imprisoned, but the consul failed to act.[47]

In a message to Blaine on November 23, Egan called Shields's a case of "most brutal treatment without the excuse of any process of law." He enclosed a letter from Shields with a claim against the Chilean government for five thousand dollars in gold. The situation became more complicated when McCreery admitted that the roster of the steamer showed Shields born in Ireland and consequently a subject of Britain. Egan resolved the problem by referring to consular instructions that in a case where a national of another nation shipped under the U.S. flag, "the crew will find their protection in the flag."[48]

The Shields case reinforced the assertion that the Chilean police used undue force towards U.S. sailors and lacked all humanitarian instincts. Moreover, there was never a categorical denial of Shields's claim by the Chilean authorities.[49] Their professions of ignorance or attempts to make the incident trivial were unconvincing.

Egan notified Matta that when Shields came to the consulate he was taken to the intendencia so that Arlegüi might witness his deplorable state. The intendente refused to view Shields's injuries. Egan concluded that the injuries inflicted on the fireman were due to "some laxity or defect in the police system which permits the retention and compulsory employment at menial labor of persons without the sanction of the judicial power."[50] On November 25, Matta charged Egan with claiming censurable conduct by the judge of crimes worse than that of Shields's assailants. He summed up the Chilean position by observing, "In all the series of grave charges against the police, against the judge, and against the Intendente of Valparaiso there are not, besides the information of Shields, any other evidence than that of persons of the consulate and of the North American ship." This, he declared, did not prove that the acts complained of could be considered established. If they wished to discuss the commission of a "criminal error or forget-fulness" by responsible Chilean authorities, Matta asked that the United States provide reports on ill treatment of Shields, how and when he was put in prison, what judicial investigations were made or omitted on shore or on board the *Keweenaw,* and "peculiar cir-cumstances."[51] Piqued, Egan replied on December 4 that the "cir-cumstances of the case are all peculiar."[52]

On November 23 the *Keweenaw* left for the United States, and a few days later Shields wrote Consul McCreery of his own concerns, as well as he was able to articulate them:

Dear Sir I take the favourable oppertunity to write you those few lines hoping the may find you in good health which I cannot Say this leves me at present from the ill treatment I recieved in Valparaiso I now fear it is going to be more Serious than what I expected for I am

suffering from a great pane underneath my Heart and around my
Kidneys this pain has affected me so Serious I am greatly afread I
am Paralysed Dear Sir on the evening we left the Harbour there was
a boat came along side from the Chillie autheriots ashore the had a
paper with them and the wanted to take me ashore with them but
the chief officer would not let them disturb me because I was very
poolery at the time Dear Sir I thought it would be wiser to let you
know about this boat coming as you might want to know.[53]

The case, however, was soon overshadowed by the *Baltimore* affair.
Shields was examined in December by an investigating board at
Mare Island. The Chileans insisted that Shields, intoxicated, was
taken to jail for his own protection, that his bruises resulted from
chronic drunkenness, that the matter was no concern of the United
States because Shields was a British subject. Nonetheless, in a
protocol signed at Washington on May 24, 1897, Chile presented to
the heirs of Shields (who died in California in January, 1895, of
undetermined cause) $3,500 as final settlement for his claim.[54]

5. *The Making of a Fight*

A NEW PHASE of negotiation over the *Baltimore* affair opened early in December, 1891, when President Harrison began to show irritability toward the Chileans. For more than six weeks the president had taken no active part in diplomacy, although whether or not he acted behind the scenes is difficult to assess. The Chilean government might have been confused by the conflicting sources of U.S. authority for the negotiation and might not have known where to appeal. Should it be to Egan, Schley, Tracy, Blaine, or Wharton? The Chileans could not be sure. In that sense Harrison's obvious intervention was fortunate, for as it clarified U.S. lines of authority, it also clarified the nature of the U.S. response.

IF BENJAMIN HARRISON was not the most attractive figure ever to hold the office of president of the United States, it made no difference in the exercise of his official duties. Charm and magnetism are not requirements for election to high office in the United States, and such qualities cannot insure a successful tenure. Harrison disliked adulation and never seemed to understand that a well-placed compliment was not evidence of perfidy and might even be necessary to the workings of the average human psyche. He was intensely reserved and dignified, which sometimes gave the impression he was unsympathetic. It was not true that when he entered a room the temperature dropped twenty degrees, or that he could carry a piece of ice in his pocket in the heat of July without losing a drop, or that he was as "glacial as a siberian stripped of his furs."[1] He was not the "White House iceberg."[2] But he seemed unable or unwilling to display the sort of emotional warmth that attracts the U.S. public to its leaders. John W. Foster once suggested carefully that had Harrison "possessed something of Mr. Blaine's fascinating manner, he would have made an ideal president."[3]

If achievement in U.S. politics requires ability, Harrison undeniably possessed talent. Like the ideal of the Puritan elders of New England, he seemed almost without ambition—believing himself forced by circumstance to take on the responsibility of high office. His lack of competitive drive did not indicate that he was incompetent. He was determined, loyal, hardworking, and thoughtful. Integrity was the key to his temperament, and while that may not have made him a charming individual, one had to admire his "instinct to do the polite, honest, dignified thing in every contingency."[4] Harrison's austere manner may have contributed to an image of unsolicitousness. Still, many astute contemporaries concluded that Harrison was a man of ability, "perhaps the best President the Republican Party had put forward since Lincoln's death."[5]

Like Woodrow Wilson of later years, Harrison was able to reach out more effectively to large groups of people rather than to individuals. He was an orator, which is no small attribute in U.S. politics, and if success in politics could be measured by articulateness, few nineteenth-century political figures equalled Harrison. A small man, with graying auburn hair, full gray beard, piercing blue eyes, he had a forceful, high, clear voice that projected vigorously. While he believed it was more important to be a gentleman than an orator, contemporaries agreed that he spoke extraordinarily well. He spoke earnestly, lucidly, convincingly, and demonstrated absolute confidence in himself. "If people could have just heard those splendid speeches," Senator Joseph Foraker of Ohio later wrote, "and then gone straight home and remembered how fine it was and never, never tried to shake the speaker's hand that was so like a wilted petunia—well, history might have been different."[6]

Harrison had won far less than a vote of national confidence in the election of 1888, where he received almost one hundred thousand fewer votes than the incumbent president and Democratic candidate, Grover Cleveland. His strength, instead, was in the electoral college. The grandson of President William Henry Harrison, great-grandson of a signer of the Declaration of Independence, Benjamin Harrison had enjoyed a long career in Indiana politics, due primarily to his name, his military record in the Civil War, his unshakable loyalty to the GOP, and his reputation as an orator and lawyer. With his election the Republicans controlled the presidency as well as both houses of Congress for the first time since the apogee of Grantism in 1874.

Although Harrison's victory filled an immediate national need for party leadership in 1888, the new president was unable to maintain the party harmony that produced his election. He was unskilled in the art of manipulation. He disliked patronage, logrolling, bargaining—in short, the tools of the nineteenth-century politician's trade. Although he was titular head of the Republican party, he was not its idol. His devout Presbyterianism, doctrinaire morality, and obstinate decency led some pundits to think he was "more than a little vain."[7] Others saw him as a relic of the eighteenth century. Still others concluded that he was unresponsive, erudite, a dainty aristocrat who "when sitting appeared to be a big man, and when standing a small one."[8] Easily irritable and impatient, demonstrating little sense of humor or capacity for happiness, rigidly formal, cold and distant, Harrison from the moment of his election was unsatisfactory to the professionals of the Republican party.[9]

What reasons persuaded Harrison to interfere in the *Baltimore* affair? There were several causes that moved this cold, cautious, capable U.S. political personality to action. For one, there was patriotism, the almost mystical patriotism of the late nineteenth century—a combination of excessive national chauvinism, ethnocentrism, and a romantic, gallant, sporting view of war. The bugles of the Civil War were distant and muffled by 1891; the campfires long had been cold. The ghastly bloodshed of those years was forgotten, replaced by idyllic visions of bravery, heroism, and comradeship. Like so many men of his generation, Harrison could never forget those great days. Any call to action in behalf of the nation could bring an almost instinctive response.

Harrison's patriotism surely helped persuade him to interfere in the *Baltimore* affair, but there was also his sense of duty as president of the United States, his right to order the foreign relations of the nation. As president he had a responsibility to keep an eye on foreign policy. In appointing Blaine secretary of state he had made it absolutely clear that foreign affairs was a function of the chief executive. Responding to the president, Blaine had agreed. Moroever, Blaine's health was poor. Respectful of Blaine's abilities and political influence, Harrison might not have taken a leading part in the *Baltimore* imbroglio if Blaine had not been ill and away from the State Department from May to late October in 1891.

Harrison could also have become involved in the crisis in order to help position himself against an upcoming political challenge from either Blaine within his own party or Grover Cleveland and the Democrats. The presidential election of 1892 was approaching, and although no evidence has been uncovered that explains the president's behavior or motives solely in political terms, his sudden interest and public involvement in the *Baltimore* affair might just as accurately be explained by political considerations as any other.

The obvious occasion for a presidential statement about the *Baltimore* embroilment, an occasion of political and constitutional import and an occasion that because of his own peculiar talents attracted the president, was the Annual Message on the State of the Union, delivered in December. Harrison devoted much of his annual message of 1891 to the affair. It began with mistaken remarks about the Chilean civil war's "infrequent and not important armed collisions." Having recognized the Balmaceda cause as lost, he said, he had directed Minister Egan "to recognize and put himself in communication" with the provisional government established by the victorious Congressionalists. During the civil war appeals had been made to extend belligerent rights to the insurgents and give audience to their representatives in the United States, but the Washington government, in Harrison's view, had correctly declined. The *Itata* incident occurred when an armed vessel of the insurgents was seized for violation of U.S. neutrality laws. "It would have been inconsistent with the dignity and self-respect of the Government not to have insisted that the *Itata* should be returned to San Diego to abide the judgment of the court," according to Harrison. He was sure that the *Itata*'s act of defiance was so obvious to the Congressionalists in Iquique that even before the *Itata*'s arrival they told Rear Admiral Brown they would put the vessel at the

President Benjamin Harrison. Courtesy Library of Congress.

disposition of the United States. A U.S. district court had concluded that "inasmuch as the Congressional party had not been recognized as a belligerent, the acts done in its interest could not be a violation of neutrality laws." In the president's view the United States had acted in a dignified manner, accepting the court's decision.[10]

During the Chilean civil war, Harrison continued, the U.S. government had proposed its good offices to bring a mediation of the conflict but was vastly disappointed in the effort. Instructions to naval officers and to Egan "from the first to the last of this struggle enjoined upon them the most impartial treatment and absolute noninterference." Those instructions were observed and "our representatives were always watchful to use their influence impartially in the interest of humanity." U.S. officials were mindful of international obligations and careful to maintain formal relations with the Balmaceda regime. In fact, should a revolt against the new president, Jorge Montt, take place, U.S. policy would be the same as toward Balmaceda. Yet people everywhere did not want to believe the truth. Despite the "legitimacy" of the U.S. position during the Chilean crisis, Harrison asserted, "It is a matter of regret that so many of our own people should have given ear to unofficial charges and complaints that manifestly had their origin in rival interests and in a wish to pervert the relations of the United States and Chile."[11]

The address to Congress in December, 1891, was long and detailed. Asylum, Harrison explained, was freely given by U.S. naval vessels and by the U.S. legation at Santiago because the overthrow of Balmaceda put in jeopardy the lives of many of his councilors and officers. Acting on humanitarian impulses, Egan gave asylum and Harrison refused to direct the surrender of fugitives. Chile had no right to deny asylum; the obloquy poured down upon the head of Minister Egan, "undoubtedly the result of the prevailing excitement," called for official protest.[12]

Harrison moved to a discussion of the riot, describing the event of October 16 as "so serious and tragic in circumstances and results as to very justly excite the indignation of our people and to call for prompt and decided action on the part of this Government." He recalled how the unarmed sailors were assaulted by armed men simultaneously in different parts of the city of Valparaiso. So "savage and brutal" was the assault that two sailors died, and others were wounded. The *Baltimore*'s board of inquiry concluded that the assault had been unprovoked, the sailors peaceful and orderly, and that the Chilean police participated by beating and maltreating the sailors. That they were "all discharged, no criminal charge being lodged against any of them, shows very clearly that they were innocent of any breach of peace."[13]

Up to that point the message was nothing unusual, except perhaps in its detailed treatment of the incident. Yet the president's address showed not merely interest but pique and even choler. Halfway through its exposition the speech turned provocative: "So far as I have yet been able to learn no other explanation of this bloody work has been suggested than that it had its origin in hostility to those men as sailors of the United States, wearing the uniform of their Government, and not in any individual act of personal animosity." The U.S. government formally requested Chile to present any information "that might tend to relieve this affair of the appearance of an insult to this Government." If Chile possessed none, the president confidently expected "full and prompt reparation."[14]

Details followed concerning perfidy somewhere in Chile, and the president was extraordinarily clear. He noted that the communique in October from Foreign Minister Matta was "couched in an offensive tone"; he awaited the result of the Chilean *sumario;* he expected an "adequate and satisfactory response." Harrison ended on a foreboding note: "If these just expectations should be disappointed or further needless delay intervene, I will, by a special message, bring this matter again to the attention of Congress for such action as may be necessary."[15]

Although Harrison revealed a disposition to push the Chileans because of Matta's apparent hostility and Chile's lack of etiquette in diplomacy, the annual message did not make much of an impression on the U.S. public. For some reason few people noticed it. The *New York Times* was one of the only papers that mentioned Chile in its coverage of the speech; Harrison's message contained one paragraph, it reported, that was "really sensational in its suggestiveness":

The intimation of the President plainly means that unless Chile apologized for its assault upon our sailors and makes an explanation satisfactory to our Government, Congress will be asked to authorize the President to employ the military and naval forces of the United States to compel reparation. The assumption is, among observers of naval movements, that the President does not expect any expression of regret from Chile, and that he will be compelled to sustain the respectful demand already made by a display of force. . . . There is no doubt about what the Congress will do, if the Administration can make a clear case of unprovoked assault and refusal to apologize against the Chileans, and considerations of economy will not be weighted against the importance of asserting the national self-respect and sense of justice.[16]

Was the *New York Times* correct in assuming Harrison meant to employ force against Chile? The issue received more public recognition later, when Secretary Tracy devoted a full ten pages to it in his annual report, describing at length the details of the riot, especially the death of Riggin, the brutality used to arrest the sailors, the wounds suffered by the crew. Not unexpectedly his conclusions were similar to Harrison's. Believing the conduct of the navy during the Chilean civil war "fair, just, and temperate," Tracy insisted that his instruction to preserve absolute fairness and impartiality was carried out to the letter. In a narrative of great length Tracy dismissed the Chilean accusations concerning the *Itata*, the cable, and the Quinteros Bay episodes. He concluded that it was impossible to account for the "outrages perpetrated" on the *Baltimore*'s crew except to believe that "those who concerted them were influenced by the calumnies which had been actively circulated, . . . aided and abetted by a police guard which should have suppressed them." None of the U.S. sailors had been indicted for misconduct, and it was certain that on the night of October 16 innocent men without weapons had sought only to defend themselves and were "driven by police to a Chilean prison because they wore the uniform of American sailors."[17]

IN A FIT of miscalculation and what U.S. officials interpreted as deliberate insult, the Chileans began to call attention to President

Harrison's message and thus raised it to prominence both in Chile and the United States. Foreign Minister Matta's response was immediate and direct. Egan on December 12 cabled Blaine the copy of Matta's response printed in the *Diario Oficial,* as well as the usual translated version, explaining that he was sending both "to avoid errors or misunderstanding." Beyond that he had written the Chilean Ministry of Foreign Relations for verification that the published text was correct.[18]

Intended to answer Harrison's and Tracy's messages, Matta's response set out its point: "Having read the portion of the report of the Secretary of the Navy and of the message of the President of the United States, I think proper to inform you that the statements on which both reports and messages are based are erroneous or deliberately incorrect." Matta first directed attention to the asylum issue: "With respect to the persons to whom an asylum has been granted, they have never been threatened with cruel treatment, nor has it been sought to remove them from the legation, nor has their surrender been asked for. Never has the house nor the person of the plenipotentiary, notwithstanding indiscretions and deliberate provocations, been subjected to any offense." He was most concerned with the *Baltimore* affair, "With respect to the seamen of the *Baltimore,* there is, moreover, no exactness nor sincerity in what is said at Washington." He chose to make public what the judge of crimes long before had told Egan: "The occurrence took place in a bad neighborhood of the city . . . among people who are not models of discretion and temperance. When the police and other forces interfered and calmed the tumult, there were already several hundred people there, and it was ten squares or more from the place where it had begun."[19]

Matta turned to Egan, suggesting that his note of October 26 was "aggressive in purpose and virulent in language" and that the *sumario* had been delayed "owing to undue pretensions and refusals of Mr. Egan himself." He went on, leaping from a listing of the diplomatic problems of U.S. behavior during the Chilean civil war and the *Baltimore* affair to an indictment of Tracy and President Harrison. The Chilean Ministry of Foreign Relations had not been provocative or aggressive, only firm and prudent. Chile would never be humiliated, no matter what erroneous views were held in Washington. "Mr. Tracy and Mr. Harrison have been led into error in respect to our people and Government," he asserted. The minister's conclusion was arrogant and insulting: "Deny in the meantime everything that does not agree with these statements, being assured of their exactness as we are of the right, the dignity, and the final success of Chile, notwithstanding the intrigues which proceed from so low a source and the threats which come from so high a source."

Matta's communication was meant for the Chilean minister, Pedro Montt, in Washington and was never sent to Egan, Tracy, Blaine, or Harrison. Supposedly it was the private correspondence of a minister of foreign relations to his representative. But, as Egan noted, the telegram was read in the Chilean senate, published in the *Diario Oficial* and Chilean newspapers, and forwarded to Chilean legations in Europe. Matta unconvincingly insisted that the telegram was an act of the government communicating instructions to a minister, and so no explanation about its contents, meant as a guide for Pedro Montt, would be given.[20] Just how he expected the U.S. government to respond to his circular is unknown. It was later learned that he had read the message to the senate with the approval of President Jorge Montt and after consultation with the president's cabinet.

Egan knew a response was warranted and was, perhaps unwisely, unwilling to await instructions from the State Department. To capitalize on the situation he labeled the circular "offensive" and declared that until it was withdrawn he would avoid communicating with the Chilean government.[21]

Matta's circular made no effort to conceal his own hostility to the United States and could only be regarded as insulting. And so, U.S. observers began to argue, the message indicated that patience toward Latin American countries was not always the best way to inculcate charity, humility, and justice. U.S. officials would not retreat now from a position of superiority; blame undeniably resided with Chile. Harrison had reacted to what he considered the Chilean government's lack of initiative; he had demonstrated his dissatisfaction. Nevertheless, up to the time of Matta's circular, U.S. diplomacy had been fairly restrained.[22]

IN THIS WAY—the presidential message of Harrison and the circular of Matta—the issue of the *Baltimore* was joined. In the nineteenth century, especially in the last years of that century, national honor was no idle phrase and, indeed, could be the measure of peace or war. It was a time when the government and the people of the United States had enjoyed about a generation of peace and unparalleled economic growth. Ideas and institutions had sometimes failed to keep up with the unprecedented changes the country had experienced. Yet improvements in transportation and communication as well as complicated political changes would influence foreign policy.

As secretary of the navy, Tracy well knew that the U.S. Navy that had arisen during the 1880s was a symbol of power—evidence that the United States was not easily to be insulted. The United States had acquired a new mission in the 1890s: to win prestige and persuade other nations to recognize that a great power existed in the New World. Clearly in possession of the attributes of a great world power but feeling neglected or at least underrated, the United States gained an opportunity in the *Baltimore* affair to display national strength.

In such a time it was bad judgment for the government of Chile to engage the national honor of the United States. Chile was in no position to dictate to the United States, whatever the justice of its position. As the *New York Daily Tribune* put the case early in 1892, with some exaggeration, "It was as undiplomatic and offensive a note as was ever written by a Minister . . . these opening and closing sentences were insolent affronts. When Minister Matta intimated that what the President and Secretary Tracy had written was 'deliberately' untrue, he cast a wanton slur . . . upon them." As for a motive for such insolence, the *Tribune* suggested, "Instructions were apparently sent in a gust of temper which was wholly unprovoked, since the earliest dispatches from Washington respecting the Baltimore outrage were diplomatic in tone and temperate in language."[23]

The issue was joined, and it rose to a crisis. Egan on December 22, 1891, wrote the State Department to ask if he should attend the inauguration of President Montt, to take place on December 26. For lack of a response (the telegram arrived on December 26), he did not attend. The Chileans took the minister's absence as an insult.[24] Pedro Montt met with Blaine on December 28 and reported in a long cable that he discussed U.S.-Chilean relations in detail. Blaine said the United States had several complaints: the Matta circular; delay in the *sumario;* the harassment of the legation in Santiago, as well as the Shields incident. "Mr. Blaine concluded telling me that the U.S. Government had a right to an apology and an indemnization for the deaths of the two Baltimore sailors," Montt noted.[25]

In its calculation or lack of calculation concerning the events of 1891, the Chilean government disregarded a parallel to the *Baltimore* affair that might well have been kept in mind, especially because it occurred almost concurrently with the incident at Valparaiso. In New Orleans, on October 15, 1890, Superintendent of Police David C. Hennessy was murdered. Just before he died, Hennessy told an accompanying friend, "The Dagoes did it."[26] The theory behind the assassination was that the Mafia had resolved to kill Hennessy because of his energetic work in exposing them and bringing them to justice. Since all Italians were suspected members of the Mafia, orders went out to the entire New Orleans police force to arrest any "Italians" they found. After numerous postponements and quashed indictments, on December 13, 1890, a grand jury indicted eleven Italians for murder and conspiracy to commit murder.

The trial of the alleged assassins began on February 16, 1891. There was intense popular interest. It took eleven days to select a jury, and over 1,300 people were questioned in the process. The state of Louisiana called sixty-seven witnesses between February 27 and March 11, and each day as the prisoners were transported to the trial in mule-drawn trucks, the suspected assassins were subjected to the taunts of children who yelled, "Who killa de chief?" The case went to the jury on March 12, and the next day it was all over. The jury was unable to reach a verdict on three of the Italians, and the remaining six were found not guilty.

From the outset the press had helped create the impression that the jury would be intimidated by the Mafia or Italian community. At the same time, the press also contributed to resentment and disapproval of the verdict. As a result, a vigilance committee was formed to rectify the court's decision not to punish the Italians. The committee announced a mass meeting for March 14, at which a crowd estimated at eight thousand assembled, listened to inflammatory speeches, and then rushed the prison in which the Italians were still held. There was no apparent effort by the police or prison officials to stop the mob, and one hour later, the eleven Italians were dead, some shot, others hanged.

After the murders of March 14, Baron Fava, the Italian minister in Washington, wrote Blaine to protest the conduct of the authorities in New Orleans, whom he accused of remaining passive during the riot.[27] Blaine called the incident a "deplorable massacre" and assured Baron Fava that the riot had not been directed against Italians as a race but against criminal elements. Fava replied with two demands: he sought assurance by the U.S. government that the guilty would be tried and he sought official recognition that an indemnity was due to the relatives of the victims. Blaine refused the demands, explaining that the federal government could not guarantee indictments or convictions. Neither could the federal government interfere to protect foreign citizens. The Italians could only appeal to state and local authorities. Whereupon Blaine and Fava began a series of heated debates. Failing to obtain reparation Fava was recalled, the two nations severed diplomatic relations, and correspondence was halted for about a year.

The Harrison administration became irritated by Italy's stand. Blaine wrote that the United States could not be "unduly hurried" or answer demands until the established authorities had ascertained all the facts. Rumor then spread that Italy was sending a warship to New Orleans. Tempers eventually cooled, especially when the Italian Foreign Office learned that only three of the victims had been Italian citizens. In his annual message to Congress on December 9, 1891, in the midst of the *Baltimore* controversy, President Harrison referred to the New Orleans riot as a "most deplorable and discreditable incident . . . an offense against law and humanity." He insisted that the mob's action had not meant any disrespect for Italy, and notwithstanding Fava's absence from Washington the president hoped for a "friendly conclusion." He refused to act further, however, until Italy returned its minister to the United States.[28]

In early April, 1892, the State Department began to discuss the payment of an indemnity. On April 12 the Italian government agreed to accept 125,000 French francs or $24,330.90. Harrison's critics thought it wrong that he settled the controversy without the advice or approval of Congress. They feared, or so they said, that the president was setting a dangerous precedent by working around Congress. But Harrison was mostly censured because Blaine made the indemnity payment out of a diplomatic emergency fund that critics insisted should not have been used. Harrison did not understand why it was necessary to ask Congress for special appropriation or authorization to draw on the emergency fund and ignored the critics.

Apparently, no one in the United States or Chile saw any lessons that might be drawn and applied to the *Baltimore* affair, and in fact the U.S. press went to great lengths to protest any possibility of comparison.[29] In Chile the possibility of imitating the Harrison administration's stand on the protection of foreigners was never considered, even though in May and June of 1891 the *Chilian Times* gave extensive coverage to the New Orleans incident—photos and stories taken from *Frank Leslie's Illustrated Newspaper*. In April, 1891, Balmaceda's minister in the United States wrote a forty-eight page despatch to the Chilean Ministry of Foreign Relations concerning the New Orleans incident and the subsequent diplomacy between Baron Fava and Blaine. Lazcano's concluding remarks indicated complete agreement with the U.S. government's position: "Only in the case of some grave negligence . . . on the part of the authorities could one accord an indemnity through diplomatic channels." The Chileans in 1892 might well have remembered Lazcano's position and reasserted it in the *Baltimore* affair, claiming that as the U.S. government denied negligence in protecting Italians in New Orleans, so the Chileans could deny responsibility for the incident in Valparaiso. They did not, perhaps not desiring to do anything that might serve to credit a member of the defeated Balmaceda administration. Later, Anibal Cruz, minister to the United States (replacing Pedro Montt), wrote the Chilean Ministry of Foreign Relations to announce that the difficulty between the Italian and U.S. government had been successfully settled, but no one in the Jorge Montt administration ever used the U.S. position in the New Orleans riot to support Chile's position in the *Baltimore* affair.[30]

Meanwhile there was a new U.S. naval presence in Valparaiso. After the *Baltimore*'s departure from Chilean waters on the very day of the publication of the Matta circular, U.S. interests in Chile were guarded by the gunboat *Yorktown,* under Commander Robley D. Evans, who was a man to defend U.S. interests in ways that the Chileans—and Evens' countrymen—would clearly understand. By 1891 "Fighting Bob's" visage did not yet have the hardened look of determination and irritability that it bore years later, when he was much photographed as the commander of the Great White Fleet. But he was a man to reckon with. Years before, during the Civil War, he had taken part in the Peninsular Campaign and been shot in both legs. Later, lying helpless in a hospital, he was approached by a Union surgeon who suggested amputation. Evans pulled out a pistol and said he would shoot at the first sign of a surgeon's saw, and the surgeon concluded Evans would die. He survived, although for the rest of his life he walked stiff-legged. That was the man who replaced Schley at Valparaiso.

Fortunately for history, Evans at the time kept a diary, later published as *A Sailor's Log: Recollections of Forty Years of Naval Life,* and in it one can read about both his feelings and his actions while at Valparaiso. He considered himself the epitome of forbearance in the presence of the inferior Latins of South America. He hoped to quell anti-American feelings by good behavior, but his job was not easy. A diary entry for December 4, 1891, made clear his good intentions: "Strongly as I feel on the subject, I can not see any good reason why I should not be perfectly civil and polite to them, even if I have to shoot them tomorrow." On December 13 he noted, "The feeling to-day is very unsettled, owing to Matta's foolish and insolent letter published yesterday." Days later he sought to take advantage of the Christmas spirit by accepting an invitation to a party for Chilean children, an assemblage that ended in fiasco: "The grown people were as nasty a mob as I ever met . . . one after another had something disagreeable to say about the United States. One and all of them hated the officers of our navy . . . and they did not hesitate to tell me so. . . . I returned to my ship feeling as no Christian ought to feel on Christmas ever."[31]

Evans cut a dramatic figure in Valparaiso harbor, and before long he turned nasty, which was not difficult for him. He soon learned that sailors going ashore for supplies were followed, scowled at, and stoned in Valparaiso. With great courtesy he apparently notified the commander of the Chilean squadron in the harbor that unfriendly action would cause him to conclude that the civil populace was beyond the control of local authorities, and he would have to arm his boats and order anyone insulting or harming his sailors to be shot. According to his diary, while he himself was ashore on December 30, three "villainous-looking scoundrels" followed him at a distance, "muttering about damned Yankees."[32]

About that time Evans began to comment on the political dimensions of the *Baltimore* negotiations in the United States. He was perturbed that some U.S. leaders were suggesting the dispute be mediated or arbitrated by a disinterested third party. The last day in December he wrote, "When the United States is willing to submit the question of the murder of her sailors in uniform to arbitration, I must look for other employment—the navy won't any longer suit me." As for Egan, Evans was certain the minister was doing only as he had been instructed, "and he has done it capitally well. The Chilean Secretary of State has found himself outclassed every time he has tackled the little Irishman, who really writes clearly, forcibly, beautifully."[33]

During a New Year's Eve celebration the Chileans caused Evans great trouble:

As the Cochrane [a Chilean warship] fired the first gun of her salute she sent off a flight of rockets. One of them, a war rocket, just missed the Yorktown. We were in plain view on account of the beams of the numerous search lights from the Chilean war vessels, and it seemed that the rocket must have been purposely aimed at us; but there was room for doubt. . . . I at once hoisted a large American flag and turned both my search lights on it, so that if anyone really wanted to hit me he could know just where I was.[34]

That incident was followed by another, more provocative, perhaps apocryphal, involving torpedo boats. Ordered to practice drills in the port and seeming to use the *Yorktown* as a target, Chilean ships passed so close to the vessel they nearly collided. Evans protested, and legend has it that he received a sneering reply that Chilean ships could travel in water belonging to the Chilean government. To that he replied that the *Yorktown* was the property of the U.S. government and that if the ship's paint was so much as scratched he would blow the bottom out of the offending torpedo boat. To Evans, the "conduct of the authorities seemed like madness . . . almost as if they intended to force us into war." While Evans did not sense the imminence of war, his diary entry for the new year noted his apprehension:

Taking all this into consideration, the crew of the Yorktown *will sleep at the loaded guns to-night, and every night until I get some better news. While I can not deny to myself that things are on the "ragged edge," so to speak, yet I can not conceive of the Chileans being stupid enough to allow it to come to blows—it seems incredible folly, and yet it may come.*[35]

A FIGHT WAS LOOMING, and now Evans was at the center. In the event of violence President Harrison would be backing him against the pretensions and impertinences of Foreign Minister Matta and the Chilean government. They had insulted the president, the secretary of state, the secretary of the navy, the U.S. minister in Santiago, not to mention the uniform of the U.S. sailors, which was equivalent to the U.S. flag. In the last decade of the nineteenth century those were issues that could lead to war.

6. Harrison and the Jingoes

BY THE END of the year it was evident that U.S. relations with Chile would be directed by President Harrison, who had decided that his nation's prestige, dignity, honor, and indeed international reputation were being tested by the imprudence, impudence, and contempt of an unimportant little country in the Southern Hemisphere. Less important, but bearing on the president's initiative, Harrison personally felt challenged by the Matta circular, which, aside from discourteous and even offensive language, denied and denigrated the president's own position on the origin and course of the *Baltimore* imbroglio. The situation would no longer continue under Blaine's rather casual guidance. Prompted by advisors and friends who, like Tracy, might have been anxious to test the expanding navy, and perhaps in an election year suspicious of the immense popularity of Blaine, Harrison now guided the *Baltimore* affair himself, carrying out his presidential pledge of 1889 to take command of foreign policy.

IT IS A LITTLE-KNOWN FACT that as relations reached their lowest point, Dr. John Trumbull traveled to Washington to see Blaine on behalf of his native Chile. He apparently was invited to Blaine's house for some occasion, and on December 4 the two men talked for an hour and a half. Trumbull found the secretary exceedingly cordial and summarized Blaine's remarks for Chilean officials:

I have known you long by name, Mr. Trumbull. I am pleased to find myself with a descendant of one of the most illustrious men of our war of independence. You carry a name the Americans much respect. I am glad to know you are a deputy in the Chilean congress, and I have wanted to speak with you because I believe that when you return to your country you can lend an important service.

Blaine lamented the diplomatic controversy, insisting that his government had only cordial feelings for Chile. The secretary, Trumbull reported, made much of the ending of the civil war, congratulating Trumbull on the "triumph of the best men."

During the initial meeting Blaine made some sensitive inquiries of his Chilean-American guest: did he not think the victors were proceeding with too much rigor toward the defeated? They had arrested thousands of people, and that increased discontent. Would it not be more important to make former enemies brothers? The victory had been a great one for liberty and the new government could afford to be generous. Persecution always brings bad consequences. A generation earlier the United States fought the greatest war ever known, and the conduct of the North toward the South afterward was one of tremendous generosity. The benefits of benevolent politics were well known. Trumbull should do all in his power to achieve the same generosity toward the defeated former government and in that way lend great service to Chile.

Trumbull thanked Blaine for the advice but warned that the secretary was poorly informed about what had happened following the Chilean revolution. Blaming exaggeration and misrepresentation in the press, he insisted that U.S. newspapers had created a false impression:

There haven't been persecutions, sir. It is certain that there have been many arrests, but this was inevitable given the initial confusion in the wake of the victory. I think, sir, that there is no other case in history which would indicate that in circumstances so difficult, the men invested with rule have acted with more indulgence and good judgement.

The Chilean situation had no parallel with the U.S. Civil War because the cause of the U.S. conflict had not been a reign of terror, presidential tyranny, Northern persecution or assassination. For the good of Chile it would be necessary to punish criminals. The new president and his ministers were just men and would proceed rationally. Responding to Blaine's intimation that climatic characteristics influenced the temperament of peoples around the world, Trumbull assured him that Chileans, like their climate, were temperate, "It is wrong to think that we are 'fire eaters' as the United States press indicates."

Blaine expressed belief that U.S. foreign policy had been operating under the influence of "decided ill will" and without proper guidance from the secretary himself, due to his illness and absence from Washington. He had, he believed, returned in time to calm emotions.

The secretary turned to the issues. Pointing to the asylum granted by Egan to partisans of the defeated regime, he emphasized that most other legations did likewise, and that they all obtained safe conducts for refugees while such documents were denied the refugees of Egan, who had been badgered:

It is not possible, Mr. Trumbull, to tolerate that the United States is treated worse than other nations. We cannot permit that you insult our dignity, and you should not abuse of the fact that we are so powerful . . . and you so weak in comparison. We want to maintain friendly relations with you. For us there would be no glory in war with you. If a powerful nation had dealt with us as you have done—England, for example, I can assure you that we would have easily gone to war, as easily as lifting a hat.

Trumbull placed the blame on U.S. partiality toward Balmaceda in the civil war, and although Blaine insisted that the United States had had to continue to recognize Balmaceda as head of the government, Trumbull argued that Balmaceda had not been the legal president but a usurper, considered so by the Chilean congress and judiciary. Blaine then bluntly refused to discuss Chile's internal political problems. Trumbull returned to the issue of neutrality, insisting that Congressionalists had sought nothing more. If the U.S. government had wished to observe neutrality, its agents in Chile clearly did not know how to implement the instruction. The behavior of those partisan agents created ill will among the Chilean masses but had no influence on officials, who wanted only friendly relations with all nations. The officials admired the United States, some had been educated there; they viewed the great republic to the north with affection.

To illustrate his point Trumbull referred to the *Baltimore* affair, remarking that all Chileans "lament and deplore this unfortunate occurrence." Blaine took the opportunity to mention that the Chilean government had made no statement of regret or indeed any explanation. Trumbull was sure Egan had received manifestations of regret, and the lack of explanation was due to judicial delays in clarifying issues. Someone appeared to be trying to make a controversy out of the kind of insignificant event that frequently occurred with sailors on liberty. It certainly had been imprudent of Captain Schley to permit so many sailors on shore so soon after the establishment of a new government, especially since he knew that the Chilean population was irritated by U.S. naval conduct during the revolution. Trumbull insisted that the charges against the United States "however unjust you esteem them, are not all unfounded."

Because most Chilean ill will seemed to be directed toward Egan, the Anglophobe Blaine tried to suggest that "British influence is responsible for all this." Trumbull, however, while acknowledging Egan's hatred for the English, refused to accept a British connection in the Chilean-American controversy.

Discussion ended on an interesting note. Blaine asked Trumbull if a treaty of extradition existed between Chile and the United States. To Trumbull's negative reply, Blaine asked if there was any reason not to negotiate one. Trumbull could think of none. Blaine then asked Trumbull his feelings about reciprocity, and Trumbull responded that anything increasing commerce was desired, although the difficulty was that the United States produced almost everything Chile produced, with the exception of nitrates. Blaine, cajoling the Chileans to conclude the *Baltimore* affair rapidly, strongly hinted there could be further talks about reciprocity.

The above account of the talk with Secretary Blaine was set down by Trumbull in a memorandum to the Chilean Ministry of Foreign Relations.[1] He ended his communication by remarking on the poor physical appearance of Blaine, who in response to a polite query about his health curtly responded, "I'm very well, thank you." Trumbull thought that if Blaine could convince the U.S. public that his health was fine, he surely would be the next Republican candidate for the presidency.

Trumbull's second talk with Blaine came on December 26, the

day designated in Chile for the inauguration of Jorge Montt as president. The Chilean minister to the United States, Pedro Montt, invited guests to his Washington house in honor of the event, and among them were Secretary and Mrs. Blaine, together with Trumbull. As the latter afterward recalled in a memorandum to Matta:

I was placed next to Mrs. Blaine and was surprised at her beginning a conversation relative to the difficulties between Chile and the United States. She was very well informed as to everything and told me that she had read all the correspondence on the subject. She spoke very frankly and gave me to understand that she was very much troubled at the seriousness of the situation. She told me also that Mr. Blaine was very anxious to avoid war.

After dinner the men, in Victorian fashion, passed into the smoking parlor, and Trumbull had the opportunity to speak again with Blaine. Blaine expressed delight to see Trumbull but also regret that the latter had not yet returned to Chile to help bring a peaceful settlement of pending questions. Blaine spoke frankly, "You know how anxious I am to have matters settled amicably, but I am afraid that if Chile does not give us some satisfaction the situation will become more critical than it is; there is considerable feeling about Chile's action and much as I desire peace I fear the dangers of the situation."

Trumbull agreed that he would like to achieve a peaceful solution and was convinced of the secretary's "earnest desire" for settlement. He asked Blaine to suggest a course that might be acceptable to the United States and Chile. Blaine, careful to preface his remarks, "You understand, of course, Mr. Trumbull that I am not to be cited officially in the matter," recommended that Chile should express regret for the attack on the sailors, explain the event based on the conclusions of the Chilean court of justice, and if the court considered Chile not bound to pay an indemnity, offer to submit the question to arbitration. "This would be perfectly satisfactory and Chile by so doing would 'spike our guns,'" he concluded.

Blaine showed annoyance with events since his last conversations with Trumbull:

Chile has not been very considerate in her treatment of us, and the ill will which you entertain for us has been very clearly manifested. The note addressed by Señor Matta to your foreign representatives was very harsh and our President regarded it as insulting; it created much ill feeling and augmented the dangers of the situation.

Trumbull replied that the Matta circular had been wrongly interpreted, referring not to Harrison but to agents who had misinformed him. At that point Blaine cut off what he deduced would be a lecture and stated, "I am very sorry it was sent." Trumbull now demonstrated his own irritation, regretting not that the Matta telegram was sent but that it caused such ill feeling. He promised to suggest Blaine's proposal of arbitration in hopes it would bring settlement. At that juncture the discussion was interrupted by the approach of a senator who wished to speak with Blaine, and the evidence suggests it was Trumbull's last meeting with Blaine.[2]

There is no way to measure how much Trumbull's two conversations with Blaine influenced either the United States or the Chilean position in the *Baltimore* controversy—especially considering Harrison's ever-increasing control over diplomacy. Yet Trumbull considered the interviews important enough to describe them in detailed messages to Matta.

Available evidence suggests that Manuel Matta was primarily responsible for Chilean foreign policy in the *Baltimore* affair. There is no evidence that President Montt or specific members of the Chilean senate ever formally interceded. Whether because of internal circumstances following the civil war, the order of domestic Chilean politics, or the personal ambitions of Matta, what is clear is that as minister of foreign affairs he was responsible for policy. Surely it would be reasonable for him to assume that his counterpart in the United States, Secretary of State Blaine, was responsible for U.S. foreign policy. If Matta supposed Blaine to be the major force behind U.S. policy, then perhaps Blaine's pacifism, his pleadings for peace as reflected in Trumbull's two memoranda, his repeated efforts for the settlement of all questions, may have led Matta to assume he had not yet pushed the United States to the brink. If it was logical for Matta to conclude that his counterpart had as much power and authority as he, that Blaine's position as communicated to Trumbull demonstrated an unwillingness to make a show of force, perhaps it was logical also for Matta to conclude that Chile could, with impunity, respond to the bluster of the United States president in kind. It is unfortunate that Trumbull's two memoranda may have led the Chilean government to unsound and dangerous conclusions.

THE CHILEAN INVESTIGATION of the riot ended on December 19, taking far too long, so most U.S. observers thought. The *sumario*'s procedures never had been satisfactory to the United States, and understandably neither were the conclusions, which most likely reflected domestic concerns. The procedures were supposed to be confidential but they were not. The Harrison administration was disturbed by Chilean newspaper accounts relating correspondence between officials conducting the inquiry. U.S. officials protested that the *Baltimore* sailors should testify in English and provide their own interpreters. They were dismayed by their inability to obtain a signed copy of each sailor's testimony.

The United States should have been prepared for the *sumario*'s findings. Commander Evans of the *Yorktown* had cabled Tracy on January 4, summarizing a publication by Judge Foster Recábarren: the Chilean judge of crimes had decided the riot was caused by drunken sailors from the *Baltimore* who attacked drunken Chilean sailors; Riggin was killed by a pistol fired by an unknown party; evidence of the officers and crew of the *Baltimore* was being disregarded because of contradictions; the Chilean police were innocent; four Chileans found guilty of taking part would be imprisoned. Evans concluded, "General feelings there [Santiago] and at Valparaiso are unfriendly to the United States; new cabinet conservative but noncommittal."[3]

Egan reported similarly about the judge's report—that the police commander saw an "insignificant quarrel, the cause of which is not known to him." The Chilean doctor was insisting that all of Turnbull's wounds should have been curable in a month, insinuating that his death was not due to his wounds; Riggin's death was caused by a pistol, not a rifle. The *sumario* omitted the testimony of important witnesses, and Egan considered many of the charges against the *Baltimore* crew unjustifiable.[4]

Pedro Montt communicated with the State Department and explained that the *sumario* had been sent to a prosecuting attorney, who examined it and framed an indictment against Chileans and U.S. sailors who were judged responsible. The chief prosecuting attorney of Valparaiso concluded, Montt said, that the riot originated in a brawl between drunken sailors and reflected the character of the neighborhood in which it occurred—a place that is "inhabited by people of disreputable habits and abounds in places for the sale of liquors." From the first moment the police did everything possible to restore order, and all witnesses, including the *Baltimore*'s crew, attested to the admirable conduct of the police. Those who were sentenced to prison were Carlos Gómez, three to five years; Federico Rodríguez, 61 days to 541 days; José Ahumada, 541 days to three years; and to the shock and disbelief of State Department officials, Seaman John Davidson of the *Baltimore*, 541 days to three years. Montt promised that on receiving the official attorney's report he would send it to Blaine, although it exceeded three hundred pages. He concluded that he had received instructions that the "Government of Chile has felt very sincere regret for the unfortunate events which occurred in Valparaiso on the 16th of October." Although incidents of this character are not infrequent in ports receptive to sailors of various nationalities, he continued, the fact that deaths and injuries occurred to persons employed in the service of a friendly nation, "and the frank desires for American cordiality which my Government entertains have led it to cordially deplore the aforesaid disturbance and to do everything in its power toward the trial and punishment of the guilty parties."[5]

The Chilean half-apology did not suffice. Harrison had not tempered his wrath of early December, and he told Blaine to ask Egan whether the Chileans had withdrawn the "personally offensive" parts of the Matta circular. But by that time, because of domestic politics, Matta had been replaced by Luis Pereira, considered friendly to the United States.[6]

An amicable solution might have been close, but the Chilean government now chose an inappropriate moment to express longtime displeasure with Minister Egan. That move can only be viewed as a blunder, no matter how valid the Chilean argument. Pedro Montt told Blaine on January 20 that he had received instructions from his government asking that, "in a desire to cultivate cordial and friendly relations," Egan be removed. Montt declared that Egan was persona non grata and assured Blaine that "the desire of the Government of Chile to draw closer its relations with that of the United States is its motive for taking this step."[7]

Harrison's personal reaction can only be surmised, but it cannot be coincidence that in a strongly worded telegram, unlike any other he had ever sent, Blaine instructed Egan to say that in view of the palpable insult of the Matta circular he did not "deem it necessary to make any present response thereto." If relations did not improve by the withdrawal of the offending telegram and an apology for the entire *Baltimore* episode, no minister in Chile would be needed at all.[8]

Blaine's previously tranquil attitude now changed, and Harrison's hand seems evident. The secretary reminded Montt of complaints about the length of the Chilean judicial proceedings, that the court had taken over eighty days to consider a matter that the United States would have disposed of in two weeks, and the Matta note had not yet been apologized for "by a frank withdrawal":

In regard to Mr. Egan, you complained many times and very bitterly to me. Especially was he deserving of censure, you thought, for not communicating to his Government the brutal murder of some young men who were slain by order of Balmacdea. When on the next day I showed you the dispatch of Mr. Egan, speaking of the incident in severe and proper terms, you acknowledged that you were mistaken. I thought you would be satisfied, but you again spoke disparagingly of Mr. Egan, and I said somewhat impatiently, "Why do you not demand his recall, instead of constantly disparaging him?" intending thereby not to favor his recall, but to put a stop to the frequent mention of Mr. Egan's name.[9]

The request for the recall of Egan raised tempers at the White House to a point where discretion was of secondary importance. Blaine now had to send a harsh and provocative message from the president. He informed Egan on January 21 that the U.S. position was that the riot was an attack on the uniform of the U.S. Navy, caused by hostile feeling toward the United States; the Valparaiso police "flagrantly failed" to protect the sailors, participating in the unprovoked assault, and Riggin was most likely killed by them. The United States, he said, demanded a "suitable apology" and "adequate reparation" for the injury to the sailors and the government.[10]

Blaine was careful to make clear whose opinion he was expressing and how serious the president considered the situation, "You will assure the Government of Chile that the President has no disposition to be exacting or to ask anything which this Government would not, under the same circumstances, freely concede." The president regretted that from the start "the gravity of the questions involved has not apparently been appreciated" by the Chileans, so that an imbroglio in which two U.S. seamen were killed and sixteen seriously wounded and only one Chilean hurt was not distinguished from an ordinary brawl in which the provocation was personal and the participation limited. Blaine continued, "No self-respecting government can consent that persons in its service, whether civil or military, shall be beaten and killed in a foreign territory in resentment of acts done by or imputed to their Government without exacting a suitable reparation." The United States always had recognized that principle and acted on it when injury was done by its people, and furthermore, "in such case the United States has not sought for words of the smallest value or of equivocal meaning in which to convey its apology, but has condemned such acts in vigorous terms and has not refused to make other adequate reparation."

Harrison had told Blaine to have Egan again call attention to the imprudent Matta circular and affirm that the words ascribing untruth and insincerity to Harrison and Tracy "are in the highest degree offensive to this Government." Blaine therefore instructed Egan that although the president had been disposed to regard the circular as indicating a Chilean desire to suspend relations, he had not done so in view of the fact that a reorganization of the Chilean cabinet had been pending. Now the president directed him to say, "If the offensive parts of the dispatch of the 11th of December are not at once withdrawn, and a suitable apology offered, with the same publicity that was given to the offensive expressions, he will have no other course open to him except to terminate diplomatic relations with the Government of Chile."

Harrison had decided to act. When he learned that in response to Egan's attempt to have the new regime disavow the Matta circular, the Chileans had answered evasively, he seems to have revised a bland reply drafted by Blaine into a note in the tenor of an ultimatum. It is possible that the president actually drafted his harsh note earlier but delayed sending it, first on Blaine's appeal, and then because Blaine again fell ill and was away from the department. In fact, at a cabinet meeting where the president's desire for action had begun to prevail against Blaine's pleas for appeasement, the secretary, perhaps coincidentally, suffered a nervous attack and fainted, breaking up the meeting just before the group reached a consensus on Harrison's more aggressive diplomacy. Most likely Harrison held up the ultimatum hoping for a response that would defray the necessity of sending it. Now he could find no reason for delay.

The Chileans did not receive the U.S. note until 10:00 A.M. on Saturday, January 23, apparently because Egan was modifying and translating it into Spanish. Fenton R. McCreery, the young secretary at the legation, had a hand in the work and commented in his diary:

Mr. Egan and myself worked until 2 a.m. and arose again at 6 to continue work on a telegram received from the Secretary of State. The United States Government presented through this Legation an ultimatum to Chili which was delivered at 10 a.m. the 23d. . . . The fact is that Mr. Egan had been so clever in avoiding the diplomatic pitfalls set for him that the Chilian Government would like another man less practiced in his diplomacy. . . . An answer to the ultimatum is promised tomorrow. They are fools enough to provoke a war here. Since my arrival January 6 school boys could not have lost more ground in diplomatic matters than this Chilian Government and the fall of Spanish pride is awful for it is forced up to such an abnormal height.[11]

Although it is impossible to know how the communication was handled in the Chilean Ministry of Foreign Relations, or by whom, it is credible that on a hot summer weekend, another high-handed

Fenton R. McCreery, Secretary of the U.S. Legation at Santiago. Courtesy Michigan Historical Collections, Bentley Historical Library, University of Michigan.

protest from the United States might not have received the highest priority. Either the message was not recognized as an ultimatum, or the people required to translate and deal with it were not available, or the need to respond was simply deferred.[12] Whatever the cause of the delay, and the Chilean archives offer no clue, the Chilean response was not drafted on January 23.

When on Monday morning, January 25, 1892, Harrison personally had not yet obtained the Chilean reply, he threw all caution to the winds. He transmitted to Congress all the correspondence relative to United States–Chilean relations, together with a message reviewing the situation.

His communication of January 25 was described by some contemporary observers as a "masterly message" that "won world approval," and stirred—as it had not been stirred in years—the pride of the United States. Patriots chose to view the statement as indicative of a "powerful yet generous people, who conscious of their own strength, will firmly assert their rights and maintain their dignity, without any disposition to despoil or humiliate their weaker neighbors."[13] Despite histrionics, it is clear that the message intended to provoke a final confrontation. The president had yanked and not simply guided diplomatic maneuvering out of the State Department and delivered it into the hands of Congress.

In his December message Harrison had briefly set out the *Baltimore* affair, and now in his new message of Janaury 25 he recalled his promise to bring the matter to the attention of Congress "for such action as may be necessary."[14] The time had come to present the diplomatic correspondence to Congress, from the Balmaceda revolution to the Mare Island investigation. Instituted by the secretary of the navy on January 7, the Mare Island inquiry examined seventy-two witnesses and throughout January transmitted the accumulating testimony to the president. The fact that the *Baltimore* sailors' testimony differed essentially from the Chilean *sumario,* and did not differ from Schley's or his officers' inquiry, established its truthfulness in the eyes of the president and much of the public. Considering the international questions paramount and emphasizing why Chilean responses were unsatisfactory, the president hoped to convince Congress of the justice of U.S. demands.

Harrison defended Egan, stating that none of his acts proved him unworthy of his position or justified serious criticism. "He has, I think, on the whole, borne himself, in very trying circumstances, with dignity, discretion, and courage, and has conducted the correspondence with ability, courtesy, and fairness." He supported Egan's decision to grant asylum to members of the former Balmaceda government and reprimanded the Chileans for the denial of safe-conducts for the refugees. He pointed out the disrespect "manifested toward this Government by the close and offensive police surveillance of the legation premises" and castigated the secret police, who "offensively scrutinized persons entering or leaving the legation, and on one or more occasions arrested members of the minister's family." On one occasion police agents sought to invade the legation, "pounding upon its windows and using insulting and threatening language towards persons therein." Even the Argentine minister, he said, considered the offense so flagrant that he protested on behalf of the United States.

The president turned to the *Baltimore* affair. Reminding Congress that in his annual message he had concluded that the "bloody work" took its origin in hostility "to these men as sailors of the United States, and not in any individual act or personal animosity," he now explained that an abstract of the Chilean *sumario* had just arrived in Washington. He regretted he could not modify the conclusion announced in his annual message: "I am still of the opinion that our sailors were assaulted, beaten, stabbed, and killed, not for anything they or any one of them had done, but for what the Government of the United States had done, or was charged with having done." The riot was brutal, cowardly, and the president reaffirmed that the *Baltimore* was in Valparaiso by virtue of an invitation that friendly nations extend to one another. He was aware that not every personal collision or injury involving sailors visiting ports raised international questions, but this one had. In cases where sailors were assaulted by residents "animated by hostility to the Government whose uniform these sailors and officers wear, and in resentment of acts done by their Government, not by them," their country was compelled to "take notice of the event as one involving an infraction of its rights and dignity . . . as if its minister or consul, or the flag itself, had been the object of the same . . . assault."

On and on, relentlessly, went the president's message, recounting the circumstances of the riot, the granting of shore leave, the orderly and sober conduct of the men, the unsatisfactory Chilean conclusion that it was impossible to know the cause of the melee, the failure of the Chilean police to arrive quickly at the scene, the fact that unarmed U.S. sailors were pursued by a mob and fought "only to aid their own escape from death" or to succor some mate whose life was in peril, and the brutal stabbing and beating of eighteen U.S. sailors.

The president expressed disapproval of the Chilean response, complaining that Chilean communications had not "taken the form of a manly and satisfactory expression of regret, much less of apology." The event was so serious that even if the *Baltimore* crew's injuries had been entirely the result of an accident, the incident would still have called for some public expression of sympathy and regret:

It is not enough to say that the affair was lamentable, for humanity would require that expression, even if the beating and killing of our men had been justifiable. It is not enough to say that the incident is regretted, coupled with the statement that the affair was not of an unusual character in ports where foreign sailors are accustomed to meet. It is not for a generous and sincere government to seek the words of small or equivocal meaning in which to convey to a friend- ly power an apology for an offense so atrocious as this.

Complaining of unreasonable delay in the Chilean investigation and the "undiplomatic, but grossly insulting" Matta circular, Harrison asked for "grave and patriotic consideration which the questions involved demand." He made clear that the issues raised by the *Baltimore* affair went far beyond the death of two U.S. sailors. If the dignity, prestige, and influence of the nation were not to be sacrificed, "we must protect those who, in foreign ports, display the flag or wear the colors of this Government against insult, brutality, and death, inflicted in resentment of the acts of their Government, and not for any fault of their own."

Harrison concluded his message to Congress abruptly: "I have as yet received no reply to our note of the 21st instant, but, in my opinion, I ought not to delay longer to bring these matters to the attention of Congress for such action as may be deemed appropriate."

HARRISON'S COMMUNICATION to Congress on January 25 was not a war message, since he did not deliver it in person and never used the word "war." But it was a commitment to action. During the middle of January, 1892, even before the ultimatum, Harrison's private secretary recorded in his diary that the president had assured him, "All the members of the Cabinet are for war."[15] The message of January 25 passed on the entire *Baltimore* imbroglio to the only organization with the power to declare war, and with a suggestion that it take "such action as may be deemed appropriate."

The effort to whip up enthusiasm for a military solution to the crisis met with much less enthusiastic approval than Harrison anticipated. The Democratic press lobbied against humiliating Chile through acts of arrogance or shame, and the Republican press demonstrated little energy in supporting the action of the party's president. It rightly interpreted Harrison's message as an invitation to war but counseled instead consideration of consequences. "It is worth a hundred million dollars," the *New York Sun* wrote, "to have the world understand that there is a country, and a united country, behind the flag." However vigorous the condemnation of Egan or Blaine, the Republican press never denied the necessity of demanding apology and compensation from Chile. Yet most editorial writers simply recommended that the Chileans yield to superiority of force before it became necessary to demonstrate it.[16]

Some Republican papers, like the *New York Daily Tribune*, had been commenting on the possibility of war since early December. While they did not advocate it, the *Tribune* contended that war should not be shunned "when it becomes necessary to fight for the honor of the flag and the safety of American citizens against outrage, violence and murder." Although supporting the administration's determination to bring a halt to Chile's procrastination; agreeing that the gravity of the situation had been clearly defined; and defending the demands made on Chile as sensible, businesslike, and dignified; few papers offered jingoistic cries for an immediate call to arms. The nation's papers agreed that Chile must give satisfaction, that U.S. honor and pride were at stake, and that the president's harsh tone was warranted. The problem was Chilean arrogance and how best to combat it. Complaints against Chile were defended as just, the shooting and stabbing of the *Baltimore*'s sailors were pictured as horrible and bloody, cruel and cowardly. The press made this position clear as well as its belief in the need "to bear ourselves, or else abandon all pretense of protecting our own flesh and blood on foreign soils." That should be "the conviction of every person who is capable of reasoning as a man and not as a woman." A certain restraint existed; the feverlike pitch of Harrison's message was not contagious.[17]

The *Baltimore* affair was not a partisan political issue. Republican and Democratic newspapers shared a characteristic tone: "The fact that Chile is a small power and we a great one necessarily affected the expectation of naval or military glory to be achieved in any contest we might have with her." But "we are not hunters of glory," they wrote in an attempt to temper recklessness and counsel self-control: "Disparity of size does not diminish the gravity of an injury on the one part or preclude the necessity of retaliation on the other. But that disparity undoubtedly should favor a peaceful settlement in the present case."[18] It was the disparity of size and "civilization" that increased the chances that misunderstandings would arise between the two nations.

Congress at once addressed the situation. Senator William Breckinridge of Kentucky noted that it was not too great a presumption to believe that the "President of a great and free people, dealing with a free but feeble people, would not have used such language . . . if he had not had some intimation of what the answer would be." Recognizing that war was the necessary but ultimate resort in protecting the "honor, the glory, the dignity of the Republic, the safety and security of its seamen," Breckinridge proposed a resolution requesting more information from the president so that Congress could discuss the question with more knowledge and thought. The chairman of the House Committee on Foreign Affairs, James Blount of Georgia, reminded Congress of the importance of his committee, promising that after careful deliberation, which would avoid the "confusion provoked by instantaneous discussion," the committee would make its recommendations to the Congress based on serious, earnest, calm deliberation.[19]

While Congress deliberated, editorial writers debated, and the public watched, the United States considered war. On January 7, 1892, even before the president's ultimatum, the U.S. government had learned through a military attaché in Austria that its Hirten-berg factory had purchase orders from Chile for three million cartridges and forty thousand Mannlicher magazine rifles. At Valparaiso heavy Krupp guns were reportedly arriving, and news reached the secretary of state that Chile sought the services of a Prussian major to supervise their mounting.[20]

There certainly was military talk. The press began to wonder if Chile's small but modern fleet was capable of ravaging California or other parts of the West Coast, and public figures wrote each other to express varying concerns. John Hay advised Henry Adams early in January that Brooks Adams and Theodore Roosevelt were "profoundly disgusted" with Harrison for not declaring war, and Roosevelt "goes about hissing through his clenched teeth that we are dishonest. For two nickels he would declare war himself."[21] Other administration opponents protested that Secretary of War Stephen B. Elkins was helping Harrison plunge the country into war.[22] But Congressman Nelson Dingley of Maine pressed his colleagues to support Harrison in maintaining the "dignity and honor of this country, even to the extent of war if that should be clearly necessary."[23] The great industrialist Andrew Carnegie thought war so likely that he traveled to Washington to see if he could persuade Harrison to be patient. As he recorded the conversation, he did not get much reassurance from the president:

AC: *Mr. President, if I were going to fight, I would take some one of my size.*

BH: *Well, would you let any nation insult and dishonor you because of its size?*

AC: *Mr. President, no man can dishonor me except myself. Honor wounds must be self-inflicted.*

BH: *You see our sailors were attacked on shore and two of them killed, and you would stand that?*

AC: *Mr. President, I do not think the United States dishonored every time a row among drunken sailors takes place. . . . I would be disposed to cashier the captain of that ship for allowing the sailors to go on shore when there was rioting in the town and the public peace had been already disturbed.*[24]

"A Warning. Uncle Sam.—Look here, Sonny; it might n't look well for a big fellow like me to lick a little fellow like you,—but if you rile me too much, I'll have to do it." Cover of *Puck*, January 27, 1892.

Commander Evans of the *Yorktown*, still at Valparaiso, looked for war and noted in his diary that if it came, his ship "would give their navy a drubbing in two hours, and when the *Boston* comes we could shell the town into ruins and never be hurt." At one point, as early as December 21, he apparently received a telegram ordering him to keep his ship full of coal, an order that led him to wonder if "they regarded me at the Department as some kind of an idiot. Of course I was full of coal and everything else I should need when the time for action came." By January 5, Evans believed war was probable, noting in his diary, "I don't see how war can now be avoided." The weight of responsibility frightened him, interfered with his sleep, and, so he wrote, was telling on his temper.[25]

Some people worried about the administration's disposition for war and chose a novel way of expressing themselves. The English press in Valparaiso reprinted these sarcastic assaults on U.S. arrogance in order to malign war hysteria in the United States. In a veiled attack on Commander Evans on February 20, 1892, an English newspaper in Valparaiso made fun of the United States' military qualities:

CHILE, BEWARE!
Our venerable Uncle Sam
Is slow to wrath, but when he starts
Out on the warpath
It takes a continent to hold him
Be careful how you get
His dander up.
'Tis quite a little trip around the Horn
To get in good position for a kick
At you, but if he undertakes the trip,
He'll get there!
And mark you, Chile,
There is a bird—a large, tough, healthy bird
That has been known to fly
From Washington to Africa
And come back home with both his talons full
of wool.

It wouldn't take him very long to make
A flying visit anywhere
In South America.
He's harmless if he's let alone, but don't
Throw stones at him
Or poke him with your cane, for then
He's dangerous. This tough old fowl still roosts
Upon the flag-pole's topmost end
Below him wave the stars and stripes,
We call him, Chile,
The American
Eagle. And
You'd better
Not stir
Him
Up.

There were other samples of doggerel, such as that published on
March 11, 1892, in the Valparaiso English press:

What's to pay? The papers say
  "War with Chile!"
Guess not much! Bet my crutch,
    Agin a pair o'shoes,
    It's only bunkum news.
Our buntin' can't be huntin'
For glory, down that way,
    With neighbor Chile.
War is done,—sixty-one
Sorter fixed this generation.
What's the matter? All this clatter
    About Chile? . . .
Who's to blame? S'pose we claim
    'Tis Chile?
There's neither right nor glory there to win.
    Our dignity won't spile
    By keepin' it a while,

Forgivin' and forebearin' isn't sin.
Can't we afford to wait
For time to arbitrate?
There's where the "dignity" comes in
For us an' Chile.
What a shame, to hack and maim
Plucky, little, untamed Chile!
Just as if, in a tiff,
A big "cop" with a club
Says: "Ax my parding bub,
Or wack
I'll crack
Yer pesky bantam head with my new bully!
Your folks have had a row
With some o'mine, an' now
I'll lick you if you don't apologize;
I'm spilin' for a fight
(you know I'm allus right),
Especially with one about your size
Sassy Chile!"[26]

Unknown to the Chileans, perhaps, the USS *Baltimore* itself represented a special effort by the United States to build a new navy of impressive size—in fact, second to none. That effort did not originate with the Republican administration that took office in March 1889, but the ability to summarize and articulate older principles and organize public and political opinion distinguished President Harrison and Secretary Tracy as founders of the "new navy" and leaders of the growing movement for political and economic expansion.

Along with a renewed recognition of the influence of sea power on history and an awareness of the nation's improving international position came the realization that many nations of lesser status and potential, like Chile, had warships that could embarrass the United States. At midcentury Senator Eugene Hale of Maine admitted "a sense of shame. . . . There is nothing whatever to prevent Chile or any other South American power which has in its possession . . . a second or third-rate ironclad from steaming along the Pacific coast and laying our towns under contribution, and burning and destroying."[27] In 1881 Secretary of the Navy William H. Hunt noted that unless Congress took action the navy would dwindle into insignificance: "We have been unable to make such an appropriate display of our naval power abroad as will cause us to be respected. The exhibition of our weakness in this important arm of defense is calculated to detract from our occupying in the eyes of foreign nations that rank to which we know ourselves to be justly entitled." U.S. ships stood "in such mean contrast" to those of lesser powers.[28] And so the U.S. Navy was revived, beginning with appropriations in 1882–83 and construction of such ships as the *Baltimore* in the latter part of the decade.

Measured by tonnage, the U.S. Navy at the beginning of the 1890s fell far behind the navies of Britain, France, Russia, and Germany and such lesser powers as the Netherlands, Italy, Spain, Turkey, China, Norway-Sweden, and Austria-Hungary. Yet when the administration of Benjamin Harrison came to an end in March, 1893, the U.S. Navy had advanced in tonnage and number of ships from twelfth to about fifth place.

The transition from weakness to strength at the beginning of the 1890s occurred under the leadership of the secretary of the navy, Benjamin F. Tracy. With Tracy, a sixty-year-old New York lawyer, maneuvering to increase building programs, something later described as a revolutionary change or rebirth occurred within the Navy Department. Tracy reveled in responsibility, although he had no naval experience, and came to Harrison's attention mostly as a sop to New York Republican rivalries. He of course had the political credentials necessary for appointment. Beginning in New York as a Whig county district attorney, he had helped organize the New York Republican party, served as assemblyman, received the Congressional Medal of Honor for military service in the Civil War, gained national recognition for the defense of Henry Ward Beecher in Beecher's adultery trial, and served as a judge in the New York Court of Appeals.[29] Independent and strong-willed, he gained backing and friendships. Conservative and efficient, he demonstrated vigor and competence in management, gaining the loyalty of subordinates and the trust of the navy. Aware of the importance of public approval, he cleverly attempted to stimulate interest and support by initiating a policy of naming new battleships after states and new cruisers after cities, a policy followed thereafter.

Among other innovations, Tracy rejected the prevailing theory of limited coastal defense and commerce destruction for the idea of strategic control of the seas. He sought to replace the old wooden ships of the Civil War era with steel-armored cruisers with offensive capabilities. Whether Captain Alfred T. Mahan or Rear Admiral Stephen B. Luce created that bold new doctrine for Tracy to exploit or merely served as propagandists, whether naval growth stimulated or reflected the dramatic economic transformation of the time, the Harrison administration and the general public willingly came to support the labors of the secretary of the navy, who popularized a sense of national pride and a desire for risking involvement in international affairs when he insisted that only a navy that could carry war to an enemy could maintain peace. "War is a great calamity," he noted, "but it is not the greatest calamity that can befall a free, intelligent and self-respecting people."[30] The secretary sought to make the navy the strong arm of diplomacy.

Tracy may also have reckoned that a large navy would increase pressure for territorial control or acquisition—perhaps just for coaling stations and naval bases, or for the support of commercial expansion.[31] Whatever the motive for a larger navy, the fact is that when the War of the Pacific broke out in 1879 between Chile and the combined forces of Peru and Bolivia, two new British-built Chilean ironclads were considered superior to the best U.S. warship then in existence.[32] Later, in 1885, the new Chilean steel cruiser *Esmeralda* was esteemed by the Navy Department to be the "most perfect ship of her class ever built."[33] Theodore Roosevelt in 1888, just before he arrived in Washington as civil service commissioner, wrote Harrison, "It is a disgrace to us as a nation that we should have no war ships worthy of the name, and that our rich seaboard cities should lie at the mercy of a tenth rate country like Chili."[34]

Whether the United States really feared Chile or viewed it as a likely rival, or whether proponents of a big navy merely tried to

Benjamin F. Tracy, Secretary of the Navy. Courtesy The Huntington Library.

advance their cause by pointing to the nearest third-rate country with a superior navy is unclear. Tracy even realized that when all the plans of expansion of the previous seven years were completed, the United States would still be "absolutely at the mercy of states having less than one-tenth of its population, one-thirtieth of its wealth, and one-one hundredth of its area."[35] And despite Tracy's successes, midway in his term of office many U.S. observers were still lamenting the weakness of U.S. naval power. "We have no navy worthy of the name, and nearly all our seaports are without proper defenses," whined *Scientific American*. U.S. ports were "at the mercy of any single piratical boat that chooses to enter. This is a very humiliating position for a country like ours to be placed in."[36] By exaggerating the inferiority of the U.S. world position—pointing out incidents like the *Virginius* affair of 1873 and the Samoan conflict of 1888–89, in which the navy was considered humiliated, noting the possibility of a French canal across Panama, and recognizing that a tremendous increase in the volume of exports during the last decade had created an international race for commercial supremacy that the United States wished to dominate—politicians made naval expansion a respectable, even necessary, goal.

Whatever his public logic, Tracy saw to it that new ships like the *Baltimore* were designed for a fight. Tracy projected a fifteen-year construction program of new ships for the Pacific and Atlantic and plans for more than coastal defense. His proposed armadas would total forty-two ships; seagoing battleships, first-class coastline battleships, monitors, armored cruisers, harbor defense rams, dispatch boats, protected cruisers, gunboats, torpedo boats, and dynamite ships, all carrying new weaponry. That collection of ships would certainly have improved upon the thirty-one unarmored cruisers and the three armored cruisers with seventeen guns that together constituted the U.S. Navy when the ambitious Tracy took office.[37]

In view of the talk both in Chile and in the United States, the Navy Department in 1891 made certain preparations. As early as December, Secretary Tracy had sent for Democratic House member Hilary A. Herbert of the Naval Affairs Committee, told him war was imminent, and sought his help. Tracy intended to fit out a repair ship to attend to the fleet and no law authorized such expenditure. Herbert promised support but went to see Blaine and found him "quite as cold as Mr. Tracy was hot. Mr. Blaine said there was no danger whatever, and he pooh-poohed the idea that there would be any war."[38]

The navy huffed and puffed about war uncertainly, like Congress and the press. Earlier Captain Alfred T. Mahan was ordered to Washington, and he arrived on December 17 only to find Tracy gone for the Christmas holidays. Mahan returned to consult the secretary on December 27 and was asked about ships moving against the Chilean nitrate port of Iquique in the north or against the Chilean coal port of Lota in the south.[39]

Tracy at last got busy. From Rear Admiral Brown he received a list of the U.S. vessels that would be ready in case of war. The North Atlantic Squadron under Rear Admiral Bancroft Gherardi had the *Philadelphia* and the *Concord* with 524 men, eighteen main battery guns, twenty-six secondary guns. Admiral Gherardi was certain of the success of U.S. war plans, at least according to Fenton R. Mc-Creery, who noted in his diary that the admiral had told him "that within thirty days he could have concentrated seventeen ships of all classes in front of the nitrate coast where he would have established a blockade hoping thus to cut off the principal source of Chili's government revenue—rather than move upon the Capital from a point near Valparaiso."[40]

The South Atlantic Squadron under Acting Rear Admiral John G. Walker had five ships (the *Chicago, Atlanta, Bennington, Essex,* and *Yantic*) with 1,081 men, thirty-eight main battery guns, and thirty-nine secondary guns. The Pacific Squadron under Rear Admiral George Brown had five ships ready (the *San Francisco, Baltimore, Charleston, Boston,* and *Yorktown*) and 1,339 men, forty-four main battery guns, and sixty-six secondary guns. The *Miantonomah, Newark, Vesuvius, Kearsarge, Mohican,* and *Iroquois* were in reserve with 1,040 men, forty-three main battery guns, and forty-four secondary guns.[41]

Brown, on December 31, 1891, sent Tracy a long memorandum that he devised after a cruise down the coast of Chile. He identified from north to central Chile the ports of Arica, Pisagua, Iquique, Antofagasta, Caldera, and Coquimbo and suggested that in event of war they could be subdued by four or five modern ships, stopping commerce from the outside and thereby cutting off customs collections, which would injure the credit of Chile. Brown discovered that Arica was defended only by a few old guns and Pisagua by two short-range rifles of small caliber, which could be silenced, he thought, by two ships, effectively stopping the shipment of nitrates. The railroad leading to the nitrate works would have to be destroyed, but that could be accomplished by shelling or by a small landing party.[42]

Iquique, the most important port in Chile for customs revenues, was defended only by a "few rifle guns of small calibre and inferior range." Iquique could be blockaded, all shipments of nitrates stopped, and the harbor cleared of merchant ships. The railroad could be destroyed by shelling, the guns silenced by three or four ships. Antofagasta could be taken "without firing a gun." As for Caldera, Brown found it "practically undefended," and ships could land marines at almost any place. He considered Coquimbo the most desirable place to construct a U.S. base: "The port is defended by but one large obsolete gun, which could be silenced in ten minutes." It was a fine port with good water and a supply of beef, with a large expanse of fertile, level country between the sea and foothills. There, he noted, a "large force could rest and recruit with security from an attack."

In the event of war with Chile, Brown argued in his memorandum to Tracy of December 31, the port of Valparaiso should be blockaded by the largest force of ships available. For the southern ports of Talcahuano, Lota, and Coronel he had no information, although he learned that the Chileans had Krupp field pieces there and about twenty-five thousand Mannlicher rifles and an abundance of ammunition in all of Chile. Most Chilean ships were run-down and in need of repairs because of the hard service required during the Balmaceda uprising. The *Esmeralda,* for example, Chile's most formidable ship, would probably be sent to France for repairs. Chilean Captain Fuentes of the *Lynch* informed him, Brown concluded, that both his ship and the *Condell* required extensive repairs.

Along with U.S. war preparations came the unexpected offer of aid from Chile's neighbor and longtime rival, Argentina. The Argentine minister in the United States, Vicente Quesada, suggested to Blaine the transit of U.S. forces through Argentine territory, promising to supply U.S. ships with coal. Pressed by Blaine about the compensation Argentina would exact, Quesada demurred but ultimately confessed that his country was seeking the entire southern part of Chile. In the meantime the Argentine minister in Chile,

Estanislao Zeballos, sent information about Chilean armaments to the United States.[43]

In further preparation for war, an informal naval strategy board was formed with officers from the Office of Naval Intelligence and other naval bureaus, and it placed orders for war matériel. Work at navy yards increased, coal and supplies were rushed to the Pacific Squadron. Tracy made it his business to prepare the navy and kept his work no secret. Barely two weeks after the *Baltimore* riot, the press began discussing the number and quality of U.S. warships available in the event of war with Chile, noting the general air of preparation at the navy yards.[44]

Admirals and other naval officers were asked about ships, arms, coaling problems, and the general strength of U.S. forces in case of emergency. The *New York Daily Tribune* presented a detailed analysis of the Chilean Navy and the condition of its fighting force, and the *New York Times* wrote of the "renewed activity that is being displayed in fitting out all the vessels" at the Brooklyn Navy Yard. Apparently orders had been received to overhaul, modify, and prepare all ships there for action "at the shortest notice." When interviewed, Admiral John Irwin, commander at Mare Island, assured his questioner that the United States could "handle Chili easily without additional work or preparation. We have ships enough in fighting trim. Valparaiso is the key to the entire situation, and I do not apprehend any difficulty in capturing the key." At Mare Island repairs were in progress on the *Omaha, Mohican, Thetis,* and *Ranger.* Hasty preparations were similarly reported in Chicago and Boston.[45]

By late December the press was reporting war preparations with an air of certainty. The *New York Times* covered those arrangements in earnest, talking of single-turreted monitors, modern breech-loading guns, smooth-bore guns and mountings, and the daily work at the Bureau of Ordnance as well as the activities at East Coast ordnance shops, where it was assumed guns and projectiles were being prepared in anticipation of war with Chile. On December 29 the *Times* reported that prominent army officers were being called to Washington, and certain industries were being consulted about armor and the building of deck plates.[46]

In January preparations intensified. An order was issued for the shipment to San Francisco of 45,000 pounds of powder for the navy's big guns. At the same time the press reported the shipment of 2,200 pounds of gun cotton. The work of the Navy Department continued to be reported throughout the month, including a "hurried preparation of torpedoes for active service, the training of apprentice gunners, the fitting out and movement of ships." By midmonth the *New York Times* was reporting the training of the National Guard and other militiamen. According to the *Times*, Brigadier General John H. Mullen, Adjutant General of Minnesota, reported to the War Department at Washington the number of men he could send to the field in the event of war with Chile. Apparently he assured Secretary Elkins that he could have 1,400 men prepared for active warfare in a week. The adjutant general of the state militia in St. Louis was also reported to have issued a general order for all companies of the First Regiment to be recruited without delay to their full strength. He too was reported on his way to Washington for consultation with Elkins. The *New York World* similarly reported, "Blustering colonels are drilling militia with great ado in some parts of the country." The Women's Christian Temperance Union introduced petitions signed by 500,000 women "praying for a peaceful solution" of the Chilean controversy, and Naval Post 400 of the Pennsylvania Grand Army of the Republic passed a resolution on January 22 "sustaining the President's demand for an apology from Chili, failing in which he is urged to inflict salutary punishment, and tendering their services to a man."[47]

By January 25, the Irish-Americans of Philadelphia were reported ready to serve against Chile if war should be declared. Colonel John D. Murphy, Commander of the Hibernian Rifles and Chief Signal Officer of the Irish-American Military Union, offered Harrison the services of his command. Finally, the *New York Daily Tribune* of January 26 devoted most of its first three pages to the issues of the *Baltimore* affair and a substantial section to how a war might be fought. The National Guard of New York was readied; the mayor held a press conference to explain New York's part in case of hostilities; and merchants, shippers, and freight-handlers formed companies of volunteers. The paper's entire third page was devoted to explaining how an attack by Chile on the United States would be met.[48]

Such were the considerations of administration officials, military advisors, and public advocates of preparedness. Were they acting preemptively or irrationally? The most cautious and concerned observers thought not, whether they agreed or disagreed about the causes of U.S.-Chilean conflict. But the real questions for contemporaries, as well as for historians seeking to understand the evolution of U.S. diplomacy, were whether the *Baltimore* affair was worth the costs of war and, even more important, whether U.S. honor or prestige were at stake in the effort to seek redress from Chile. Under what circumstances would war or a demonstration of military power enhance national solidarity or international reputation? Were domestic needs in line with diplomatic interests? Were U.S. policymakers astute enough to understand the need to align means and ends in considerations of foreign policy? Those were not easy questions in early 1892. Those were not easy times.

7. Bang to Whimper

DESPITE THEIR MARKEDLY DIFFERENT but clear version of the origins and significance of the *Baltimore* affair, the Chilean government failed to sense that in challenging the claimed rights of U.S. sailors on shore leave they were courting trouble. Perhaps Chilean authorities should have better calculated the wisdom of doing so, because by late January 1892, President Harrison's indignation and Chilean imprudence had transformed the unfortunate incident into a serious crisis. There was little time now for careful assessment, but to the great advantage of the United States, war was averted and the confrontation came to an end. Actually, the resolution of the affair had nothing of the drama of its unfolding. A change in the foreign ministry in Chile brought in the astute Luis Pereira, who skillfully determined accommodation was in his nation's best interest. The Chileans acquiesced so quickly that Harrison's ultimatum soon appeared anticlimactic.

BECAUSE OF THE HIGH REGARD with which most Western nations held Chile, European diplomats watched with concern as President Harrison bullied his way to the end of the *Baltimore* affair. The Chilean minister in Paris, Augusto Matte, reported that the European press attributed the affair in Valparaiso to the asylum the United States had granted to Balmaceda's supporters.[1] Matte himself was overwrought by not being able to cooperate more directly in a solution to the affair and informed the Ministry of Foreign Relations that he considered it his duty to remain active and would help the foreign minister even from his distant post in France. He sent cables to Chile from the end of October through mid-January, seeking to explain U.S. policy as he learned it from the U.S. minister in Paris, Whitelaw Reid, whom he described as "a person of great influence." It soon became evident that Matte considered the whole affair, especially Egan's lack of "greater prudence" during the civil war, inspired by the electoral hopes of Secretary Blaine.[2]

Believing in the "influence that the European press exercises on public opinion in the United States," Matte took steps to see that the principal European newspapers favored Chile. In doing so, he took advantage of the Continent's general sympathy for Chile and of the "disfavor that the United States has in Europe due to its economic policies." He wrote the Chilean ministers in London, Berlin, and Rome to see that they obtained press coverage that would offer the "true" circumstances of the imbroglio: "You will see that the press of those countries manifest themselves in favor of Chile. . . . If, as we do not expect, the events become grave, we will try to give even more impulse to this press movement than we have initiated."[3] In mid-November he wrote that he was arousing European favor for the cause. He continued to speak with Reid, whom he now identified as a "close friend" of Harrison's. Reid was said to have asserted that the conflict would be resolved and Chile could count on the "strict discretion" of the United States.[4]

Matte arranged to meet James Gordon Bennett, owner of the *New York Herald,* who lived in Paris, hoping to use the opportunity to call attention to the way in which newspapers affected international relations.[5] His conversation proved ineffective, and he had little more success with the press of governments of Europe. Despite the sympathy that Europe offered, Matte was forced to admit that European governments all advised Chile to avoid conflict with the United States. Although *Le Temps, Les Debates, La Justice,* and *Le Soir* published editorials damning U.S. diplomacy, Matte received word that the French would not carry their sympathy further.[6]

In addition, the Europeans, however concerned, would not mediate, and certainly the United States was not seeking mediation. Matte reported Britain would not because of "accented animosities" toward the United States, Germany refused because of serious differences with the United States, and Italy was unavailable because of questions pending in the New Orleans lynching. Spain was unacceptable since it was well known that the former parent country looked "with vivid repugnance on United States intervention in South America."[7]

The Chilean minister in Berlin, Gonzalo Bulnes, met with Baron Marschall von Bieberstein, German minister of state, who in a reserved manner read a communication from the German minister in Washington that war between Chile and the United States was imminent. Bieberstein confided, with an impression of utmost gravity, that the United States was moved by a desire for commercial domination of South America, that the *Baltimore* affair was a pretext to exclude European commercial activity. Bulnes argued that Chile in defending its own commercial freedom defended European interests. But Bieberstein was not moved and made clear that Chile alone would have to end the conflict, that since the United States was clearly "seeking the pretext for a war," Chile should not provide it.[8]

Perhaps the Chilean minister in Berlin had expected that Germany would help Chile because of what the former chancellor, Otto von Bismarck, had said about the *Baltimore* affair. In a meeting with Bennett of the *Herald,* the great statesman showed amazement that "a nation as powerful as the American Union did not show more moderation and respect for a nation as small as Chile, that had just come out of a civil war and that insisted in imposing on it the same qualities that they condemned in the riot." Those remarks were relayed to the Chilean Ministry of Foreign Relations, in hope that Bismarck's opinion would be useful.[9] The Chilean consul in Berlin, Carlos Krauss, reported that a single voice was heard in the German empire—condemning the policies of Egan, sympathizing with Chile.[10]

The British Foreign Office at first believed that the trouble originated with Egan, whose appointment it had regarded with displeasure.[11] Or that it stemmed from the action of U.S. naval personnel over whom he had no control.[12] In the immediate aftermath of the *Baltimore* affair the Foreign Office did not regard the controversy as threatening a war. It saw the conflict as nothing more than a Yankee tendency to belligerence even in trivial matters. The *London Times* reported on October 30 that "little or no excitement has been caused in official circles."[13] The British minister to Chile, John

G. Kennedy, called the *Baltimore* affair, "merely a question of temper."[14] Still, by November the British were concerned about Egan's role in the imbroglio, and Kennedy wrote perceptively to Lord Salisbury at the Foreign Office:

Mr. Egan and Captain Schley have changed their previous prudent attitude for one of defiance; this may be explained by their conviction that patience and prudence under direct insults to the United States Flag have been in vain and that the best way to put an end to the systematic annoyance to which they have been subjected was by obtaining authority to defy and threaten the Chilean Government.[15]

Kennedy was so worried about Captain Schley's "probably exaggerated language to his foreign colleagues at Valparaiso" that he endeavored to persuade the German and French admirals to postpone their departures from Valparaiso, and he recommended the return to the coast of ships of the British fleet.[16] He earlier reported that Schley had told the commanding officers of British, German, and French ships in the port that the situation was critical and they must be prepared for anything.[17]

By New Year's Eve the Foreign Office was correctly reporting the seriousness of the situation, suggesting that unless Matta was removed from office, war between the United States and Chile could be expected. Kennedy noted significantly that from the beginning he had endeavored to persuade Matta to use less forcible language and introduce good will or friendship into notes to the United States. His efforts were in vain, and he concluded that Matta's successor would "certainly be compelled to drop the defiant attitude hitherto observed toward the United States and also to make concessions to the demands of that country."[18]

The British minister in Chile actually thought well of Egan, had never joined the campaigns against him or against the United States, and frequently noted in cables to the Foreign Office that Egan's attitude had been uniformly correct. "By the exercise of patience and prudence," Kennedy wrote, "Mr. Egan has managed to turn the tables on the Chilean Government, who have placed themselves in the wrong by a ridiculous display of defiance and discourtesy towards the United States and its representatives here." Egan deserved credit for his display of firmness and ability.[19] Kennedy appeared so favorably disposed toward Egan that he even rejected the claim that U.S. action was moved by a desire to break the British commercial hegemony in Chile. Kennedy consistently praised Egan, reporting that during the period when he was under attack—the object of hatred by the Chilean government and populace—Egan showed "great serenity, astuteness and fortality [sic] of resource, and has enabled the United States Government to emerge from a position of embarrassment and to formulate serious charges of offense against the dignity of the Government officers of the United States."[20]

WHATEVER THE VIEWS of the British minister, the administration of Jorge Montt remained convinced that Chile was not responsible for the riot of October 16, insisted that the U.S. ultimatum was unjust, and surmised that the entire crisis had been inspired by Harrison's political aspirations. Nevertheless, Chilean authorities probably decided that without outside support the *Baltimore* affair was not worth a war.[21]

Chile's reply to Harrison's ultimatum arrived the same day that the president laid the issue before Congress, Monday, January 25. Fenton R. McCreery, the young secretary at the U.S. legation in Santiago, noted that it was "a very humiliating letter for these proud people to send. It was transmitted immediately to the secretary of state in Washington in the original Spanish so that if there are any slight mistakes in translation the Washington folks will have to take the responsibility."[22] In the reply Foreign Minister Pereira expressed a willingness to pay reparations for the dead and injured sailors. The reply suggested that an arbitral tribunal or the U.S. Supreme Court should decide the amount. The new foreign minister deplored the parts of the Matta circular considered offensive to the United States and agreed to withdraw them with the same publicity the original telegram received. Pereira stiffly regretted the lack of judgment in sending it. Finally, Chile promised not to move on the recall of Egan until the Chilean government could show cause to the satisfaction of the United States.[23] The tone of the reply differed enormously from the correspondence communicated by Matta's envoys. President Montt and Foreign Minister Pereira clearly appreciated the risks of challenging the United States.

The timing of Harrison's subsequent message to Congress and the Chilean accommodation made them an object of much comment. The Chilean note was dated January 23, and it appeared not to have been delivered to the president until after Harrison sent his address to Congress on January 25. The administration later claimed the translation was not complete until after Harrison's remarks had gone in, but many contemporaries suggested that the president knew of the note and decided to send his address anyway.

As early as October 30, Pedro Montt in Washington had hinted that the controversy was fabricated by Harrison, because the election of 1892 was nearing and he feared he would not be reelected.[24] The *Chilian Times* stated that the "hectoring" of Harrison and Blaine ("these doughty fire eaters") had occurred because they were "within a few days of political election and they hope that by a cheap and comparatively safe display of spread-eaglism they may gain."[25] Some U.S. pundits saw Harrison's behavior as a maneuver for reelection under conditions of high political liabilities: his uninspiring personality, the McKinley Tariff, and his exceedingly large budget. Some perceived the president's position as a device to extract larger naval appropriations from Congress. He hoped, some said, to present the Republican party as the defender and protector of U.S. citizens and interests.

The president did not transmit the Chilean note to Congress until January 28, a delay which, considering his hurry in handing the issue to Congress, was impossible to justify. He concluded that the Chilean note was so conciliatory and friendly that he was sure the remaining differences could be reconciled on terms satisfactory to the United States, through normal diplomatic channels and without special Congressional action.[26]

A note dated January 29 went to Egan the following day, and the end was in sight. The new note directed the minister to announce that Chile's acquiescence had given the United States great pleasure, and that relations between the two republics could now be restored to a basis of cordiality, with a full and honorable adjust-

"Thank goodness, the cruel war is over. Now what next?"
Cover of *Puck*, February, 10, 1892.

ment of all matters. The president assured the Chileans that Pereira's expressions of regret for and condemnation of the attack were gratifying, and he congratulated the Chilean government for the "frank and ample withdrawal" of the Matta circular. Egan was instructed to assure the Chileans that Harrison was ready to respond to friendly overtures in a spirit of generosity.[27]

Nothing more happened until the summer of 1892, when Egan's displeasure with the continuing Chilean attacks on him caused him to devise methods to discredit his most vocal Chilean opponents. On June 22, he wrote to Consul McCreery in Valparaiso:

Cannot you get in Valparaiso from some friends full and reliable particulars about old Doctor Dave Trumbull [John Trumbull's father]; deal in the undertaking line with full details of their stealing of the coffins—the dates and the names of the prominent Chilian citizens who were left without their shrouds; also some good sound reliable data about the worthy Doctor's little deals in exchange and the various other little negocios [businesses] in which he was said to have engaged during the brief hours that he was able to spare from soul saving. . . . A number of good solid facts on those subjects would knock these two impudent rascals John and Dave sky high. . . . Get right down to work and see what you can do.[28]

Apparently nothing came of Egan's attempt, but in late March, Egan reminded Blaine that the Chilean claims had not yet been settled.[29] When a new Chilean cabinet was elected in mid-June, Egan sensed the time was right and cabled that the Chileans now desired to make a prompt settlement. By that time Secretary Blaine had resigned and had been replaced by John W. Foster, who responded to Egan in July that the president hoped the indemnity would be proportional to the offense.[30] In a confidential telegram Foster told Egan the United States would accept fifty thousand dollars in gold "if you could not do better." Egan was able to do better and sent word that the Chileans had offered seventy-five thousand dollars. He recommended acceptance.[31]

The indemnity was handed over on July 16, 1892, and Egan sent the draft to the department. To the families of Riggin and Turnbull, killed in the riot, went ten thousand dollars each. To the two sailors most seriously injured, Anderson and Hamilton, five thousand dollars each. To the remaining injured sailors, from seven hundred dollars to four thousand dollars apiece. The twenty-three others arrested and detained received from three hundred to five hundred dollars each.[32]

In late July the governments of Chile and the United States, having resolved all questions arising from the *Baltimore* affair, agreed to arbitrate their remaining diplomatic differences—that is, everything on the diplomatic docket at that moment. Claims made by the citizens of both nations pertaining to corporations, companies, or private individuals against either government, and complaints about acts committed by civil or military authorities of either country, could be submitted. A three-member board, one from each nation and the third named by the president of Switzerland, convened beginning in January 1893, and for several years resolved claims for injuries done to life and property.[33]

MANY U.S. SAILORS have died in service to their country, and most are remembered or mourned by family and friends, but time erodes the individual identities of countless men whose collective contribution is unmistakable and whose individual legacy is small. Only a few great leaders or controversial figures leave a more permanent imprint, thanks to biographers, historians, journalists, and maritime aficionados.

That natural or at least predictable course of events has an interesting exception in the *Baltimore* affair. There the diplomacy of the imbroglio and the personalities and ploys of Harrison, Blaine, Wharton, Tracy, Egan, and Schley have obscured the equally fascinating public reaction to the unfortunate and unproductive death of Boatswain's Mate Charles W. Riggin. Patriotic defender of flag and country or instigator of a drunken brawl, Riggin was, for a short time, so celebrated and honored that his death outside the True Blue Saloon in Valparaiso was elevated to heroic proportions.

Riggin and Coalheaver William Turnbull were buried with military honors in the Cementerio de los Disidentes, or English Cemetery as it was known, situated on the crest of a steep bluff overlooking the port, with cobblestone roads leading up to it lined with picturesque but poor shanties that, nearly a century after the *Baltimore* riot, still appear typically nineteenth-century. The dead sailors' shipmates commissioned a large, handsome marble stone to mark the graves, and while it has been impossible to determine its cost, its appearance suggests it was a monument of exceptional quality. Decorated with a large marble cross and sculptured marble ivy climbing round, it stands on a massive marble block, on which is engraved:

> *Sacred*
> *To the Memory of*
> *C. W. Riggin*
> *Boatswains Mate U.S.N.*
> *Born in Philad U.S. of A.*
> *Feb 10 1863*
> *Killed in Valparaiso*
> *Oct 16 1891*
> *Age 28 Y 3 months*

The opposite side bears an appropriate legend for Riggin's dead comrade:

> *and*
> *W. Turnbull*
> *Coal Heaver U.S.N.*
> *Born in P.E. Island*
> *Oct 14 1867*
> *Died Oct 25 1891*
> *Of Wounds Received*
> *Oct 16 1891 in Valparaiso*
> *Aged 24 Years 11 Days*[34]

The honor paid to the two young sailors did not end with the sentimentality of engraving an ornate, expensive tombstone, the absolution given the entire crew of any wrongdoing or bad conduct while on shore, or the apparent willingness of the president to go to war for the perceived premeditated assault on the honor and dignity of the United States. Several months after news of Riggin's death reached the United States, the *New York Recorder* suggested a fund

Memorial to Charles W. Riggin and William Turnbull, Valparaiso, Chile. Photo by author.

be raised by dime contributions, mostly from school children, from which three silver statuettes of Riggin were molded and presented to Harrison, Blaine, and Tracy.[35] One of them is today still on exhibit at the Benjamin Harrison Memorial Home in Indianapolis as the "Riggin Testimonial." Although its legend is partly inaccurate (in Indianapolis the ship is erroneously referred to as the *Charleston*), the testimonial faithfully represented the mood that soon surrounded the martyred sailor:

The statuettes were intended as testimonials from the American people, showing their appreciation of the prompt and patriotic action taken by the National Administration to uphold the rights of the United States. The statuettes were also designed to serve as momentos of the attack upon American sailors in the streets of Valparaiso, Chile, October 19, [sic] 1891. Boatswain's Mate Riggin was chosen as the model for the statuettes because he was the only native of the United States who lost his life in the affray. In addition, Riggin was considered by his superior officers as a model seaman and his record of twelve years in the service was untarnished.[36]

Fund raising started with the *Recorder*'s article of January 31, and closed on March 27, after 25,274 contributions had been received. The closing did not stop the flow of dimes, which eventually brought the total to 26,382. According to the Riggin Testimonial, "No fund had ever before received one-fifth the number of subscriptions in the same time." The model for the statuettes was sculpted by Alexander J. Doyle of New York, who did so as a "gratuitous contribution to the patriotic sentiment they embody."[37]

Another memorial marked the final disposition of Riggin's body, which did not rest long in Valparaiso. In February, 1892, Secretary Blaine cabled Egan that Riggin's brothers and sisters desired to bring his remains back to Pennsylvania "for interment by the side of his mother." Blaine instructed Egan to inquire what was necessary to obtain a permit of exhumation.[38] At first there was some problem with the sanitary laws in Chile. Then, after Grace and Company agreed to attend to details, the new secretary of state, John W. Foster, was scandalized in July, 1892, by a telegram from Egan stating that "Grace house Valparaiso insultingly refuse to receive the body of Riggin."[39] With the financial and organizational aid of the *Philadelphia Inquirer* the remains were ultimately sent to Panama on the Chilean *Cachapoal,* and from there to New York on the U.S. steamer *Progress,* at a cost to the government of $528.69.[40]

It appears that the *Inquirer* hoped its efforts on behalf of Riggin would help increase circulation, which already exceeded eighty-two thousand. Between July 21 and August 15, 1892, Riggin, alive or dead, was front-page news, illustrated with sketches of him and his curly-haired nephew, who was always appropriately dressed in a sailor suit. In anticipation of new obsequies, grand plans were made to demonstrate the nation's sympathy and gratitude. "The demonstration in this city . . . will be not merely a local affair," observed the Republican newspaper: "There is no longer any question as to the character and extent of the honor that will be paid to the memory of Boatswain's Mate Charles W. Riggin—the murdered American sailor."[41] The proposed patriotic interment would be extraordinary in many respects. Secretary Foster approved military honors to surround Riggin's return but hoped "nothing will be said or done by the public oration or demonstration which would revive the unfortunate diplomatic incident and cause [ill] feeling among the Chilean authorities."[42] The *Inquirer* and most of Pennsylvania's patriotic organizations agreed on the treatment the hero would receive:

It will be the grandest demonstration in honor of the memory of a poor but brave American seaman that has ever been witnessed in Philadelphia. It will be one that will put to shame some carping critics and mousing owls that I find are disposed to assail the Grand Army of the Republic, the Patriotic Sons of America, the American Mechanics and other patriotic organizations . . . simply because they wish to pay all the respect that within them lies to the man who lost his life at the hands of a foreign mob for no other reason than that he wore the navy blue of the United States.[43]

The *New York Times* of Thursday, August 11, 1892, reported that Consul William McCreery and his daughter accompanied the body from Valparaiso and at New York made formal transfer of the remains to a committee of representatives from the Navy Yard, various naval posts, the Patriotic Sons of America, Grand Army of the Republic, Sons of Veterans, United American Mechanics, and the deceased's brother, John L. Riggin. Reporters at the scene from the *Inquirer* wrote, "Sunshine made the morning of the dead sailor boy's homecoming a bright one."[44]

The affray in Valparaiso had so elevated popular emotions that the return of Riggin's remains became akin to the return of a martyred saint. "By his death," the *Inquirer* explained, "a great principle has been vindicated—that the flag of the Union is to be respected everywhere, on land and sea alike . . . and no right-minded American citizen will object to paying due honor to the body of the seaman who fell at the hands of the mob that this great principle might be maintained before . . . the world."[45] Praise for Riggin reached such a height that on request by a large number of military and civil associations and the *Inquirer,* the mayor of Philadelphia consented that his body should lie in state under the Liberty Bell in Independence Hall.

Public opinion concerning that apotheosis was not unanimous, but the doubters were few. Such journals as the *Nation* and newspapers as the *Philadelphia Press* questioned the propriety of an honor previously given in death only to extremely famous historical figures such as Benjamin Franklin, Henry Clay, and Abraham Lincoln. Critics contended that a mere boatswain's mate did not deserve such high honors. But the *Inquirer* insisted that calling Riggin only a boatswain's mate was an insult to flag and country. It was impossible to pay too much respect "to the man who in his country's service was dragged from a car by a foreign mob and cruelly stabbed in the back and shot to death because he wore the American Navy blue. . . . Everything goes to show he was a faithful, sober man, and whether admiral or seaman his fellow citizens cannot honor him too highly." Theodore Roosevelt agreed. He and his supporters thought the arrangements in Philadelphia a fitting climax to the dead sailor's life.[46]

Whatever the appropriateness, the ceremonies of Sunday, August 14, 1892, were altogether impressive. The *New York Times* recorded that at Independence Hall "when the spectators, who had gathered in large numbers, were finally admitted they were allowed to file past the coffin, which was buried beneath the drapery and surrounded by the guard with fixed bayonets." The *Inquirer* was more emotional, emphasizing that the 28,140 spectators

taught to sneering critics of the American seaman, in the very cradle of liberty—beneath the very bell that proclaimed freedom from kingly rule; within a dozen yards of the very spot from which the Magna Charta was read—that they, the many—not the few— must rule; that governments derive their just powers from the consent of the governed; that the poor and lowly as well as the rich and mighty, have rights which must be held inviolate.[47]

Six thousand representatives from Pennsylvania's naval, military, civic, and patriotic organizations joined in the funeral procession, and according to one estimate "at least 300,000 others silently watched the cortege as it moved from Independence Hall to Woodlands Cemetery, where several thousand listened to the funeral oration and sermon and witnessed the religious services at the grave." Among those present was a military escort of 125 men from the First Regiment of the Pennsylvania National Guard, 200 from the Third Regiment, 50 from the Gray Invincibles, 72 from Company D of the New Jersey National Guard, a long line of Grand Army Veterans, Sons of Veterans, Sons of America, Junior Mechanics, and naval veterans, along with several bands. A firing squad of marines preceded the hearse, with several dozen seamen and petty officers acting as an honor guard. Drawn by six black horses the hearse was draped with a cloth of blue with white stars, in the middle of which was a cluster of shields surrounding a gold eagle. An Episcopalian minister read the service, after which the former assistant district attorney William W. Ker, of Pennsylvania, described how Riggin was killed, emphasizing, "Every wound that he received was given in the hatred, not of him, but of the country in whose service he was enrolled." The assembled people then sang "My Country 'Tis of Thee," and the Reverend Duncan MacGregor of the Centennial Baptist Church of Philadelphia, who had postponed a trip to the mountains to officiate at the ceremony, paid a glowing tribute to the dead seaman and to U.S. patriotism. Together with

Riggin's relatives, Dr. MacGregor repaired to the grave, which was lined with evergreen and ivy. After a brief service, and after the casket had at last been lowered, the firing squad fired three volleys.[48]

History can sometimes be made by great men whose mere presence or conscious response to situations has important consequences for society; accidental events can set forces in motion that alter society. Although it would be simplistic to say that Boatswain's Mate Charles Riggin became a hero because he died, he was, nonetheless, a symbol of heroism—revered not for his own accomplishments but rather for what people wanted to think was his self-sacrifice. His meteoric rise to popularity in death had no basis in any achievement in life.

The forces that enlarged Riggin's heroism might be explained by political opportunism: a few months prior to the presidential election the Republican party sought to associate the sailor's memorial with the incumbent president's successful foreign policy. Riggin's heroism also might be explained by the national psychic crisis theory of Richard Hofstadter—that societies in stress seek out some person or thing, real or symbolic, to protect them. The United States in the late nineteenth century was in the midst of profound change. Perhaps U.S. society in 1891–92 adopted Riggin as a talisman for the values of a golden past.[49] Or maybe the sanctification of Riggin's death shows no more than that heroism is in the eye of the beholder.

If short-lived heroes like Riggin personify the historical event, it should not be surprising that a parallel to Riggin's heroism exists in Chilean history. In the aftermath of the political and social upheaval of the Chilean civil war of 1891, followed by the humiliation of having to acquiesce to the U.S. perception of the riot outside the True Blue Saloon, the legend of Carlos Peña may have served the same needs within Chilean society in the last decade of the nineteenth century that Riggin's death did in the United States.

Following the Chilean accommodation in 1892 and payment of the seventy-five thousand dollars indemnity for the injuries and deaths during the riot, the U.S. government considered demanding a salute to the Stars and Stripes in a U.S. port. The prevailing

Chilean belief is that that was so humiliating a gesture that no Chilean government dared fulfill the obligation until 1902, and then only after vitriolic debate and considerable hesitation. Finally, at that time, so the story goes, the Chilean warship *Chacabuco* was ordered to San Francisco to put an end to the entire *Baltimore* affair. There, according to Chilean legend, a pathetic drama took place. The *Chacabuco*'s commander assembled the crew, and as a Chilean band aboard the ship played the U.S. national anthem, he asked for a volunteer to perform the humiliating task of lowering the Chilean flag in expiation of the supposed insult of 1891. Naturally no one responded and the situation grew tense. At last the youngest officer aboard ship, Carlos Peña, stepped forward and stood at attention before his captain, indicating he was willing. While the band continued to play the "Star Spangled Banner," Peña with tears in his eyes began to lower the Chilean flag until it lay on the ship's deck. Mortified that the single star of the Chilean flag lay prostrate, Peña turned toward the band and ordered them to play the Chilean national hymn. The band began, as if electrified, and as it did so Peña reached down, caught the flag, clutched it to his breast, and shot himself in the head. According to one account, "Over the planks of the deck, the body of the lieutenant and the insignia of the republic became confused in one intimate embrace."[50]

According to the above story, there is, in an obscure corner of the Chilean Naval Academy in Valparaiso, a bust of a young naval officer. On the pedestal is reputed to be the simple inscription:

> *Navy Lieutenant Carlos Peña*
> *Death with honor and glory.*

It is said that by an unwritten code of silence nobody in the academy ever speaks of Carlos Peña or the deed that brought him singular fame. Yet somehow the cadets always learn of Peña's heroic act— now long obscured by the passage of time.

The Chilean story varies, but its outline bears a resemblance to the emotionalism demonstrated in the United States by Riggin's apotheosis. The fact that no bust of Carlos Peña stands on a pedestal in the Naval Academy is unimportant. The fact that no such name as Carlos Peña is recorded in the annals of the Chilean naval academy or navy is irrelevant. The knowledge that the U.S. government considered but rejected a Chilean salute to the flag is long forgotten. The fact that no ship named *Chacabuco* sailed to any U.S. port in 1902 or any year is ignored.[51] The legend of Carlos Peña indicates that the *Baltimore* affair had an equally profound effect on Chilean society as it had on that of the United States.

What is most important about the *Baltimore* affair from the Chilean perspective is the impact it had on international relations. Some historians point out that throughout most of the late nineteenth century Chilean foreign policy reflected an awareness of a system of power politics in the Western Hemisphere—one in which Chile sought a favorable position. Within that hemispheric system, Chile hoped to defend and advance its national interests, augment its power, and compete for influence.[52] The Chileans abhorred the arrogance and impatience of the United States in the *Baltimore* affair—the insulting way in which they were forced to capitulate, not so much from fear as from expediency. While Americans have largely forgotten this minor flap with a small country, Chileans remember it as major confrontation with a great power. From the perspective of Chilean domestic politics, the *Baltimore* affair may have served as something of a balm in healing the wounds of the Chilean civil war, but Chilean acquiescence in the face of U.S. threats of military hostility also demonstrated that the South American republic would not be accepted on equal terms with the great powers outside the limited international system in South America. Although nations like the United States, Britain, or Argentina could have an enormous impact on Chile's internal politics or exercise great influence on its foreign relations, the *Baltimore* affair demonstrated that resistance to such intervention was not easy, profitable, or even respected in dealing with the United States.

Resentment probably induced the Chileans to refuse participation in the Columbian Exposition held in Chicago in 1893. It likely influenced Chile's decision to side with Spain in the War of 1898. Even now, Chileans remain suspicious, resentful, often confused by what they perceive to be U.S. condescension toward its Latin neighbors. While this suspicion, resentment, and confusion about hemispheric relations has resulted from many different experi-

ences, the *Baltimore* affair is surely a most significant and neglected historical precedent contributing to the attitude of Chile.

THE *BALTIMORE* AFFAIR was an extraordinarily important episode
in U.S. diplomatic history. Along with the Hawaiian revolution, the
Samoan problem, and Venezuela boundary dispute, and several
other diplomatic events of the late nineteenth century, it fits into the
longer sweep of the United States' accumulation of power and influence—the complex of events that marked the prelude to greater
assertion of U.S. ambitions in the Spanish-American War. In view
of the *Baltimore* affair, that conflict now emerges as considerably
less a cause of the United States' new world status than an expression or affirmation of a power and role that the United States
had achieved earlier. Nearly the leading industrial power in the
world, with the settlement of the continent completed, the nation
now possessed the wealth, military potential, and ambition that
gradually made international political activity necessary and
desirable.

Whether the United States consciously or unconsciously willed
international involvement remains an intriguing historical debate.
But incidents like the *Baltimore* affair do reveal that, however
vaguely, the U.S. populace was beginning to feel a growing and
moralistic world responsibility that made noninvolvement and pas-
sivity in the face of international turmoil an intolerable evasion of
duty instead of a virtue. That crude, adolescent sense of responsibility drove the nation to intervene, sometimes with methods and
manners that reflected the nation's unsophisticated and unclear
understanding of what its wealth, power, and ambition entailed.

The U.S. populace sensed but did not really comprehend the
drift of events, and the administration reflected some of the same
confusion in its often inappropriate responses to international incidents. For his part, Secretary of the Navy Benjamin F. Tracy worked
to revitalize U.S. naval forces, not specifically because of the *Baltimore* affair, but because such crises happened to parallel a perceived need for a dramatic display of strength to gain the attention
and serious consideration of foreign governments. To Tracy, Harrison, and their followers, the *Baltimore* imbroglio provided the

opportunity to convince the nation of the importance of military might. In addition, the crisis afforded the opportunity to win prestige and great power status by taking an assertive stand, backing it with moralistic rhetoric, and assuring it with military strength. The United States, it was implied, would thereafter be taken seriously by the community of leading European powers.

European nations were not impressed by those motives, although they could not deny the new strength of the U.S. Navy and indicated that by their refusal to support the Chilean position in the *Baltimore* affair. They were not administered the diplomatic "awakening jolt" that the United States hoped to deliver because Europe had, in fact, already conceded the great power status of the growing U.S. republic. Britain, for example, was the predominant economic power in the world in the late nineteenth century, and its commercial strength, supported by a powerful navy, increased British political influence. That was a phenomenon the U.S. government had always found annoying and threatening yet also respected and admired. Still, British economic expansion in the Western Hemisphere was not accompanied by the type of political influence the United States feared. Britain actually acquiesced in U.S. hemispheric preeminence, and its diplomats determined "not to upset the susceptibilities of the United States."[53] In any case, the British desired the same things the United States did: peace and prosperity with little effort and minimal expense.

Since U.S. diplomacy before 1898 often belied the fact that its great power status had been unquestioned for years, the U.S. government often exaggerated the need for assertive or forceful action. A transformation in U.S. foreign policy would not come until the U.S. ascent was recognized by its own populace—when the public stopped being apathetic about U.S. diplomacy and increased national awareness helped develop a determined, consistent policy for international relations.[54] Until that time, the narrow-minded nationalism and diplomatic bullying demonstrated in the *Baltimore* affair annoyed the very powers the United States wanted to impress. They interpreted it as rude, unnecessarily belligerent, and undignified behavior.

In adapting to the status of a world power, the United States undoubtedly made some mistakes. With Tracy's navy to back the nation, the administration of Benjamin Harrison sought to impose its beliefs on others, whatever the resistance or however much patience and discretion would have proved the wiser course. Ultimately, that display of unilateral, moralistic, aggressive diplomacy would have a more easily recognizable and indelible imprint in the Spanish-American War of 1898. But in 1891 and 1892 the crisis did not lead to war, and consequently, despite all the bravado surrounding questions of honor and the imminence of war, the *Baltimore* affair was as much a national catharsis for contemporary currents in U.S. diplomacy as a catalyst for future assertions of U.S. power. The *Baltimore* affair both reflected and contributed to a sense of urgency and impatience in U.S. diplomacy that would characterize it long after the crisis with Chile had faded from memory.

ABBREVIATIONS

AN	Archivos Nacionales, Santiago
FO	British Foreign Office
FRUS	*Papers Relating to the Foreign Relations of the United States*
H. Exec. Doc.	*House Executive Document*
NARS	National Archives and Record Service
RE	Chilean Ministry of Foreign Relations (Ministerio de Relaciones Exteriores)
RG	Record Group

Notes

PREFACE

1. See, for example, William Appleman Williams, *The Tragedy of American Diplomacy* (Cleveland: World Publishing Co., 1959) and *The Roots of the Modern American Empire* (New York: Random House, 1969); Walter LaFeber, *The New Empire: An Interpretation of American Expansion, 1860–1898* (Ithaca, N.Y.: Cornell University Press, 1963); Thomas J. McCormick, *China Market: America's Quest for Informal Empire, 1893–1901* (Chicago: Quadrangle, 1967).

2. James A. Field, Jr., "American Imperialism: The Worst Chapter in Almost Any Book," *American Historical Review* 83 (June, 1978): 644–68. On the importance of chance, see Carl von Clausewitz, *On War,* ed. Michael Howard and Peter Paret, Book 1, Chapter 7 (Princeton: Princeton University Press, 1976).

3. Charles S. Campbell, *The Transformation of American Foreign Policy, 1865–1900* (New York: Harper & Row, 1976); Ernest R. May, *Imperial Democracy: The Emergence of America as a Great Power* (New York: Harper & Row, 1961).

4. See Robert L. Beisner's reply to James A. Field, Jr., *American Historical Review* 83 (June, 1978): 673.

5. Ibid., 677. See also Robert L. Beisner, *From the Old Diplomacy to the New, 1865–1900* (Arlington Heights, Ill.: Harlan Davidson, 1975).

1. THE RIOT IN VALPARAISO

1. Benjamin F. Tracy, January, 1890, Benjamin F. Tracy Papers, Letter Book II, vol. 24, Manuscripts Division, Library of Congress. On the *Baltimore,* see Log Book of the USS *Baltimore,* preface, n.d. Navy Department, NARS; Memorandum 3276, August–November, 1891, file 10, Tracy Papers; Benjamin F. Tracy, "Our War-Ships," *North American Review* 152 (June, 1891); 655; Thomas Campbell Copeland, *Harrison and Reid: Their Lives and Record* (New York: Charles L. Webster,

1892), 181; *Chilian Times* (Valparaiso), April 11, 22, 1891. The dynamite cruiser was the largest-gunned warship the U.S. was able to construct before the invention of battleships a few years later.

2. Harry Thurston Peck, *Twenty Years of the Republic, 1885–1905* (New York: Dodd, Mead, 1906), 624; Winfield Scott Schley, *Forty-five Years under the Flag* (New York: D. Appleton, 1904), 192; Richard S. West, Jr., *Admirals of the American Empire: The Combined Story of George Dewey, Alfred Thayer Mahan, Winfield Scott Schley, and William Thomas Sampson* (Indianapolis: Bobbs-Merrill, 1948), 98–99, 295–96.

3. Schley, *Forty-five Years*, 212. An unproved suggestion that Schley asked to be sent to Chile is found in West, *Admirals of the American Empire*, 166. There is no evidence to corroborate the assertion or to show that even if true, Tracy would have been influenced by Schley's request. On the *Baltimore*'s orders see Blaine to Egan, March 23, 1891, *FRUS 1891*, no. 86, p.107; Egan to McCann, April 3, 1891, Miscellaneous Correspondence of Patrick Egan, RG 59, NARS.

4. McCann to Tracy, April 29, 1891, Letters Received by the Secretary of the Navy, RG 45, area file 299, no. 32, NARS.

5. Brown to Tracy, September 9, 1891, Naval Correspondence, "Message of the President of the United States Respecting the Relations with Chile, Together with the Diplomatic Correspondence; the Correspondence with the Naval Officials; the Inquiry into the Attack on the Seamen of the U.S.S. Baltimore in the Streets of Valparaiso; and the Evidence of the Officers and Crew of the Steamer Keweenaw Respecting the Ill Treatment of Patrick Shields by the Chilean Police," *H. Exec. Doc. 91*, 52d Cong., 1st sess., 1891–92, p. 288 (hereafter cited as *H. Exec. Doc. 91*); Brown to Tracy, September 20, 1891, ibid., pp. 289–90; Brown to Tracy, October 11, 1891, ibid., p. 292; Schley to Tracy, September 23, 1891, ibid., p. 290; Ramsey to Schley, September 26, 1891, ibid., p. 290. No documentation concerning why Tracy's and Schley's numerous requests to withdraw were ignored has been discovered.

6. *Baltimore* Log, Friday, October 16, 1891; Schley, *Forty-five Years*, 221–22.

7. Schley to Tracy, October 2, 1891, Naval Correspondence, *H. Exec. Doc. 91*, p. 292; Schley to Tracy, October 4, 1891, ibid. On Schley's changing observations of the political climate of Chile and Valparaiso, see Deposition of Winfield Scott Schley, Inquiry, *H. Exec. Doc. 91*, pp. 586–91; Schley to Tracy, September 25, 1891, series 2, Benjamin Harrison Papers, Manuscripts Division, Library of Congress; Osgood Hardy, "The United States and Chile: A Study of Diplomatic Relations with Especial

Emphasis on the Period of the Chilean Civil War of 1891" (Ph.D. diss., University of California, Berkeley, 1925), 290; Harold Lindsell, "The Chilean-American Controversy of 1891–92" (Ph.D. diss., New York University, 1942), 84; Allan Burton Spetter, "Harrison and Blaine: Foreign Policy, 1889–93" (Ph.D. diss., Rutgers University, 1967), 219–20.

8. Although there are countless versions of the riot that took place on October 16, 1891, the official U.S. position is presented in the inquiry conducted at Mare Island, California, contained in *H. Exec. Doc. 91*, pp. 341–610. I have reconstructed and interpreted the account from that inquiry.

9. Deposition of Winfield S. Schley, Inquiry, *H. Exec. Doc. 91*, p. 592.

10. Deposition of Uriel Sebree, ibid., pp. 572–73.

11. Deposition of John William Talbot, ibid., pp. 342–43.

12. Ibid., p. 344.

13. Ibid., p. 348.

14. Deposition of James Martin Johnson, ibid., p. 356.

15. Ibid.

16. Ibid., p. 357.

17. Ibid.

18. Deposition of Charles Langen, ibid., p. 369.

19. The official Chilean version of the Valparaiso riot, conducted October 17–December 19, 1891, known as the *sumario,* cannot be located. Apparently an official copy was never sent to the State Department and none can be found in the Archivos Nacionales in Santiago or in any of the other Chilean juridical or military archives. Reconstruction of the Chilean account can be surmised from press reports in the United States and Chile. The version presented here is taken from Egan to Blaine, January 18, 1892, enclosures 1 and 2, no. 263, *FRUS 1891*, pp. 289–305. Included are accurate translations of a review of the judge's report published originally in *El Progresso* (Talca, Chile) and a review of the prosecutor's report taken from the *Chilian Times*, October 26, 1891, *La Patria*, October 17, 1891, and *La Unión*, October 17, 1891. All three were Valparaiso newspapers.

20. "Opinion of the Fiscal in the Baltimore question," from the *Chilian Times*, December 31, 1891, in Egan to Blaine, no. 263, *FRUS 1891*, p. 293. See also *La Unión*, vol. 7, no. 1934, January 2, 1892, pp. 2–4.

21. Ibid., p. 297.

22. Ibid., p. 298.

23. Ibid.

24. Ibid., p. 299. The Chileans invited two of the physicians from the *Bal-*

timore to examine the corpse. Assistant Surgeon Stitt and Passed Assistant Surgeon Stephen S. White concluded the wound was caused by a rifle bullet. The *Baltimore*'s weapons expert, Lieutenant Henry McCrea, reported that "holes in the said uniform must have been made by a rifle of moderate caliber."

25. Ibid.
26. Deposition of James Martin Johnson, Inquiry, *H. Exec. Doc. 91*, p. 366.
27. Deposition of John B. Larson, ibid., p. 396.
28. Deposition of John H. Hamilton, ibid., p. 389.
29. Deposition of A. J. Stewart, ibid., p. 421.
30. Deposition of Patrick McWilliams, ibid., p. 489.
31. "Opinion of the Fiscal in the Baltimore question," from the *Chilian Times,* December 31, 1891, in Egan to Blaine, no. 263, *FRUS 1891,* p. 300.
32. USS *Baltimore* Medical Journal, October 22–October 24, 1891, Navy Department, NARS, pp. 214–16.
33. Deposition of E. R. Stitt, Inquiry, *H. Exec. Doc. 91*, p. 560.
34. *Baltimore* Medical Journal, October 25, 1891, Navy Department, NARS, p. 217; *Baltimore* Log, October 25–26, 1891, Navy Department, NARS.

2. OLD WOUNDS

1. On early U.S.-Chilean relations see Eugenio Pereira Salas, *Los primeros contactos entre Chile y los Estados Unidos, 1778–1808,* Historia de las relaciones internacionales de Chile (Santiago: Editorial Andrés Bello, 1971). Carlos Mery Squella continues in *Relaciones diplomáticas entre Chile y los Estados Unidos de América, 1829–1841,* Historia de las relaciones internacionales de Chile (Santiago: Editorial Andrés Bello, 1965). He calls early U.S. commercial relations with Chile "prudent and irreproachable" without resort to "ostentatious show of force" (pp. 23–24). See also Daniel Martner, *Estudio de política comercial Chilena e historia económica nacional,* 2 vols. (Santiago: Imprenta Universitaria, 1923); Brian Loveman, *Chile: The Legacy of Hispanic Capitalism* (New York: Oxford University Press, 1979); Robert N. Burr, *By Reason or Force: Chile and the Balancing of Power in South America, 1830–1905* (Berkeley: University of California Press, 1965); Arthur P. Whitaker, *The United States and the Southern Cone: Argentina, Chile, and Uruguay* (Cambridge: Harvard University Press, 1976) and *The United States and the Independence of Latin America, 1800–1830* (New York: W. W. Norton, 1941); Henry Clay Evans, Jr., *Chile and Its Relations*

with the United States (Durham, N.C.: Duke University Press, 1927); William Roderick Sherman, *The Diplomatic and Commercial Relations of the United States and Chile, 1820–1914* (Boston: Gorham Press, 1926).

2. Quoted in Evans, *Chile and Its Relations with the United States*, 67.

3. Quoted in Evans, *Chile and Its Relations with the United States*, 76–77. See also Mario Barros, *Historia diplomática de Chile: 1541–1938* (Barcelona: Ediciones Ariel, 1970), 16. Barros agrees that diplomatic relations between Chile and the United States were not cordial after 1860 and suggests that the United States was developing a role "unfavorable to what was then our international policy."

4. Kilpatrick to Seward, April 2, 1866, *FRUS 1866*, vol. 2 (Washington, D.C.: GPO, 1867), 386–93.

5. The literature on the War of the Pacific is enormous and partisan. The standard Chilean version presented here is reconstructed from Barros, *Historia diplomática;* Luis Galdames, *A History of Chile* (Chapel Hill: University of North Carolina Press, 1941); Anson Uriel Hancock, *A History of Chile* (Chicago: Charles H. Sergel, 1893); Gonzalo Bulnes, *La Guerra del Pacífico* 3 vols. (Santiago: Imprenta Universo, 1912–19); Burr, *By Reason or Force;* Sir William Laird Clowes, *Four Modern Naval Campaigns: Historical, Strategic, and Tactical* (New York: Unit Library, 1902); David M. Pletcher, *The Awkward Years: American Foreign Policy under Garfield and Arthur* (Columbia: University of Missouri Press, 1962); Frederick M. Nunn, *Yesterday's Soldiers: European Military Professionalism in South America, 1890–1940* (Lincoln: University of Nebraska Press, 1982).

6. *New York Daily Tribune,* November 2, 1891. On the early mediation attempts of the United States see Pletcher, *Awkward Years,* 42–43; Bulnes, *Guerra del Pacífico,* vol. 2.

7. David Saville Muzzey, *James G. Blaine: A Political Idol of Other Days* (New York: Dodd, Mead, 1935), 84; Fenton R. McCreery, October 31, 1891, diary, March–November, 1891, box 5, 5868, McCreery Family Papers, Bentley Historical Library, Ann Arbor, Mich.

8. *Chicago Times,* January 29, 1893.

9. *Washington Post,* January 30, 1882. Blaine later contradicted himself about who had instigated the conflict, remarking, "To blame England would be childish." Quoted in Edward P. Crapol, *America for Americans: Economic Nationalism and Anglophobia in the Late Nineteenth Century* (Westport, Conn.: Greenwood Press, 1973), 81.

10. On the suspected British connection in the War of the Pacific see Walter

LaFeber, *The New Empire: An Interpretation of American Expansion, 1860–1898* (Ithaca, N.Y.: Cornell University Press, 1963), 130; Sherman, *Diplomatic and Commercial Relations,* 131–32; Pletcher, *Awkward Years,* 9, 41; Crapol, *America for Americans,* 81; Harold Blakemore, *British Nitrates and Chilean Politics, 1886–1898: Balmaceda and North* (London: Athlone Press, 1974), 18–19.

11. Hurlbut's meddling is discussed in Pletcher, *Awkward Years,* 46–58; Whitaker, *United States and the Southern Cone,* 360–61; Herbert Millington, *American Diplomacy and the War of the Pacific* (New York: Columbia University Press, 1948) 85–95, 106–35; Charles S. Campbell, *The Transformation of American Foreign Relations, 1865–1900* (New York: Harper & Row, 1976), 94–98.

12. The Trescot fiasco is presented in Millington, *American Diplomacy,* 95–126; Pletcher, *Awkward Years,* 73–94; Bulnes, *Guerra del Pacífico,* vol. 3; Campbell, *Transformation of American Foreign Relations,* 94–98; Russell H. Bostert, "Diplomatic Reversal: Frelinghuysen's opposition to Blaine's Pan American Policy in 1882," *Mississippi Valley Historical Review* 42(1956): 653–71.

13. Patricio Estellé, *La controversia chileno-norteamericana de 1891–1892* (Santiago: Editorial Jurídica de Chile, 1967), 161–62; Barros, *Historia diplomática,* 16–17. U.S. historians agree: see Crapol, *America for Americans,* 181; Millington, *American Diplomacy,* 142; Pletcher, *Awkward Years,* 40; Sherman, *Diplomatic and Commerical Relations,* 142; Foster Rhea Dulles, *Prelude to World Power: American Diplomatic History, 1860–1900* (New York: Macmillan, 1965), 40–41; Frederick B. Pike, *Chile and the United States, 1880–1962* (Notre Dame, Ind.: University of Notre Dame Press, 1963), 49, 59; Alice Felt Tyler, *The Foreign Policy of James G. Blaine* (Minneapolis: University of Minnesota Press, 1927), 128.

14. Joseph Pulitzer to William Walter Phelps, February 14, 1889, General Correspondence and Miscellaneous, box 2, Phelps Collection, Huntington Library, San Marino, Calif.

15. Muzzey, *James G. Blaine,* 424–25.

16. The best study of Blaine's anti-British attitude is Crapol, *America for Americans,* 68, 85–87, 186, 206. See also Pletcher, *Awkward Years,* 14; Tyler, *Foreign Policy of James G. Blaine,* 113; William Appleman Williams, *The Roots of the Modern American Empire: A Study of the Growth and Shaping of Social Consciousness in a Marketplace Society* (New York: Random House, 1969), 136. On British commerce with Chile see J. Fred Rippy, *British Investments in Latin America, 1822–*

1949 (Hamden, Conn.: Archon Books, 1959), 25, 32–40; Joseph Smith, *Illusions of Conflict: Anglo-American Diplomacy toward Latin America, 1865–1896* (Pittsburgh: University of Pittsburgh Press, 1979), 4–5, 22–23, 27.

17. Blakemore, *British Nitrates*, 11, 22; Loveman, *Chile*, 147; Millington, *American Diplomacy*, 52; Allan Burton Spetter, "Harrison and Blaine: Foreign Policy, 1889–93" (Ph.D. diss., Rutgers University, 1967), 213–14. Commerce statistics for Chile may be culled from William E. Curtis, "Our Commercial Relations with Chili," *North American Review,* no. 424 (March, 1892): 359–64; Martner, *Estudio de política comercial chilena,* 2:475; Crisóstomo Pizarro, *La revolución de 1891: la modernización* (Valparaíso: Ediciones Universitarias de Valparaíso, 1971), 52; "Chili's Commerce and Finances," *The Nation* 46 (May 31, 1888): 442–43; Brian R. Mitchell, *Abstract of British Historical Statistics* (Cambridge: Cambridge University Press, 1962), 321–22; Department of Commerce, Bureau of the Census, *Historical Statistics of the United States* (Washington, D.C.: Government Printing Office, 1960), 550–53. See especially Thomas F. O'Brien, *The Nitrate Industry and Chile's Crucial Transition, 1870–1891* (New York: New York University Press, 1982).

18. U.S. commercial ties with Chile are discussed in a note sent from the Chilean minister to the United States, E. E. Varas to RE, October 15, 1889, vol. 415, AN; C. Maude to Salisbury, March 24, 1892, FO, no. 27, 16/268. On British nitrate investments, the best source is Blakemore, *British Nitrates,* 1, 7, 14, 22. See also Rippy, *British Investments in Latin America,* 36, 38, 58–61, 133. Pike, *Chile and the United States,* 10; Whitaker, *The United States and the Southern Cone,* 57, 65–67; Albert Bushnell Hart, *Practical Essays on American Government* (New York: Longmans, Green, 1893), 103; Curtis, "Commercial Relations with Chili," 359–64; "Chili's Commerce and Finances," 442–43; Horace N. Fisher, "Notes," *New England Magazine* 8 (March, 1893): 96–115; Smith, *Illusions of Conflict,* 27.

19. W. E. Curtis to Henry [?], February 26, 1890, box 1, 5868, Correspondence 1890, McCreery Family Papers, Bentley Historical Library.

20. Smith, *Illusions of Conflict,* 3, 25.

21. *New York Daily Tribune,* January 22, 1891.

22. There is no adequate study of Egan, and information about his life and personality is scarce. Sources pertaining to him before he became minister to Chile are Allen Johnson and Dumas Malone, eds., *Dictionary of American Biography* (New York: Charles Scribner's Sons, 1931), 51–

52; *Nebraska State Journal,* October 1, 1919; Arthur Bradley Hayes and Sam D. Cox, *History of the City of Lincoln, Nebraska* (Lincoln: Nebraska State Journal Co., 1889), 299–301, 309–12; William O'Brian, *Recollections* (New York: Macmillan, 1905), 135–36; F. Hugh O'Donnell, *A History of the Irish Parliamentary Party,* (New York: Longmans, Green, 1910) 2:270; Thomas N. Brown, *Irish–American Nationalism, 1870–1890* (Philadelphia: J. B. Lippincott, 1966), 117, 141, 158.

23. Johnson and Malone, *Dictionary of American Biography,* 51.

24. Fenton R. McCreery, June 15, 1890, diary, March–June, 1890, box 5, 5868, McCreery Family Papers, Bentley Historical Library.

25. E. E. Varas to RE, April 8, 1889, no. 36, vol. 415, AN: "Although in general republican newspapers approve the election and consider Mr. Egan a person dignified of the position and able to carry out the charge, many of them have expressed the opinion that perhaps the appointment of someone else would have been better accepted, given the present political situation and the fact that this gentleman only recently obtained his naturalization in this country, and where, until now, he had preferred to promote Irish Land League causes, fighting the politics of the present British government." For an earlier indication of Chilean discontent over Egan's appointment see Varas to RE, March 28, 1889, no. 33, vol. 415, AN. The National British-American Association passed a resolution protesting the appointment in June, 1889. See the *New York Times,* June 22, 1889. The British minister in Chile, John G. Kennedy, wrote Foreign Secretary Lord Salisbury, "Mr. Egan's appointment to Chile was not relished by his own countrymen or by the Chilean government. . . . Baron Gütschmid [Felix von Gütschmid, German minister to Chile] believes Mr. Egan is actively working against British and German commercial and political interests in Chili so as to establish the influence of the United States." Kennedy to Salisbury, April 12, 1891, FO, General Correspondence, Chile, 1823–1897, no. 33, 16/264. On the wisdom of Egan's appointment see also José Miguel Barros Franco, *El caso del "Baltimore": Apuntes para la historia diplomática de Chile* (Santiago: Escuela de Ciencias Jurídicas y Sociales, 1950), 19; Harold Blakemore, "The Chilean Revolution of 1891 and Its Historiography," *Hispanic American Historical Review* 45 (August, 1965): 404–5; Estellé, *Controversia chileno-norteamericana,* 167–68; John A. S. Grenville and George Berkeley Young, *Politics, Strategy, and American Diplomacy: Studies in Foreign Policy, 1873–1917* (New Haven, Conn.: Yale University Press, 1966), 96; Hart, *Practical Essays,* 107–8; Harold Lindsell,

"The Chilean-American Controversy of 1891–1892" (Ph.D. diss., New York University, 1942), 151–52; LaFeber, in *New Empire,* 130–31, asserts that the appointment "openly declared war upon British influence in Chile."

26. Balmaceda remains a controversial and enigmatic figure even for U.S. historians. Hancock, *History of Chile,* 348, characterizes him as "rather an Andrew Johnson than a Robespierre"; Muzzey, *James G. Blaine,* 414, calls Balmaceda a man of "Bismarckian audacity." An incisive contemporary comment came from Minister Kennedy, "Balmaceda was tall and thin, with effusive manners and great faculty of speech; consumed by political ambition and personal vanity." Kennedy to Salisbury, December 31, 1891, FO, no. 145, 16/266.

27. Blakemore, *British Nitrates,* 43. See also O'Brien, *Nitrate Industry,* 111–12, 128–29; Michael Monteón, *Chile in the Nitrate Era: The Evolution of Economic Dependence, 1880–1930* (Madison: University of Wisconsin Press, 1982), 31.

28. Blakemore, *British Nitrates,* 71–99, 121–25, 152, 193. See also "Chilean Revolution of 1891" and "Los agentes revolucionarios chilenos en Europa, en 1891," *Mapocho* 5 (1966): 101–17. Blakemore decisively shows that Britain was officially impartial during the conflict and unofficially less than neutral. Whatever the British position, Blakemore insists, the conflict leading to the revolution was a struggle of the aristocracy, between Balmaceda and the Chilean congress, one in which the masses played a small part. See Barros, *Historia diplomática,* 454, who believes the revolution was not social, economic, or political but one of temperaments—a "psychological explosion of the Basque aristocracy"; Barros Franco, *El caso del "Baltimore,"* 15; Clowes, *Four Modern Naval Campaigns,* 135–36; Estellé, *Controversia chileno-norteamericana,* 162, asserts Blaine and Balmaceda conspired to limit British activity in Chile; Pike, *Chile and the United States,* 41–46; Whitaker, *The United States and the Southern Cone,* 69–70; Osgood Hardy, "The United States and Chile: A Study of Diplomatic Relations with Especial Emphasis on the Period of the Chilean Civil War of 1891" (Ph.D. diss., University of California, 1925), 99–109; Frederick M. Nunn, *The Military in Chilean History: Essays on Civil–Military Relations, 1810–1973* (Albuquerque: University of New Mexico Press, 1976), 108–10; Maurice Zeitlin, *The Civil Wars in Chile* (Princeton, N.J.: Princeton University Press, 1984), 80–84, 92–117; Monteón, *Chile in the Nitrate Era,* 26–47.

29. "Manifesto to the Nation," January 1, 1891, *Diario Oficial de la Re-*

pública de Chile, vol. 16, no. 4221 (Santiago: Oficina de la Imprenta Nacional, 1891), 1; see also Pedro Montt, *Exposition of the Illegal Acts of Ex-President Balmaceda Which Caused the Civil War in Chile* (Washington, D.C.: Gibson Bros., 1891); John Bassett Moore, "The Late Chilean Controversy," *Political Science Quarterly* 8 (1893): 467–94.

30. Lazcano to Blaine, January 16, 1891, *FRUS 1891,* p. 313; Lazcano to Blaine, June 20, 1891, *FRUS 1891,* p. 320; Blaine to Lazcano, January 30, 1891, *FRUS 1891,* p. 313.

31. Egan to Blaine, January 17, 1891, *FRUS 1891,* pp. 93–94. See also State Department Notes from Patrick Egan to the Chilean Government, 1889–1893, January 16, 1891, RG 59, NARS. Blaine to Tracy, January 19, 1891, Naval Correspondence, "Message of the President of the United States Respecting the Relations with Chile, Together with the Diplomatic Correspondence; the Correspondence with the Naval Officials; the Inquiry into the Attack on the Seamen of the U.S.S. Baltimore in the Streets of Valparaiso; and the Evidence of the Officers and Crew of the Steamer Keweenaw Respecting the Ill Treatment of Patrick Shields by the Chilean Police," *H. Exec. Doc. 91,* 52d Cong., 1st sess., 1891–92, p. 233 (hereafter cited as *H. Exec. Doc. 91*).

32. J. F. Van Ingen to Blaine, January 14, 1891, State Department Consular Despatches from Talcahuano, RG 59, no. 122, NARS.

33. Tracy to McCann, January 24, 1891, Naval Correspondence, *H. Exec. Doc. 91,* p. 233.

34. Tracy to McCann, March 4, 1891, ibid., p. 237.

35. McCann to Tracy, March 10, 1891, enclosure 1 (February 22, 1891) and enclosure 2 (March 10, 1891), Naval Correspondence, *H. Exec. Doc. 91,* pp. 238–39.

36. Egan to Mrs. Frank Sharp, January 17, 1891, and Egan to Mr. McCrer and Brother, February 5, 1891, State Department Consular and Miscellaneous Correspondence of Minister Patrick Egan, 1889–93, RG 59, NARS.

37. Montt to Blaine, May 16, 1891, State Department Notes from the Chilean Legation in the United States to the State Department, RG 59, NARS. Barros Franco, *El caso del "Baltimore,"* 479, asserts Egan responded to Montt's request saying, "We can't deal with insurgents." Lazcano was, of course, deeply grateful for the action and thanked the United States for its "prompt and friendly action" in enforcing the "most rigid execution of its neutrality laws." Lazcano to William F. Wharton (acting secretary of state), June 22, 1891, State Department Notes from the Chilean Legation, RG 59, NARS. The press was quick to note the

likely problems this definition of recognition would cause. See *New York Daily Tribune,* June 12, 1891; *New York Times,* June 25, 1891; ibid., June 28, 1891; ibid., June 30, 1891; ibid., August 30, 1891.

38. Egan to Pitkin, January 12, 1891 and February 12, 1891, Miscellaneous Correspondence of Patrick Egan, RG 59, NARS.

39. Egan to J. W. Merriam, April 22, 1891, ibid.

40. Egan to Blaine, March 17, 1891, no. 143, *FRUS 1891,* p. 107. Egan to Blaine, June 3, 1891, no. 171, *FRUS 1891,* pp. 134–35. Egan to Blaine, July 16, 1891, no. 181, *FRUS 1891,* p. 146.

41. Quoted in Egan to Blaine, February 13, 1891, no. 129, *FRUS 1891,* p. 104.

42. McCann to Tracy, March 24, 1891, Naval Correspondence, *H. Exec. Doc. 91,* p. 244; McCann to Tracy, May 17, 1891, ibid., p. 289.

43. Fenton McCreery, March 19, 1891, diary, March–November, 1891, box 5, 5868, McCreery Family Papers, Bentley Historical Library.

44. Kennedy to Thomas Sanderson (British undersecretary of state), September 15, 1891, FO 16/266. Kennedy later wrote the Foreign Office, "Relations between Chile and the United States are strained in consequence of hostility shown the congressional party by the latter," October 2, 1891, FO, no. 42, 16/267. See also Kennedy to FO, October 8, 1891, FO, no. 105, 16/267; Kennedy to Sanderson, September 4, 1891, FO, 16/266.

45. Wharton to Egan, July 3, 1891, State Department Instructions to the Minister in Chile, RG 59, no. 112, NARS. See also Osgood Hardy, "Was Patrick Egan a 'Blundering Minister'?" *Hispanic American Historical Review* 8 (1928): 78, and "United States and Chile," 285–86; Moore, "The Late Chilean Controversy," 467–68. In Chile the rumor even spread that it would be the *Baltimore* that would be sold. See *La Unión,* vol. 7, no. 1856, October 2, 1891, 2.

46. Joaquín Rodríquez Bravo, *Balmaceda y el conflicto entre el congreso y el ejecutivo,* 2 vols. (Santiago: Imprenta Gutenberg and Imprenta Cervantes, 1921 and 1925), 2:226–27.

47. "The attitude of my father, as Minister of the United States Government requires no defence," wrote Egan's son Francis, the twenty-five-year-old clerk of the U.S. legation in Chile. For other defenses, see the *Chilian Times,* October 17, 1891, no. 845, and *El Ferrocarril,* October 16, 1891. Still, the charge of corruption was constantly made. See John Trumbull, *A Challenge: Chili's Vindication* (Valparaiso: Imprenta del Universo de G. Helfmann, 1892); *Harper's Weekly,* September 12, 1891, vol. 25, no. 1812; *New York Times,* September 12, 1891; *London Times,* September 7, 1891. President Harrison dismissed the charges as "vague and gener-

al. . . . I do not believe they are true." Harrison to H. K. Carroll, April 16, 1892, Albert T. Volwiler Papers, box 7 (August 6, 1891 to May 4, 1892), Lilly Library, Indiana University.

48. Egan to Blaine, March 17, 1891, no. 143, *FRUS 1891*, p. 107. See also Blakemore, *British Nitrates*, 181–82, 199; Trumbull, *A Challenge*, 9–10; William Howard Russell, *A Visit to Chile and the Nitrate Fields of Tarapacá* (London: J. S. Virtue, 1891), 42, 82; Alberto Fagalde, *La prensa estranjera y la dictadura chilena* (Santiago: Imprenta Santiago, 1891), vii.

49. Kennedy to Sanderson, September 15, 1891, FO, 16/266.

50. Blakemore, *British Nitrates*, 193–97, 204, 210. See also Blakemore, "The Chilean Revolution of 1891," 420, and "Los agentes revolucionarios chilenos," 103–5, 112; Burr, *By Reason or Force*, 193; Hancock, *History of Chile*, 349–50. Historians agree that Osgood Hardy, in "British Nitrates and the Balmaceda Revolution," *Pacific Historical Review* 17 (May, 1948): 165–80, overstated the relation of the British nitrate interest to the Balmaceda uprising.

51. Harlow to Harrison, June 11, 1891, Benjamin Harrison, Papers, series 1 (December 2, 1889 to January 10, 1890), Manuscripts Division, Library of Congress.

52. Barros Franco, *El caso del "Baltimore,"* 20; Hernán Ramírez Necochea, *Balmaceda y la contrarevolución de 1891* (Santiago: Editorial Universitaria, 1969), 163; Campbell, *Transformation of American Foreign Relations*, 168–69.

53. Kennedy to Salisbury, May 25, 1891, FO, no. 49, 16/264; Kennedy to Salisbury, June 23, 1891, FO, no. 62, 16/265.

54. *London Times*, September 3, 1891, p. 3.

55. Trumbull, *A Challenge*, 5–15, 31.

56. "The Chilian Situation," *The Nation*, 52 (June 18, 1891): 492–93; "Our Treatment of Chili," ibid., 53 (October 29, 1891): 326–27; untitled commentary, ibid., December 3, 1891, p. 426.

57. "It is safe to say without any undue criticism of Mr. Egan that if we had had a trained diplomat in Chile . . . there would have been no 'Chilean imbroglio,'" Freeman Snow, "The Chilean Imbroglio," *Harvard Monthly* 13 (February, 1892): 184. Estellé, in *La controversia chileno-norteamericana,* 166, similarly complains that the great defect of nineteenth-century U.S. foreign policy rested with representatives "without any preparation and only occupying said office as a way of compensating their political services." See also Smith, *Illusions of Conflict,* chapter two, on the training of U.S. diplomats in the late nineteenth century.

1. Lazcano to Blaine, March 10, 1891, *FRUS 1891*, p. 314. Blaine to Lazcano, March 13, 1891, *FRUS 1891*, pp. 314–15; see also Waldo Silva Barros Luca to Blaine, March 22 and March 24, 1891, ibid., p. 315.

2. Lazcano to Blaine, May 5, 1891, ibid., p. 316.

3. *Chilian Times,* July 18, 1891, no. 824, p. 2. The *New York Times* also posed and answered the same question: "It will be seen that if there had been any neglect or delay on the part of our Government to take action upon this information our position would have been precisely analogous to that of Great Britain in the matter of the *Alabama,* and our own doctrine, which was sustained by the tribunal of arbitration, might have been quoted against us by Chile with overwhelming effect." *New York Times,* May 7, 1891. See also the *New York Times,* May 11, May 14, and May 15, 1891.

4. Charles Mason Remey, ed., *Life and Letters of Rear Admiral George Collier Remey: United States Navy, 1841–1928,* 10 vols. (Washington, D.C.: Charles Mason Remey, 1939), 3:771. See also Tracy to Remey, May 8, 1891, Naval Correspondence, "Message of the President of the United States Respecting the Relations with Chile, Together with the Diplomatic Correspondence; the Correspondence with the Naval Officials; the Inquiry into the Attack on the Seamen of the U.S.S. Baltimore in the Streets of Valparaiso; and the Evidence of the Officers and Crew of the Steamer Keweenaw Respecting the Ill Treatment of Patrick Shields by the Chilean Police," *H. Exec. Doc. 91,* 52d Cong., 1st sess., 1891–92, p. 250 (hereafter cited as *H. Exec. Doc. 91*). Tracy's words were: "If *Itata* is found seize her and accompany her into port. If *Itata* is convoyed by Chilean war vessel explain circumstances and demand restoration to possession of United States. If demand refused, enforce if your force is clearly sufficient; if not sufficient, follow *Itata* till you fall in with Admiral Brown . . . who has been ordered to intercept her." See also *Chilian Times,* May 13, 1891, no. 804, p. 1.

5. Brown to Tracy, May 14, 1891, enclosure 1, Naval Correspondence, *H. Exec. Doc. 91,* pp. 253–54. See also McCann to Tracy, May 16, 1891, Naval Correspondence, *H. Exec. Doc. 91,* p. 255.

6. Errázuriz to Blaine, June 5, 1891, *FRUS 1891*, p. 317.

7. McCann to Tracy, May 12, 1891, Naval Correspondence, *H. Exec. Doc. 91,* p. 252. See also Remey to Tracy, July 4, 1891, Naval Correspondence, *H. Exec. Doc. 91,* p. 274; Patricio Estellé, *La controversia chileno-norteamericana de 1891–1892* (Santiago: Editorial Jurídica de

Chile, 1967), 204–5. The Balmaceda regime, however, expressed gratitude to the United States. See Lazcano to RE, February 26 and July 18,
1891, no. 43 and 66, Chilean Legation in the United States, AN.

8. Mario Barros, *Historia diplomática de Chile: 1541–1938* (Barcelona:
Ediciones Ariel, 1970), 39; Harold Lindsell, "The Chilean-American
Controversy of 1891–1892" (Ph.D. diss., New York University, 1942),
50–55; Osgood Hardy, "The United States and Chile: A Study of Diplomatic Relations with Especial Emphasis on the Period of the Chilean
Civil War of 1891" (Ph.D. diss., University of California, 1925), 186–
210.

9. Francisco Valdés Vergara to Ismael Valdés Vergara, May 15, 1891, in
Benjamín Valdés Alfonso, ed., *Una familia bajo la dictadura* (Santiago:
Editorial Francisco de Aguirre, 1972), 172. Francisco Valdés Vergara to
Ismael Valdés Vergara, May 30, 1891, ibid., 181; Francisco Valdés Ver-
gara to Ismael Valdés Vergara, June 24, 1891, ibid., 189–90.

10. John Trumbull, *A Challenge: Chili's Vindication* (Valparaiso: Imprenta
del Universo de G. Helfmann, 1892), 24–25.

11. *La Patria,* September 14, 1891, no. 809, p. 2.

12. McCann to Tracy, June 17, 1891, General Area File, 1775–1910, RG 45,
NARS.

13. Remey, *Rear Admiral Remey,* 3:776.

14. McCann to Tracy, June 22, 1891, Naval Correspondence, *H. Exec. Doc.
91,* p. 272.

15. Wharton to Egan, June 17, 1891, State Department Instructions to
Ministers in Chile, RG 59, NARS; Wharton to Egan, June 19, 1891, ibid.;
Wharton to Egan, June 20, 1891, ibid.; Central and South American
Telegraph Company to McCann, July 10, 1891, Naval Correspondence,
H. Exec. Doc. 91, p. 276; McCann to Central and South American
Telegraph Company, July 11, 1891, ibid., p. 277; McCann to Merriam,
July 12, 1891, ibid., p. 278; McCann to Tracy, July 14, 1891, ibid., p. 276.

16. Trumbull, *A Challenge,* 23–24.

17. Brown to Tracy, August 19, 1891, Naval Correspondence, *H. Exec. Doc.
91,* p. 280.

18. Brown to Tracy, August 20, 1891, Naval Correspondence, *H. Exec. Doc.
91,* p. 281; Brown to Tracy, August 31, 1891, ibid., p. 282.

19. *La Patria,* September 10, 1891, vol. 39, no. 8434, p. 2. *El Mercurio,*
September 11, 1891, vol. 64, no. 19239, p. 2. *El Ferrocarril,* June 22,
1892, no. 11424, p. 2. *La República,* June 29, 1892, p. 3.

20. Trumbull, *A Challenge,* 25–27. "Hitherto the United States Navy was
obeying orders; but not so in Admiral Brown's trip to Quinteros. There

the naval officer assumed the responsibility of his action, though even in that Mr. Egan was probably the suggestor of the trip. . . . Admiral Brown, in his 'distinct denial of the odious charges' that he brought back 'most important information to the Government authorities at Valparaiso,' seeks to make out that everything was known on shore. This is not so . . . even after Admiral Brown left the harbor, the authorities did not know the force of the enemy nor whether the landing was effective, nor whether the attack might not eventually come from the South; but no sooner had Admiral Brown's flag lieutenant been to the Intendente, and given the result of the *San Francisco*'s observations than the whole aspect changed, for the Dictator's supporters then knew what to expect, and sent out all the men they could possibly spare."

21. Ibid.

22. Brown to Egan, September 8, 1891, *FRUS 1891*, p. 164.

23. Brown to Tracy, August 30, 1891, Naval Correspondence, *H. Exec. Doc. 91*, p. 281. See also Egan to Blaine, August 30, 1891, no. 195, *FRUS 1891*, p. 156, and Egan to Blaine, October 8, 1891, *FRUS 1891*, p. 184. Jorge Dupouy Grez, *Relaciones chileno-argentinas durante el gobierno de don Jorge Montt, 1891–1896* (Santiago: Editorial Andrés Bello, 1968), 13.

24. Egan to Blaine, August 30, 1891, no. 195, *FRUS 1891*, p. 156; ibid., no. 193, p. 153.

25. Ibid., September 24, 1891, p. 166.

26. Brown to Tracy, September 5, 1891, ibid., p. 287.

27. Egan to Matta, September 23, 1891, Notes from Patrick Egan to the Chilean Government, RG 59, NARS; Egan to Matta, September 25, 1891, ibid.; Egan to Matta, September 25, 1891, ibid.

28. Wharton to Egan, September 26, 1891, State Department Instructions to Ministers in Chile, RG 59, NARS.

29. Egan to Matta, September 26, 1891, Notes from Patrick Egan to the Chilean Government, RG 59, NARS.

30. Quoted in Egan to Blaine, August 30, 1891, no. 193, *FRUS 1891*, p. 153.

31. Robley D. Evans, *A Sailor's Log: Recollections of Forty Years of Naval Life* (New York: D. Appleton, 1901), 274.

32. Harrison to Blaine, September 26, 1891, in *The Correspondence between Benjamin Harrison and James G. Blaine, 1882–1893,* edited by Albert T. Volwiler (Philadelphia: American Philosophical Society, 1940), 196.

33. Matta to Egan, October 20, 1891, enclosure 1 in Egan to Blaine, October 26, 1891, no. 213, *FRUS 1891*, p. 199; Egan to Blaine, October 26, 1891,

ibid., pp. 198–99; Wharton to Egan, October 1, 1891, State Department Instructions to the Ministers in Chile, RG 59, NARS.

34. Juan E. Mackenna, *Carta política dirijida por Juan E. Mackenna* (Valparaiso: Imprenta Mercantil, 1893), 150.

35. Quoted in Egan to Blaine, September 7, 1891, no. 198, *FRUS 1891*, p. 161.

36. Trumbull, *A Challenge,* 15.

37. Merriam to Wharton, August 31, 1891, State Department Consular Despatches from Iquique, RG 59, no. 548, NARS.

38. Egan to Blaine, September 17, 1891, no. 203, *FRUS 1891*, p. 163.

4. WRANGLING

1. Winfield Scott Schley, *Forty-five Years under the Flag* (New York: D. Appleton, 1904), 223–24.

2. USS *Baltimore* Log, October 17, 1891, Navy Department, NARS.

3. Schley to Lieutenant S. A. May, Lieutenant J. H. Sears, Passed Assistant Surgeon S. S. White, October 18, 1891, enclosure C in Schley to Tracy, October 23, 1891, Naval Correspondence, "Message of the President of the United States Respecting the Relations with Chile, Together with the Diplomatic Correspondence; the Correspondence with the Naval Officials; the Inquiry into the Attack on the Seamen of the U.S.S. Baltimore in the Streets of Valparaiso; and the Evidence of the Officers and Crew of the Steamer Keweenaw Respecting the Ill Treatment of Patrick Shields by the Chilean Police," *H. Exec. Doc. 91,* 52d Cong., 1st sess., 1891–92, p. 296 (hereafter cited as H. Exec. Doc. 91); also Schley to Tracy, October 17, 1891, Naval Correspondence, *H. Exec. Doc. 91,* p. 293.

4. Egan to Blaine, October 18, 1891, *FRUS 1891*, p. 194; Schley to Egan, October 17, 1891, enclosure 1 in Egan to Blaine, October 19, 1891, no. 211, *FRUS 1891*, p. 195. To the notion the disturbance was unprovoked and premeditated, John Trumbull remarked: "This unmitigated lie is the origin of all your difficulty with Chile. It arose from the venom of a heart that loved duplicity . . . and was filled with disappointment and bitter hatred." John Trumbull, *A Challenge: Chili's Vindication* (Valparaiso: Imprenta del Universo de G. Helfmann, 1892), 15–16.

5. *Baltimore* Log, October 18, 1891, Navy Department, NARS.

6. Witnesses to the crew's sobriety are found in Schley, *Forty-five Years,* 225; Thomas Campbell Copeland, ed., *Harrison and Reid: Their Lives and Record* (New York: Charles L. Webster, 1892), 195.

7. Schley to Egan, October 22, 1891, Naval Correspondence, *H. Exec. Doc. 91*, pp. 298–300; Schley to Tracy, October 23, 1891, Naval Correspondence, *H. Exec. Doc. 91*, pp. 293–95.

8. May, Sears, and White to Tracy, October 19, 1891, enclosure D in Schley to Tracy, October 23, 1891, Naval Correspondence, *H. Exec. Doc. 91*, pp. 296–97; also Schley to Egan, October 22, 1891, enclosures 1 and 2 in Egan to Blaine, October 28, 1891, no. 217, *FRUS 1891*, pp. 204–7.

9. *New York Times,* October 18, 1891; ibid., October 24, 1891; *New York Daily Tribune,* October 24, 1891; ibid., October 27, 1891.

10. Schley to Egan, October 22, 1891, Benjamin Harrison Papers, series 2, September 22–December 10, 1891, Manuscripts Division, Library of Congress; Egan to Blaine, October 23, 1891, *FRUS 1891*, p. 196.

11. Tracy to Schley, October 24, 1891, Naval Correspondence, *H. Exec. Doc. 91*, p. 301; Schley to Tracy, October 26, 1891, Naval Correspondence, *H. Exec. Doc. 91*, p. 302; Tracy to Schley, October 30, 1891, Naval Correspondence, *H. Exec. Doc. 91*, p. 302; Schley to Tracy, October 31, 1891, Naval Correspondence, *H. Exec. Doc. 91*, pp. 302–3.

12. Wharton to Egan, October 23, 1891, *FRUS 1891*, pp. 196–97. The *New York Daily Tribune* reported the same notions, October 25, 1891.

13. Schley to Arlegüi, October 17, 1891, enclosure A in Schley to Tracy, October 23, 1891, Naval Correspondence, *H. Exec. Doc. 91*, pp. 295–96: "I regret extremely to inform your excellency that, while my men were on liberty yesterday afternoon to enjoy the hospitality of a port with which my nation is upon the most friendly terms of amity, an unfortunate disturbance occurred, in which one of my petty officers was killed and six of my men seriously stabbed. I feel that it will only be necessary to request your excellency to institute a most searching investigation into the circumstances leading to this affair, in order to establish the culpability for this unfortunate collision. I can only say in advance that if my men have been the instigators in this affair they will be dealt with most severely under the laws of my country, and I feel certain that if it should be otherwise your excellency will bring to justice all offenders."

14. Egan to Blaine, October 26, 1891, no. 214, *FRUS 1891*, pp. 202–3; *New York Daily Tribune,* November 1, 1891. See also Jorge Dupouy Grez, *Relaciones chileno-argentinas durante el gobierno de don Jorge Montt, 1891–1896* (Santiago: Editorial Andrés Bello, 1968), 13.

15. *New York Daily Tribune,* November 1, 1891.

16. Foster Recábarren to Schley, October 17, 1891, Naval Correspondence, *H. Exec. Doc. 91*, p. 294.

17. Arlegüi to Schley, October 22, 1891, Naval Correspondence, *H. Exec. Doc. 91*, pp. 300–1.

18. Egan to Matta, October 26, 1891, enclosure 3 in Egan to Blaine, October 28, 1891, no. 217, *FRUS 1891*, pp. 208–9.

19. Matta to Egan, October 27, 1891, enclosure 4 in Egan to Blaine, October 28, 1891, no. 217, *FRUS 1891*, pp. 209–10; also Matta to Egan, October 27, 1891, enclosure A in Montt to Blaine, December 19, 1891, ibid., pp. 330–31.

20. Egan to Blaine, October 31, 1891, *FRUS 1891*, pp. 210–11.

21. *New York Daily Tribune,* October 29, 1891; ibid., October 30, 1891.

22. Fenton R. McCreery, November 10, 1891, diary, March–November, box 5, 5868, McCreery Family Papers, Bentley Historical Library, Ann Arbor, Mich.; ibid., December 9, 1891, diary, 1891–92.

23. Montt to Matta, October 30, 1891, no. 75, vol. 482, AN; Montt to Matta, November 9, 1891, no. 10, vol. 482, AN.

24. *New York Times,* October 28, 1891.

25. Arlegüi to Schley, October 20, 1891, enclosure 1 in Schley to Tracy, November 25, 1891, Naval Correspondence, *H. Exec. Doc. 91*, p. 314.

26. Schley to Tracy, October 31, 1891, Naval Correspondence, *H. Exec. Doc. 91*, pp. 302–3; Egan to Blaine, October 30, 1891, *FRUS 1891*, p. 210.

27. Egan to Blaine, October 28, 1891, no. 217, *FRUS 1891*, p. 204. Egan to Blaine, October 30, 1891, ibid., p. 210. Schley to Tracy, October 31, 1891, Naval Correspondence, *H. Exec. Doc. 91*, pp. 302–3. Tracy to Schley, November 1, 1891, ibid., p. 303. Blaine to Egan, November 1, 1891, *FRUS 1891*, p. 211. Schley to Tracy, November 2, 1891, Naval Correspondence, *H. Exec. Doc. 91*, p. 303. Schley to Tracy, November 6, 1891, ibid., p. 304. Tracy to Schley, November 7, 1891, ibid.

28. Arlegüi to Schley, November 5, 1891, enclosure 17 in Schley to Tracy, November 25, 1891, Naval Correspondence, *H. Exec. Doc. 91*, p. 319; Schley to Arlegüi, November 6, 1891, enclosure 18 in Schley to Tracy, November 25, 1891, ibid., p. 320; Schley to Arlegüi, November 17, 1891, enclosure 31 in Schley to Tracy, November 25, 1891, ibid., p. 323. See also *Baltimore* Log, November 20, 1891, Navy Department, NARS.

29. Arlegüi to Schley, October 29, 1891, enclosure 7 in Schley to Tracy, November 25, 1891, Naval Correspondence, *H. Exec. Doc. 91*, pp. 314–15; Schley to Arlegüi, November 1, 1891, enclosure 8 in Schley to Tracy, November 25, 1891, ibid., p. 315; Schley to Egan, November 1, 1891, enclosure 9 in Schley to Tracy, November 25, 1891, ibid.; Egan to Schley, November 2, 1891, enclosure 11 in Schley to Tracy, November 25, 1891, ibid., p. 316; Schley to Arlegüi, November 3, 1891, enclosure 12, in Schley to Tracy, November 25, 1891, ibid., pp. 316–17; Matta to Montt, left with Blaine, December 3, 1891, *FRUS 1891*, p. 324; Montt to Blaine, December 11, 1891, ibid., p. 325.

30. Schley to Arlegüi, November 6, 1891, enclosure 21 in Schley to Tracy, November 25, 1891, Naval Correspondence, *H. Exec. Doc. 91*, p. 320; Arlegüi to Schley, November 6, 1891, enclosure 22 in Schley to Tracy, ibid., pp. 320–21; Schley to Tracy, November 8, 1891, ibid., p. 304. On November 8 the story even spread that the Chileans had blown up the *Baltimore* with a torpedo. See the *New York Times*, November 8, 1891; see also Trumbull, *A Challenge*, 30–31.

31. Matta to Egan, October 30, 1891, enclosure C in Montt to Blaine, December 19, 1891, *FRUS 1891*, pp. 332–33. Ezequiel Lazo to Arlegüi, October 27, 1891, no vol. no., pp. 95–97, AN; Arlegüi to Matta, October 28, 1891, no. 3116, no vol. no., pp. 92–95, AN. Arlegüi contended that the *sumario* demonstrated the "extremes of inaccuracy of the charges formulated by the honorable minister of the United States against the police of this port. Thus it is entirely impossible that the police could have committed the number of brutalities and cruel excesses that are imputed to them." Like Schley, who seemed to have made up his mind, the Chilean judge of crimes apparently formulated the Chilean version of the incident even before the *Baltimore* sailors testified. Schley naturally objected to the report and in sending it to Egan on November 1 insisted that until all the information was before the intendente he could not understand how the conclusion could be reached that the charges against the police were inaccurate. See Montt to Blaine, December 19, 1891, *FRUS 1891*, pp. 326–30; Matta to Egan, October 30, 1891, enclosure 13 in Schley to Tracy, November 25, 1891, Naval Correspondence, *H. Exec. Doc. 91*, pp. 317–18.

32. Robley D. Evans, *A Sailor's Log: Recollections of Forty Years of Naval Life* (New York: D. Appleton, 1901), 259–60. See also Edwin A. Falk, *Fighting Bob Evans* (New York: Cornwall Press, 1931), 154–56. Schley to Tracy, December 18, 1891, Naval Correspondence, *H. Exec. Doc. 91*, pp. 325–27: "In defense of the good character of my men on that occasion I reassert that the difficulty was in no sense a drunken street quarrel."

33. Tracy to Schley, December 4, 1891, Naval Correspondence, *H. Exec. Doc. 91*, p. 324; Schley to Tracy, December 5, 1891, ibid., pp. 324–25; Schley to Tracy, December 6, 1891, ibid., p. 325; Schley to Tracy, December 18, 1891, ibid., pp. 325–26. The judge of crimes remanded McWilliams to Schley, expressed satisfaction at the punishment decided by the court-martial (solitary confinement of thirty days in double irons on bread and water, and loss of three-months pay), but requested that if not contrary to navy rules, the term of imprisonment be remitted.

Schley complied. Schley to Arlegüi, December 3, 1891, enclosure 40 in Schley to Tracy, November 25, 1891, ibid., p. 330.

34. Foster Recábarren to Arlegüi, November 26, 1891, *Memoria del Ministro de Relaciones Esteriores Culto i Colonización: Presentado al Congreso Nacional en—1892* (Santiago: Imprenta Nacional, 1892), 2:74. See also *La Patria,* December 9, 1891, vol. 29, no. 8508, p. 2; *La Unión,* December 2, 1891, vol. 7, no. 1908, p. 2. As if to prove that drunken U.S. sailors always cause riots, the Chilean press reported that drunken U.S. sailors had recently rioted in Montevideo. *La Patria,* December 13, 1891, vol. 29, no. 8512, p. 3.

35. Schley to Tracy, November 25, 1891, Naval Correspondence, *H. Exec. Doc. 91,* pp. 310–13 and enclosures 1–52, pp. 314–34.

36. *Chilian Times,* November 7, 1891, no. 850, p. 2.

37. Foster Recábarren to Minister of Justice, November 3, 1891, *Memoria . . . 1891,* 2:82–83. Foster Recábarren to Matta, November 3, 1891, no. 382, no vol. no., AN. Foster Recábarren to Egan, November 3, 1891, State Department Notes from the Chilean Legation to the State Department, RG 59, no. 5, NARS. See also *El Mercurio,* November 11, 1891, vol. 65, no. 19289, p. 2, which expressed the same idea.

38. This version of the Shields case is reconstructed from the testimony of Shields and thirteen others in Evidence of the Officers and Crew of the Steamer Keweenaw Respecting the Ill Treatment of Patrick Shields by the Chilean Police, *H. Exec. Doc. 91,* pp. 611–64. See also *FRUS 1891,* pp. 217–60.

39. McCreery to Arlegüi, November 4, 1891, enclosure 1 in Egan to Blaine, November 9, 1891, *FRUS 1891,* p. 222.

40. Deposition of Patrick Shields, Ill Treatment of Shields, *H. Exec. Doc. 91,* p. 621.

41. Luis Pereira to Montt, January 13, 1891, Telegrams, vol. 495, 1891–93, AN. See also Deposition of William H. Jenkins, Ill Treatment of Shields, *H. Exec. Doc. 91,* p. 632.

42. Egan to Blaine, November 7, 1891, *FRUS 1891,* p. 217. McCreery to Arlegüi, November 4, 1891, unnumbered enclosure in Egan to Blaine, November 9, 1891, no. 223, *FRUS 1891,* p. 223.

43. Arlegüi to McCreery, November 4, 1891, unnumbered enclosure in Egan to Blaine, November 9, 1891, no. 223, *FRUS 1891,* p. 223. See also Arlegüi to McCreery, November 7, 1891, unnumbered enclosure in Egan to Blaine, November 23, 1891, no. 238, ibid., p. 239.

44. Stephen S. White to Schley, November 3, 1891, enclosure 2 in Egan to Blaine, November 9, 1891, no. 223, ibid., p. 222. See also Medical Report

of Dr. S. S. White, November 20, 1891, enclosure 7 in Egan to Blaine, November 23, 1891, no. 237, ibid., pp. 242–43.

45. Egan to Blaine, November 9, 1891, no. 223, ibid., p. 221; McCreery to Egan, November 7, 1891, enclosure 4 in Egan to Blaine, November 9, 1891, ibid., p. 223.

46. Depositions of Frederick Baxter, Herbert T. Sprague, Charles R. Malcolm, Abel Blardell, Charles A. Wheeler, Ill Treatment of Patrick Shields, *H. Exec. Doc. 91*, pp. 643–60; deposition of William H. Jenkins, ibid., p. 634. See also McCreery to Egan, November 11, 1891, enclosure 2 in Egan to Blaine, November 23, 1891, no. 237, *FRUS 1891*, pp. 239–40.

47. Declaration under Oath of Patrick Shields, November 18, 1891, enclosure 3 in Egan to Blaine, November 23, 1891, no. 237, *FRUS 1891*, pp. 240–41; Declaration under Oath of Charles A. Wheeler, November 19, 1891, enclosure 4 in Egan to Blaine, November 23, 1891, ibid., p. 241; Declaration under Oath of Andrew McKinstrey, November 19, 1891, enclosure 6 in Egan to Blaine, November 23, 1891, ibid., p. 642.

48. Egan to Blaine, November 23, 1891, no. 237, *FRUS 1891*, p. 238; McCreery to Egan, November 20, 1891, enclosures 8 and 9 in Egan to Blaine, November 23, 1891, ibid., pp. 243–44; Shields to McCreery, November 20, 1891, enclosure A in Egan to Blaine, November 23, 1891, ibid., p. 243; "Claim of Patrick Shields for $5000," November 20, 1891, enclosure B in Egan to Blaine, November 23, 1891, ibid., p. 244; Egan to McCreery, November 23, 1891, enclosure 10 in Egan to Blaine, November 23, 1891, ibid.

49. Montt asked for instructions from the Ministry of Foreign Relations but only seems to have received one. On January 15, 1892, he delivered a telegram to Blaine that he had received the previous day, stating that the Chilean police had taken up Shields drunk in the street. That was the official Chilean position. Montt to Matta, December 26, 1891, vol. 482, no. 57, AN.

50. Egan to Matta, November 23, 1891, enclosure 11 in Egan to Blaine, November 23, 1891, no. 237, *FRUS 1891*, pp. 244–46.

51. Matta to Egan, November 25, 1891, enclosure 2 in Egan to Blaine, December 5, 1891, no. 246, ibid., p. 257. One Chilean writer has observed that there are no "studies of Chilean prison practices during the last century; but we esteem that the charges made by Shields cannot be rejected without deeper studies." See José Manuel Barros Franco, *El caso del "Baltimore": Apuntes para la historia diplomática de Chile* (Santiago: Escuela de Ciencias Jurídicas y Sociales, 1950), 48.

52. Egan to Matta, December 4, 1891, enclosure 5 in Egan to Blaine, December 5, 1891, no. 246, *FRUS 1891,* pp. 259–60.

53. Shields to McCrerry, November 26, 1891, box 1, 26, McCreery Family Papers, Bentley Historical Library.

54. Charles I. Bevans, ed., *Treaties and Other International Agreements of the United States of America, 1776–1949,* Department of State Publication no. 8549 (Washington, D.C.: Government Printing Office, 1971), 6:540. See also A. Bascuñán Montes, *Recopilación de tratados y convenciones celebrados entre la república de Chile y las potencias extranjeras* (Santiago: Imprenta Cervantes, 1898), 3:358.

5. THE MAKING OF A FIGHT

1. Quoted in George Harmon Knoles, *The Presidential Campaign and Election of 1892* (Stanford, Calif.: Stanford University Press, 1942), 34–35.

2. James Ford Rhodes, *History of the United States from Hayes to McKinley, 1877–1896* (New York: Macmillan, 1919), 316.

3. John W. Foster, *Diplomatic Memoirs,* (New York: Riverside Press, 1909), 2:253. Contemporaries concurred that Harrison was lacking in human appeal. Their characterizations differ only in degree. Donald Marquand Dozer, "Benjamin Harrison and the Presidential Campaign of 1892," *American Historical Review* 54 (October, 1948): 49–50, says his acquaintances found Harrison "grouchy" and a man who "generally concealed his human qualities under an austere intellectuality." Others were not so gracious. "Harrison distilled poison like an adder" according to one description quoted in David Saville Muzzey, *James G. Blaine: A Political Idol of Other Days* (New York: Dodd, Mead, 1935), 381–82. For another who considered Harrison irascible, brusque, and impatient, see Arthur Wallace Dunn, *From Harrison to Harding: A Personal Narrative Covering a Third of a Century, 1884–1921* (New York: G. P. Putnam's Sons, 1922), 1:86. One close observer, a man who came to the White House in 1889 to install the first electrical equipment and stayed because Harrison was afraid to touch the switches, called the president cold, distant, and always in control of himself, but a man who could be "extremely considerate and solicitous." See Irwin (Ike) Hood Hoover, *Forty-two Years in the White House* (New York: Riverside Press, 1934), 3, 6–8, 232, 307, 322.

4. William Allen White, *Masks in a Pageant* (New York: Macmillan, 1928), 66.

5. Henry Adams, *The Education of Henry Adams, An Autobiography* (New York: Riverside Press, 1918), 321. For another favorable contemporary view see Henry L. Stoddard, *As I Knew Them: Presidents and Politics from Grant to Coolidge* (New York: Harper & Bros., 1927), 36, 164–65. There also seems to be a consensus among modern historians that Harrison was a man of ability—intelligent, conscientious, discreet. See John A. S. Grenville and George Berkeley Young, *Politics, Strategy, and American Diplomacy: Studies in Foreign Policy, 1873–1917* (New Haven, Conn.: Yale University Press, 1966), 87–88; Walter LaFeber, *The New Empire: An Interpretation of American Expansion, 1860–1898* (Ithaca, N.Y.: Cornell University Press, 1963), 103; Harry J. Sievers, *Benjamin Harrison: Hoosier President* (Indianapolis: Bobbs-Merrill, 1968), 3:4; Foster Rhea Dulles, *The Imperial Years* (New York: Thomas Y. Crowell, 1956), 51.

6. Julia B. Foraker, *I Would Live It Again: Memoirs of a Vivid Life* (New York: Harper & Bros., 1932), 133. See also Chauncey M. Depew, *My Memories of Eighty Years* (New York: Charles Scribner's Sons, 1922), 133–34, who found Harrison "one of the most genial and agreeable of men," who had, unfortunately, a "repellent manner." He is described as a "pig blinking in a cold wind" in Edmund Morris, *The Rise of Theodore Roosevelt* (New York: Coward, McCann & Geoghegan, 1979), 399.

7. Charles Edward Russell, *Blaine of Maine: His Life and Times* (New York: Cosmopolitan Book Corp., 1931), 412.

8. Quoted in H. Wayne Morgan, *From Hayes to McKinley: National Party Politics, 1877–96* (Syracuse, N.Y.: Syracuse University Press, 1969), 289–90. Many people believed Harrison's religious devotion was the source of his personality problems, causing him to appear sanctimonious. Ike Hoover recalls that immediately after breakfast the entire Harrison family would retire to the upper floor of the White House and be closeted in a room for a half hour of prayer: "The entire atmosphere of the household was surcharged with religious feeling." Hoover, *Forty-two Years*, 8. On the possibility that Harrison's firm, doctrinal religious beliefs made him a political anomaly, see Foraker, *I Would Live It Again*, 130; White, *Masks in a Pageant*, 70, 78; Knoles, *Presidential Campaign and Election of 1892*, 35.

9. On Harrison as party harmonizer see Edward Arthur White, "The Republican Party in National Politics, 1888–1891" (Ph.D. diss., University of Wisconsin, Madison, 1941), 258–63, 313–14; Morgan, *From Hayes to McKinley*, 300; Dozer, "Benjamin Harrison and the Presidential Campaign of 1892," 49, 51; Dunn, *From Harrison to Harding*, 2:88.

One contemporary noted that Harrison did political favors "in such a way as to take all sweetness, appreciation, and gratitude" from them. See John S. Wise, *Recollections of Thirteen Presidents* (New York: Doubleday, Page, 1906), 207. Harrison expressed doubt about his own political spirit: "He said he never cared for office, felt that he had no taste for public life; felt so when Senator and if he could choose to wake up President or lawyer of Indianapolis he would choose the latter." November 22, 1889, series 15–16, Halford Diary Extracts, Benjamin Harrison Papers, Manuscripts Division, Library of Congress. He similarly stated that he had never been "possessed" by the thought of being president or had his life shaped by it. April 21, 1889, series 15–16, Halford Diary Extracts, Harrison Papers, Manuscripts Division, Library of Congress.

10. Harrison's message to Congress is reprinted in Harry J. Sievers, ed., *Benjamin Harrison, 1833–1901: Chronology-Documents-Bibliographical Aids* (Dobbs Ferry, N.Y.: Oceana Publications, 1969), 67–70 and in James D. Richardson, *A Compilation of the Messages and Papers of the Presidents, 1789–1897* (Washington, D.C.: Government Printing Office, 1898), 9:183–86.

11. Sievers, *Benjamin Harrison*, 68.

12. Ibid., 69.

13. Ibid.

14. Ibid., 69–70.

15. Ibid., 70.

16. *New York Times*, December 10, 1891. See also *New York Times*, December 23, 1891.

17. Tracy's report is printed in Department of the Navy, "Annual Report," *H. Exec. Doc. 2931*, 52d Cong., 1st sess., 1891–92, pp. 21–30.

18. Egan to Blaine, December 12, 1891, *FRUS 1891*, pp. 267–69; ibid., December 13, 1891, pp. 269–70.

19. December 11, 1891, *Diario Oficial de la República de Chile*, vol. 16, no. 4412 (Santiago: Oficina de la Imprenta Nacional, 1891), 2–3. The following quotations are also from this document.

20. Matta to Egan, December 13, 1891, unnumbered enclosure in Egan to Blaine, December 14, 1891, *FRUS 1891*, p. 270. See also Egan to Blaine, December 14, 1891, no. 251, ibid., pp. 270–72. Montt repeated the notion that the circular had been a private correspondence in Montt to Matta, December 28, 1891, vol. 482, no. 62, AN, and again to Blaine in a conference, Montt to Matta, January 9, 1892, vol. 516, no. 69, AN.

21. Egan to Blaine, December 14, 1891, no. 251, *FRUS 1891*, pp. 270–72.

22. Montt, in Washington, probably suspected something like Matta's out-

burst was forthcoming. Less than a week before, Egan had cabled Blaine with more correspondence between Schley and the intendente. Again he complained that while the *sumario* was supposed to be secret, the Chilean press had continually been publishing the interchanges between Schley, the intendente, the judge of crimes, and Matta. Egan suggested the intent was to mold public opinion against the United States. Egan must have sent a copy of the cable to Matta, because on December 8, 1891, the day before Harrison's message to Congress, Montt received a terse cable from Matta: "Egan badly informed, badly informs his government, and the *sumario*'s result is delayed by his fault. You will establish the truth of the disfigured facts." Matta to Montt, December 8, 1891, vol. 485, AN.

23. *New York Daily Tribune,* January 22, 1892; January 23, 1892; January 25, 1892. Even the Chilean expert on the *Baltimore* affair has suggested that Matta's response was constructed in "extraordinarily strong terms." See José Miguel Barros Franco, *El caso del "Baltimore"; Apuntes para la historia diplomática de Chile* (Santiago: Escuela de Ciencias Jurídicas y Sociales de Chile, 1950), 43–44.

24. Egan to Blaine, December 22, 1891, *FRUS 1891,* p. 275. Egan to Blaine, December 28, 1891, no. 256, ibid., pp. 276–78 in which Egan reports the results of his not attending: "Not having received from you any instructions . . . I did not, of course, attend the inauguration ceremony . . . and my absence was very much commented on." See also Robley D. Evans, *A Sailor's Log: Recollections of Forty Years of Naval Life* (New York: D. Appleton, 1901), diary entry December 26, 1891, p. 273: "Mr. Egan 'phoned me to-day that he had not attended the inauguration of President Montt. I suppose the press will make all sorts of a row over that. I am sure that if he had gone he would have been insulted."

25. Montt to Matta, December 28, 1891, vol. 482, no. 62, AN.

26. John E. Coxe, "The New Orleans Mafia Incident," *Louisiana Historical Quarterly* 20 (October, 1937): 1067–1110. This is one of the only works of original research on the New Orleans trouble. See also J. Alexander Karlin, "The Italo-American Incident of 1891 and the Road to Reunion," *Journal of Southern History* 8 (1942):242–44; Allan Burton Spetter, "Harrison and Blaine: Foreign Policy, 1889–93" (Ph.D. diss., Rutgers University, 1967), 411–12; John Bassett Moore, "Asylum in Legations and Consulates and in Vessels," *Political Science Quarterly* 6 (1891): 837–41.

27. The diplomatic correspondence for the New Orleans Mafia incident is published in *FRUS 1891,* pp. 658–728.

28. Sievers, *Benjamin Harrison,* 74.

29. *Harper's Weekly* 36 (January 30, 1892): 105–12; *Boston Post*, January 11, 1892; *New York Press*, January 5, 1892; *New York Daily Tribune*, October 28, 1891.

30. *Chilian Times,* no. 803, May 9, 1891, pp. 1–4; ibid., no. 814, June 13, 1891; Lazcano to RE, April 20, 1891, vol. 482, no. 58, AN; Cruz to RE, April 18, 1892, vol. 510, no. 128, AN.

31. Evans, December 4, 1891, December 13, 1891, December 26, 1891, *A Sailor's Log,* 261, 266, 268.

32. Ibid., December 30, 1891, pp. 278–79.

33. Ibid., December 31, 1891, p. 279. On troubles in Valparaiso, see ibid., pp. 271, 280, and 287.

34. Ibid., December 31, 1891, p. 279.

35. Ibid., pp. 271, 278. See also Harry Thurston Peck, *Twenty Years of the Republic, 1885–1905* (New York: Dodd, Mead, 1906), 237–38; Thomas H. Sherman, *Twenty Years with James G. Blaine: Reminiscences by His Private Secretary* (New York: Grafton Press, 1928), 189–90; *La Patria,* January 19, 1892, vol. 29, no. 8540, p. 2.

6. HARRISON AND THE JINGOES

1. Trumbull to Matta, December 4, 1891, vol. 482, AN. The account of this interview, written in Spanish, and the following, written in English, are bound upside-down, the pages of the Spanish memo mixed with the pages of the English one.

2. Trumbull to Matta, December 26, 1891, vol. 482, AN. The influence that Trumbull may have had in the course of U.S.-Chilean diplomacy may also be suggested by the existence in the National Archives, RG 59, of an article from the *World,* May 16, 1892, which wrote extensively of John Trumbull: "Dr. John Trumbull is described as being a man of striking appearance, broad shouldered and about five feet, seven inches tall. He has blue eyes and sandy hair and beard. He is said to be a man of unimpeachable character. . . . He is deservedly popular." Similarly, it is known that Trumbull corresponded with Harrison. In a long letter of March 30, 1892, found in the Harrison Papers, series 1, Manuscripts Division, Library of Congress, Trumbull wrote to establish his credibility: "By accident of birth I am Chilean. Both parents were American citizens . . . I am a graduate of Yale. My medical degree is from Harvard . . . I have an honored name to maintain, and my reputation for veracity can . . . be vouched for by those who knew me during my eleven years residence in the United States. . . . My sense of justice, love for the land

of my birth and love too for the land of my Fathers', have recently led me to do some work in ferreting out the causes of the Chilean question. . . . I firmly believe that pecuniary interests are at the bottom of all the troubles between Chile and the United States." There is no record of an answer by Harrison. Trumbull's wife was also active, writing letters to the *New York Times* and *Daily Tribune* on the various incidents that began with the Chilean civil war. Proof that the Chileans considered the work of the Trumbulls in the *Baltimore* affair significant may be found in the fact that when the Trumbull family left Chile in 1894 for an extended trip to the United States, the doctor and his family were presented with a silver-plated tray, suitably inscribed: "To John Trumbull, Esquire, M.D. from his countrymen who appreciate the services he rendered to Chile in enlightening the people of the United States on the diplomatic troubles created by Minister Egan and Consul McCreery in 1891–1892. Valparaiso, 26 September, 1894."

3. Evans to Tracy, January 4, 1892, Naval Correspondence, "Message of the President of the United States Respecting the Relations with Chile, Together with the Diplomatic Correspondence; the Correspondence with the Naval Officials; the Inquiry into the Attack on the Seamen of the U.S.S. Baltimore in the Streets of Valparaiso; and the Evidence of the Officers and Crew of the Steamer Keweenaw Respecting the Ill Treatment of Patrick Shields by the Chilean Police," *H. Exec. Doc. 91*, 52d Cong. 1st sess., 1891–92, p. 334 (hereafter cited as *H. Exec. Doc. 91*). The judge's conclusions are also found in Pereira to Montt, January 4, 1892, vol. 495, AN.

4. Egan to Blaine, January 11, 1892, *FRUS 1892*, p. 285. Somehow Tracy was led to believe that during the investigation the *Baltimore* crew approved the conduct of the Chilean police, and on January 5 he wrote Schley for verification. Schley, now in California, responded that according to Lieutenant McCrea, who accompanied the men at the *sumario,* none had approved the conduct of the police. McCrea insisted that the entire question of police conduct was "carefully evaded by the judge." See Tracy to Schley, January 5, 1892, Naval Correspondence, *H. Exec. Doc. 91*, p. 334. Schley to Tracy, January 7, 1892, ibid., p. 335. The Chileans must have received copies of the correspondence because on January 11, 1892, the Chilean foreign minister wrote Judge Foster Recábarren, asking for an "authentic and legal copy" of the *Baltimore* sailors' testimony approving the conduct of the Chilean police. Pereira to Judge of Crimes, January 11, 1892, vol. 495, AN.

5. Montt to Blaine, January 8, 1892, *FRUS 1891*, pp. 344–45.

6. Blaine to Egan, Janaury 8, 1892, *FRUS 1891*, p. 284. Egan to Blaine,

January 11, 1892, ibid., p. 285. See also Egan to Blaine, January 15, 1892, ibid., p. 287: "He [Luis Pereira] expressed an opinion that an expression of regret for such parts of that document as were considered offensive to the President and other officers of the United States would be expected to complement the withdrawal and that he received from the minister positive assurance that the Chilean minister near the United States had been instructed to express regret for all that might create unpleasantness between the two Governments." On January 21 Egan wrote to say that although Pereira had promised to consult with his colleagues of the cabinet, "this promise has not yet been discharged, and that the answer is still withheld." Egan to Blaine, January 21, 1892, *FRUS 1891*, p. 307. Although dismissed from office, Matta was apparently still a powerful political figure.

7. Montt to Pereira, January 20, 1892, vol. 516, no. 77, AN; Montt to Blaine, January 20, 1892, *FRUS 1891*, pp. 345–46.

8. Blaine to Egan, January 21, 1892, *FRUS 1891*, pp. 307–8. Egan responded less anxiously than might have been expected, assuring Blaine and Harrison that at a banquet at the house of Luis Pereira, the Chilean foreign minister had told him, with the consent of his colleagues and in the presence of the British and Spanish ministers, the "present cabinet entertained most cordial feelings for the United States and for himself personally." See Egan to Blaine, January 22, 1892, *FRUS 1891*, p. 309.

9. Blaine to Montt, January 27, 1892, *FRUS 1891*, pp. 351–52.

10. Blaine to Egan, January 21, 1892, ibid., pp. 307–8. The historian Frederick B. Pike has suggested Blaine prepared the cable of January 21, but that seems unlikely given the unprecedented tone of the message and the wording. Frederick B. Pike, *Chile and the United States, 1880–1962* (Notre Dame, Ind.: University of Notre Dame Press, 1963), 79. From November, Blaine made frequent attempts to convince Harrison of Chile's admission of guilt and expression of regret for the entire *Baltimore* incident. One of the last before the ultimatum was January 2, 1892: "I hope you will read these communications from Minister Montt, just received. They are important. . . . I do not see how we can deny their truth, for the very fact that the Chilians aver them is in effect an apology." Harrison was evidently not impressed or convinced. See Albert T. Volwiler, ed., *The Correspondence between Benjamin Harrison and James G. Blaine, 1882–1893* (Philadelphia: American Philosophical Society, 1940), 226. *El Mercurio* of Santiago wrote as early as mid-December that North Americans believed "their government should be considerate of the provisional political situation in Chile." *El Mercurio*, vol. 64, no. 19317, December 14, 1892, p. 1. *La Patria* had assured its

readers that "with patience and calm, diplomacy and patriotism on the part of our administration in Washington, there is no reason why, in due course, a satisfactory solution to the controversy cannot be reached." *La Patria*, vol. 29, no. 8540, January 19, 1892, p. 2.

11. Fenton R. McCreery, January 24, 1892, diary, 1892–93, box 5, 5868, McCreery Family Papers, Bentley Historical Library, Ann Arbor, Mich.

12. *The Nation* reported, "President Montt was absent in the mountains." There is no indication from the Chilean press, but it is likely. Chileans tried to escape the summer heat of Santiago just as U.S. residents fled the summer heat of Washington, D.C. One author describes the movement in the United States, "As August approached, the city's population decreased by almost one-third, and the tempo of government business slowed almost to a standstill." See Edmund Morris, *The Rise of Theodore Roosevelt* (New York: Coward, McCann, & Geoghegan, 1979), 406. In February, 1893, McCreery wrote to his father in Valparaiso that he had fled to a resort town "to get a little fresh air and a change from the heat of Santiago. The reason the Chileans all leave Santiago in the summer is probably because it is unhealthy at that season." Fenton R. McCreery to William B. McCreery, February 13, 1893, box 1, no. 31, McCreery Family Papers, Bentley Historical Library.

13. Charles Hedges, Ed., *Speeches of Benjamin Harrison, Twenty-third President of the United States* (New York: United States Book Co., 1892), 564–65.

14. The following discussion and quotations from Harrison's message are found in Benjamin Harrison, *Public Papers and Addresses of Benjamin Harrison, Twenty-third President of the United States, March 4, 1889– March 4, 1893* (Washington, D.C.: Government Printing Office, 1893), 174–86.

15. January 15, 1892, Halford Diary Extracts, series 15–16, Benjamin Harrison Papers, Manuscripts Division, Library of Congress.

16. For the reaction of the Republican press to Harrison's message see *Philadelphia Press*, January 26, 1892; *Albany Journal*, January 26, 1892; *New York Daily Tribune*, January 27, 1892; *New York Recorder*, January 27, 1892; *Cincinnati Commercial Gazette*, January 26, 1892; *Boston Advertiser*, January 26, 1892. For the Democratic press see *Macon Telegraph*, January 26, 1892; *Detroit Free Press*, January 26, 1892; *Boston Globe*, January 26, 1892; *Cleveland Plain-Dealer*, January 26, 1892; *Baltimore Sun*, January 26, 1892; *New York Sun*, January 28, 1892; *Atlanta Constitution*, January 26, 1892; *Philadelphia Times*, January 26, 1892.

17. *New York Daily Tribune*, January 20, 1892. See also *New York Daily*

Tribune, January 19, 1892. This is not to suggest that there was no support for Harrison. See C. C. Shayne to Harrison, October 26, 1891, Benjamin Harrison Papers, series 2, September 22–December 10, 1891, Manuscripts Division, Library of Congress. Most U.S. observers, however, did not sense the issue was truly one of national honor. The press was full of rumor and speculation and tried to arouse a war spirit or at least enough pride to produce some righteous indignation. Yet as some historians rightly conclude, "the early 1890s were a singularly unpropitious time for arousing the American people to an appreciation of world affairs. Their energies were absorbed at home." The public was generally apathetic, level-headed, and not too responsive to the war scare. See John A. S. Grenville and George Berkeley Young, *Politics, Strategy, and American Diplomacy: Studies in Foreign Policy, 1877–1917* (New Haven, Conn.: Yale University Press, 1966), 74; Harold Lindsell, "The Chilean-American Controversy of 1891–1892" (Ph.D. diss., New York University, 1942), 217–19; Osgood Hardy, "The United States and Chile: A Study of Diplomatic Relations with Especial Emphasis on the Period of the Chilean Civil War of 1891" (Ph.D. diss., University of California, Berkeley, 1925), 309, 328.

18. *New York Times,* January 26, 1892.

19. January 26, 1892, *Congressional Record,* 52d Cong., 1st sess., December 7, 1891–February 10, 1892, vol. 23, pp. 549–52. On the previous day, just after the vice president presented Harrison's message, John Sherman of Ohio moved that the message be printed but referred to the Committee on Foreign Affairs: "In view of the gravity and importance of the subject matter, I do not think it expedient to make any remarks at this time." January 25, 1892, ibid., p. 514. On January 27 another resolution was passed similar to Breckinridge's.

20. Frederick D. Grant to Blaine, January 7, 1892, Harrison Papers, series 1, December 24, 1891–March 28, 1892, Manuscripts Division, Library of Congress. See also Alfred T. Volwiler, "Harrison, Blaine, and American Foreign Policy, 1889–1893," *American Philosophical Society, Proceedings* 79 (1938): 643–44.

21. John Hay, *Letters of John Hay and Extracts from His Diary* (Staten Island, N.Y.: Gordian Press, 1969), 2:235–36.

22. J. H. Woodard to Gresham, December 20, 1891, Walter Q. Gresham Papers, no. 38, October 15, 1889–April 16, 1892, Manuscripts Division, Library of Congress.

23. Edward Nelson Dingley, *The Life and Times of Nelson Dingley, Jr.* (Kalamazoo, Mich.: Ihling Bros. & Everard, 1902), 343.

24. Andrew Carnegie, *Autobiography of Andrew Carnegie* (New York: Riverside Press, 1920), 350–52. Ten days after the *Baltimore* riot, Carnegie began counseling patience. "Chile very weak and sorely tried," he wrote Harrison: "Her giant sister should be patient, forebearing." Carnegie to Harrison, October 26, 1891, Harrison Papers, series 2, September 22–December 10, 1891, Manuscripts Division, Library of Congress.

25. Robley D. Evans, December 7, 1891, December 16, 1891, December 21, 1891, January 5, 1892, *A Sailor's Log: Recollections of Forty Years of Naval Life* (New York: D. Appleton, 1901), 262–63, 268, 270, 285.

26. *Chilian Times,* February 20, 1892, no. 881, p. 7; ibid., no. 888, March 11, 1892, p. 8. It is difficult to say what the prevailing attitude of the English-speaking community in Valparaiso was. The day after Harrison's address one paper expressed confidence that U.S.-Chilean relations would remain normal: "The demands of the United States Government were made known yesterday . . . in reality there is not the slightest danger to apprehend a rupture of friendly relations with the United States." Ibid., January 27, 1892, no. 874, p. 2.

27. Quoted in George T. Davis, *A Navy Second to None: The Development of Modern American Naval Policy* (New York: Harcourt, Brace, 1940), 33.

28. "Report of the Secretary of the Navy," *H. Exec. Doc. 2016,* November 28, 1881, 47th Cong., 1st sess., 1881–82, p. 3.

29. John K. Mahon, "Benjamin Franklin Tracy, Secretary of the Navy, 1889–93," *New York Historical Society* 44 (April, 1960): 180. See also Benjamin Franklin Cooling, *Benjamin Franklin Tracy: Father of the Modern American Fighting Navy* (Hamden, Conn.: Archon Books, 1973), and Walter R. Herrick, Jr., *The American Naval Revolution* (Baton Rouge: Louisiana State University Press, 1966).

30. Quoted in Allan Burton Spetter, "Harrison and Blaine: Foreign Policy, 1889–93," (Ph.D. diss., Rutgers University, 1967), 45. On the poor standing of the U.S. Navy see "Report of the Secretary of the Navy," *H. Exec. Doc. 2721,* 51st Cong., 1st sess., 1889–90, p. 3; Herrick, *American Naval Revolution,* 3, 55; Walter LaFeber, *The New Empire: An Interpretation of American Expansion, 1860–1898* (Ithaca, N.Y.: Cornell University Press, 1963), 126–27; Davis, *Navy Second to None,* 87.

31. On the controversy about the purpose of naval expansion see Grenville and Young, *Politics, Strategy, and American Diplomacy, 11–12, 34–37;* Mahon, *"Benjamin Franklin Tracy,"* 185, 191; Herrick, *American Naval Revolution,* 10–11, 43; LaFeber, *New Empire,* 86; Robert Seager II, "Ten Years Before Mahan: The Unofficial Case for the New Navy, 1880–

1890," *Mississippi Valley Historical Review* 40 (December, 1953): 493; Spetter, "Harrison and Blaine," 32–52.

32. "Report of the Admiral," in Navy Department, "Report of the Secretary of the Navy," *H. Exec. Doc.* 2279, 42th Cong., 2d sess., 1881, pp. 3–5. See also D. E. Worcester, "Strategy in the War of the Pacific," *Naval Journal of Inter-American Studies* 5 (January, 1963): 37; Herrick, *American Naval Revolution,* 19.

33. September, 1884, "Report of the Secretary of the Navy," *H. Exec. Doc.* 2284, 48th Cong., 2d sess., 1884–85, p. 6.

34. Henry Cabot Lodge and Charles F. Redmonds, eds., *Selections from the Correspondence of Theodore Roosevelt and Henry Cabot Lodge, 1884–1918* (New York: Charles Scribner's Sons, 1971), 63.

35. Quoted in Herrick, *American Naval Revolution,* 55.

36. *Scientific American* 64 (June 6, 1891): 358.

37. Herrick, *American Naval Revolution,* 61; Spetter, "Harrison and Blaine," 40–51; Harold and Margaret Sprout, *The Rise of the American Naval Power, 1776–1918* (Princeton, N.J.: Princeton University Press, 1939), 188–89.

38. Hilary A. Herbert, December 31, 1903, "Grandfather Talks about His Life under Two Flags," Hilary A. Herbert Papers, pp. 310–13, University of North Carolina, Southern Historical Collection, Chapel Hill.

39. Robert Seager II, *Alfred T. Mahan: The Man and His Letters* (Annapolis, Md.: Naval Institute Press, 1977), 237. Mahan preferred action against Iquique: more injury could be done because Iquique was significantly closer to California, was less well defended, and would provide a base from which to move south; Iquique was a more desirable spoil of war; Lota's coal was of poor quality and the United States already had plenty; occupation of Iquique would likely draw Peru into the war (to recover territory lost in the War of the Pacific) and that would unnecessarily complicate the situation; military operations in the south were much easier for the Chileans. Alfred T. Mahan, "Mahan's Memorandum on Chile," Benjamin F. Tracy Papers, Manuscripts Division, Library of Congress. Mahan caught the fever and wrote Rear Admiral Stephen B. Luce wondering how the government could allow matters to drag along when there was "a question of so formidable a vessel as the *Prat* thus getting the time to escape. . . . The ultimate result, I suppose can be little doubtful, but we may first get some eye openers." Mahan to Luce, January 10, 1892, Stephen B. Luce Papers, no. 9, General Correspondence, Manuscripts Division, Library of Congress.

40. Fenton R. McCreery, December 21, 1892, diary, 1891–92, box 5, 5868, McCreery Family Papers, Bentley Historical Library.

41. Brown to Tracy, Memorandum on Chile, "List of Vessels of U.S. Navy ready in view of possible service against Chile," no date, Tracy Papers, no. 31, Manuscripts Division, Library of Congress.

42. The following discussion of Brown's suggestions is found in Brown to Tracy, December 31, 1891, Memorandum, Tracy Papers, no. 328, Manuscripts Division, Library of Congress.

43. The historian Frederick B. Pike believes the Argentine offer of support was rumor, "never reliably confirmed, and indeed quite effectively denied." Pike, *Chile and the United States,* 84. The rumor began to circulate as early as February, 1892. See *La Unión,* February 17, 1892, vol. 8, no. 1972, p. 2. But was it just rumor? Chilean writer José Miguel Barros Franco made clear the Chilean disposition to believe it was more. See *El caso del "Baltimore": Apuntes para la historia diplomática de Chile* (Santiago: Escuela de Ciencias Jurídicas y Sociales, 1950), 12. Thirteen years later he strove to prove the contention, from evidence turned up in the Chilean National Archives. See José Miguel Barros Franco, "Don Estanislao Zeballos y el incidente del 'Baltimore,'" *Mapocho* 1 (July, 1963): 218, 220. Anibal Cruz to RE, December 15, 1892, vol. 516, AN. Chile learned of the Argentine offer from the Brazilian minister to the United States, who told Anibal Cruz, the Chilean minister to the United States, in late 1892. Barros Franco also notes the Chilean archives contain numerous notes from Argentina expressing sympathy with Chile in its dispute with the United States.

44. There were no official pronouncements confirming war preparations, but neither is there any question that they took place. Admirals were warned the day of Harrison's message to "keep ready," and Mahan apparently wrote, "There is not an official in the government who doesn't regard war as imminent and not a few who believe it inevitable." Quoted in Allan Burton Spetter, "Harrison and Blaine: Foreign Policy, 1889–1893" (Ph.D. diss., Rutgers, 1967), 226, 229. See also Thomas Campbell Copeland, ed., *Harrison and Reid: Their Lives and Record* (New York: Charles L. Webster, 1892), 197; Albert Bushnell Hart, *Practical Essays on American Government* (New York: Longmans, Green, 1893), 125–26; David Saville Muzzey, *James G. Blaine: A Political Idol of Other Days* (New York: Dodd, Mead, 1935), 420–21; Harry Thurston Peck, *Twenty Years of the Republic, 1885–1905* (New York: Dodd, Mead, 1906), 241; William D. Puleston, *Mahan: The Life and Work of Captain Alfred T. Mahan, U.S.N.* (New Haven, Conn.: Yale University Press, 1939), 114.

45. *New York Daily Tribune,* October 29, 1891; ibid., October 30, 1891; ibid., November 1, 1891; *New York Times,* October 31, 1891; ibid.,

November 5, 1891; see also *Denver Republican*, October 31, 1891. The *St. Louis Globe-Democrat* added an unusual editorial at the time, December 4, 1891, decrying the notion that Chileans were the Yankees or English of South America: "It must be remembered that underneath the thin coating of civilization covering the Chilean character there is a ferocity and a savagery closely akin to that of the American aborigine or the African barbarian."

46. *New York Times*, December 21, 25, 26, 27, 28, 29, and 30, 1891; January 1, 1892.

47. *New York Times*, January 2, 9, 11, 15, 16, 18, 19, and 25, 1892; *New York Daily Tribune*, January 22 and 24, 1892; *New York World*, January 27, 1892.

48. *New York Daily Tribune*, January 26, 27, and 29, 1892.

7. BANG TO WHIMPER

1. Matte to RE, October 23, 1891, vol. 483, no. 42, AN. After the success of the insurrectionists most Europeans seemed convinced that "in the last corner of America existed a civilized and free country," superior to the rest of Latin America. See Augusto Matte and Agustín Ross, *Memoria presentada a la excelentísima Junta de Gobierno* (Paris: Imprimerie et Librairie Administratives et Classiques, Paul Dupont, 1892), 19, 21, 24, 28. On the European reaction to the Balmaceda uprising see Harold Blakemore, "Los agentes revolucionarios chilenos en Europa, en 1891," *Mapocho* 5 (1966): 101–17; Alberto Fagalde, *La prensa estranjera y la dictadura chilena* (Santiago: Imprenta "Santiago," 1891); Raul Silva Castro, *Prensa y periodismo en Chile, 1812–1956* (Santiago: Universidad de Chile, 1958).

2. Matte to RE, October 30, 1891, vol. 483, no. 40, AN.

3. Ibid.

4. Matte to RE, November 14, 1891, vol. 483, no. 80, AN.

5. Ibid. See also Matte to RE, November 28, 1891, vol. 483, no. 100, AN.

6. Matte to RE, January 9, 1892, vol. 517, no. 159, AN. At this juncture Matte reported the conflict had assumed a "truly grave and threatening character" and that the United States "prepared precipitously for war"— its arsenals active and landing troops prepared. See Matte to RE, January 22, 1892, vol. 517, no. 198, AN.

7. Matte to RE, January 22, 1892, vol. 517, no. 198, AN. The Swiss legation in the United States interpreted the entire conflict as the result of misinformation by "directing circles"—Harrison, Blaine, Tracy, and Egan

(the "Irish criminal")—looking out for their own personal and professional interests, and U.S. naval officers seeking to augment the navy. The Swiss minister advised that war over the *Baltimore* affair would be an "absurdity" since the U.S. public did not want war, but neither nation's government seemed disposed to give in. Brazilian minister Salvador de Mendoça had informed the Swiss legation that he was seeking government permission to offer Brazilian arbitration. That effort was futile. January 26, 1892, no. 526, Bundesarchiv E 2/98-105, Bd. 2, "Schiedsgericht Zwischen Nordamerika und Chile, 1892–1895," Dossier 1 and 2, Bern, Switzerland. I am grateful to Peter J. Sehlinger of Indiana University–Purdue University for bringing this to my attention.

8. Bulnes to RE, January 1892, vol. 518, no. 1, AN. See also Bulnes to RE, February 5, 1892, vol. 518, no. 5, AN.

9. Matte to RE, December 26, 1891, vol. 483, no. 151, AN.

10. Krauss to RE, November 5, 1891, vol. 488, AN.

11. *South American Journal,* April 6, 1889. This was a British periodical with news and information about South America. Anti-Egan feelings in Britain were maintained throughout the Chilean civil war, the notion widely circulated that Balmaceda had declared nitrates contraband on advice by Egan, who "practically admitted" it to Kennedy. See Kennedy to Salisbury, April 12, 1891, FO, no. 33, 16/265.

12. Kennedy to Salisbury, November 8, 1891, FO, no. 123, 16/266. See also Kennedy to Salisbury, December 20, 1891, FO, no. 137, 16/266.

13. *London Times,* October 30, 1891, p. 5. On the *Times* coverage of the riot and possibilities of war, see October 27, 1891, p. 5, and November 2, 1891, p. 5.

14. Kennedy to Salisbury, November 11, 1891, FO, no. 43, 16/266.

15. Kennedy to Salisbury, November 8, 1891, FO, no. 123, 16/266. The naval attaché at the U.S. legation, Lieutenant Charles Harlow, had admitted to Kennedy, "In official despatches and letters Captain Schley is conservative and prudent—but when he talks he blows hard."

16. Ibid. See also Kennedy to Salisbury, November 9, 1891, FO, no. 93, 16/266.

17. Kennedy to Salisbury, November 8, 1891, FO, no. 122, 16/266.

18. Kennedy to Salisbury, December 31, 1891, FO, no. 142, 16/266.

19. Kennedy to Salisbury, December 31, 1891, FO, no. 143, 16/266.

20. Kennedy to Salisbury, January 27, 1892, FO, no. 7, 16/276. See also Kennedy to Salisbury, January 15, 1892, FO, no. 3, 16/276. In the United States, British observers such as Sir Cecil Spring Rice saw the matter differently. In January he wrote correspondents in Britain that the

United States was on the verge of war "owing to inconceivable stupidity" by the United States and trickery by Chile. What surprised him, however, was that Blaine, the great jingo, was now a "peacelover." He thought that Harrison and Tracy were so bent on war that even Blaine might not be able to prevent it. The U.S. Navy, he surmised, wished war to see its new ships fight and to elicit votes for more. The president, he suspected, wished war to get reelected. Of most importance was what the United States might be like if the fleet did indeed attain more power and a similar situation arose with a European nation. Perhaps, he pondered, the Bering Sea matter might cause the same turmoil between the United States and Britain as the *Baltimore* affair caused between the United States and Chile. Stephen Gwynn, ed., *The Letters and Friendships of Sir Cecil Spring Rice, A Record* (New York: Riverside Press, 1929), 1:118. It is noteworthy, although peripheral, that from January to August, 1891, the *Chilian Times* showed extraordinary concern with the Bering Sea controversy.

21. The internal Chilean conflict over the diplomacy of the *Baltimore* affair is best demonstrated in *Boletín de sessiones ordinarias en 1891, Cámara de Senadores* (Santiago: Imprenta Nacional, 1891, 1892). See especially December, 1891, and January, 1892, which included a few heated debates. As early as December 11, 1891, Foreign Minister Matta had difficulty justifying the belligerent tone of his first note to the United States. Here strong opposition to Matta's defiance was indicated. Unfortunately, little documentation of the domestic struggle exists. For a discussion of the confused political situation in Chile after the fall of Balmaceda, see Jorge Dupouy Grez, *Relaciones chileno-argentinas durante el gobierno de don Jorge Montt, 1891–1896* (Santiago: Editorial Andrés Bello, 1968), 14–17.

22. Fenton R. McCreery, January 25, 1892, diary, 1892–93, box 5, 5686, McCreery Family Papers, Bentley Historical Library, Ann Arbor, Mich.

23. Blaine to Egan, January 30, 1892, *FRUS 1891*, pp. 312–13.

24. Montt to Matta, October 30, 1891, vol. 482, no. 75, AN.

25. *Chilian Times*, December 16, 1891, p. 3. See also José Miguel Barros Franco, *El caso del "Baltimore": Apuntes para la historia diplomática de Chile* (Santiago: Escuela de Ciencias Jurídicas y Sociales, 1950), 79–81, who suggested the "ultimatum had been sent by President Harrison to serve his election interests, in opposition to the great majority of North American public opinion, and, very probably, contrary to the thinking of Blaine, who, still, appeared to subscribe to it." Patricio Estellé, *La controversia chileno-norteamericana de 1891–1892* (San-

tiago: Editorial Jurídica de Chile, 1967), similarly contends that internal U.S. politics were important to the matter: "Harrison, taking advantage of the war spirit that his Secretary of the Navy Tracy so ardently maintained, thought to assure his election." It might be noted that from early 1892 Harrison's wife lay dying of tuberculosis. She died October 25, 1892, and his devotion to her lends credence to the idea that Harrison actually had no desire to be renominated. See Edmund Morris, *The Rise of Theodore Roosevelt* (New York: Coward, McCann & Geoghegan, 1979), 455.

26. Benjamin Harrison, January 28, 1892, *Public Papers and Addresses of Benjamin Harrison, Twenty-third President of the United States, March 4, 1889 to March 4, 1893* (Washington, D.C.: Government Printing Office, 1893), 186–87. See also Albert T. Volwiler, ed., *The Correspondence between Benjamin Harrison and James G. Blaine, 1882–1893* (Philadelphia: American Philosophical Society, 1940), 238–39. Blaine to Harrison, January 30, 1892: "I have relied on Chili's good sense for reparation and I believe we will get it more easily that way than by arbitration."

27. Blaine to Egan, January 30, 1892, *FRUS 1892*, pp. 312–13.

28. Egan to McCreery, June 22, 1892, box 1, no. 27, McCreery Family Papers, Bentley Historical Library.

29. Egan to Blaine, March 24, 1892, no. 284, *FRUS 1892*, p. 52.

30. Egan to Wharton, June 23, 1892, no. 315, *FRUS 1892*, pp. 53–54; Foster to Egan, July 1, 1892, *FRUS 1892*, p. 57.

31. Foster to Egan, July 5, 1892, "Strictly Confidential," State Department Instructions to Ministers in Chile, RG 59, NARS. Egan to Foster, July 11, 1892, series 1, June 12–September 21, 1892, Harrison Papers, Manuscripts Division, Library of Congress; Foster to Egan, July 12, 1892, ibid. See also Harrison's Message to Congress, December 6, 1892, in Harrison, *Public Papers and Addresses*, 137–38.

32. Egan to Foster, July 16, 1892, *FRUS 1892*, p. 64; McCreery to Foster, September 1, 1892, no. 344, ibid., p. 67. On the apportionment of the indemnity, see the *New York Daily Tribune*, February 10, 1893.

33. The tribunal is considered in Egan to Foster, July 27, 1892, *FRUS 1892*, p. 65; Foster to Egan, July 28, 1892, ibid.; Egan to Foster, August 2, 1892, no. 335, ibid., p. 66; Egan to Foster, August 13, 1892, no. 339, ibid., pp. 66–67. The convention is reprinted in Charles I. Bevans, ed., *Treaties and Other International Agreements of the United States of America, 1776–1949* (Washington, D.C.: Government Printing Office, 1971), 6:535–39, and A. Bascunán Montes, *Recopilación de tratados y*

convenciones celebrados entre la república de Chile y las potencias extranjeras (Santiago: Imprenta Cervantes, 1894), 2:357–59.

34. Visit made by the author, April 13, 1978.

35. New York Recorder, January 31, 1892.

36. "The Riggin Testimonial," Benjamin Harrison Memorial Home, Indianapolis.

37. Ibid.

38. Blaine to Egan, February 11, 1892, State Department Instructions to Ministers in Chile, RG 59, no. 177, NARS; Blaine to Egan, February 25, 1892, ibid.; Egan to Blaine, March 5, 1892, State Department Diplomatic Despatches, RG 59, no. 281, NARS; see also Anibal Cruz to RE, July 17, 1892, vol. 516, no. 160, AN. This suggests that before Foster became secretary of state he opposed the "idea of repatriating that cadaver" and acquiesced only because "Mr. Blaine had promised it" to Riggin's relatives.

39. Egan to Foster, July 11, 1892, State Department Diplomatic Despatches, June 1–December 31, 1892, RG 59, no. 324, NARS.

40. Egan to Foster, August 2, 1892, ibid.; undated correspondence, no. 19, McCreery Family Papers, Bentley Historical Library.

41. Philadelphia Inquirer July 21, 1892, vol. 127, no. 21, p. 1; ibid., August 1, 1892, vol. 127, no. 32, p. 1.

42. Ibid., August 3, 1892, vol. 127, no. 34, p. 1.

43. Ibid., August 7, 1982, vol. 127, no. 38, p. 5. The issue included seven illustrations pertaining to the funeral, including Riggin at twenty-one years old and plot number 506, section F, of Woodlands Cemetery where Riggin was buried. "The plot wherein the former sailorboy will find a final resting place could not have been better selected in beautiful Woodlands, with its grand old trees and its magnificent vaults and monuments, its splendid avenues and its pretty general scene," the paper maintained.

44. New York Times, August 11, 1892, p. 1; Philadelphia Inquirer, August 11, 1892, vol. 127, no. 42, pp. 1–2.

45. Ibid., August 9, 1892, vol. 127, no. 40, p. 4.

46. The Nation, August 18, 1892, pp. 120–21; Philadelphia Press, August 8, 1892, p. 2; Philadelphia Inquirer, August 9, 1892, vol. 127, no. 40, p. 5. In an editorial, the Inquirer suggested that criticism of the Independence Hall honor was a "grievous blunder," not from lack of patriotism, "but simply a feeling of spiteful jealousy" against the Inquirer. The Republican paper insisted, "Independence Hall is the place of the peo-

ple, not of particular men. The Declaration of Independence was not promulgated from that hall for the benefit of half a dozen men who had rendered the nation a great service, but for the benefit of the many—of all the people." See also the *Philadelphia Inquirer,* August 10, 1892, vol. 127, no. 43, pp. 1–2, and August 12, 1892, ibid., p. 1, which included the long poem "Only a Boatswain's Mate."

47. *New York Times,* August 14, 1892, p. 3; *Philadelphia Inquirer,* August 14, 1892, vol. 127, no. 45, p. 1.

48. *Philadelphia Inquirer,* August 15, 1892, vol. 127, no. 46, pp. 1–3, 5; *New York Times,* August 15, 1892, p. 2. The Chilean minister also reported on the proceedings. See Cruz to RE, August 17, 1892, vol. 516, AN.

49. Walter T. K. Nugent, *From Centennial to World War: American Society, 1876–1917* (Indianapolis: Bobbs-Merrill, 1977), 37. For other views on the evolution of life in the United States during the nineteenth-century see Vincent P. DeSantis, *The Shaping of Modern America: 1877–1916* (Boston: Allyn and Bacon, 1973), and Morton Keller, *Affairs of State: Public Life in Late Nineteenth Century America* (Cambridge: Harvard University Press, 1977). On the psychic crisis of the 1890s, see Richard Hofstadter, "Cuba, the Philippines, and Manifest Destiny," in *The Paranoid Style in American Politics and Other Essays* (New York: Knopf, 1966), 145–87.

50. Barros Franco, *El caso del "Baltimore,"* 11n. For a different version, see Frederick B. Pike, *Chile and the United States, 1880–1962: The Emergence of Chile's Social Crisis and the Challenge to United States Diplomacy* (Notre Dame, Ind.: University of Notre Dame Press, 1963), 81.

51. Barros Franco, *El caso del "Baltimore,"* 83–84. On the idea of a Chilean salute to the Stars and Stripes see *El Ferrocarril,* January 31, 1892, and Montt to Pereira, February 9, 1892, no. 142, AN. Barros Franco indicates that one of his professors, Ernesto Barros Jarpa, suggested the legend of Carlos Peña first appeared publicly in a journal, *Lira Chilena.* On Peña's legendary existence see Mario Vergara, "El imperialismo Yankee en Chile: Resumen histórico del incidente del U.S.S. 'Baltimore'," p. 8, Santiago, 1944, AN. Typescript. To confirm Peña's nonexistence, Barros Franco wrote the director of the naval academy.

52. Robert N. Burr, *By Reason or Force: Chile and the Balancing of Power in South America, 1830–1905* (Berkeley: University of California Press, 1965), 261–62. See also Arthur P. Whitaker, *The United States and the Southern Cone, Argentina, Chile, and Uruguay* (Cambridge: Harvard University Press, 1976).

53. Joseph Smith, *Illusions of Conflict: Anglo-American Diplomacy toward Latin America, 1865–1896* (Pittsburgh: University of Pittsburgh Press, 1979), 8–14, 21–39.

54. Robert L. Beisner, *From the Old Diplomacy to the New, 1865–1900* (Arlington Heights, Ill.: Harlan Davidson, 1975), 35–39, 67–70.

Bibliographical Essay

ECONDARY SOURCES are of course far more numerous than those discussed in the present pages. Robert Jones Shafer, *A History of Latin America* (Boston: D. C. Heath, 1978), like many other well-done texts, offers a view of Chilean history within the context of Latin American history. Another starting point is the work of Chile's foremost historians—Diego Barros Arana, a nineteenth-century liberal who wrote *Historia jeneral de Chile* (16 vols., Santiago: R. Jover, 1884–1902) and provides a framework through 1933; and Francisco Encina, who offers the conservative, revisionist view in *Historia de Chile desde la prehistoria hasta 1891* (20 vols., Santiago: Editorial Nascimento, 1950).

Two surveys translated into English are Anson Uriel Hancock, *A History of Chile* (Chicago: Charles H. Sergel, 1893), a political study that concludes with the civil war of 1891, and Luis Galdames, *A History of Chile* (Chapel Hill: University of North Carolina Press, 1941), which carries Chilean history to the Great Depression. The work by Galdames is not analytical or interpretive and offers little about the War of the Pacific or the Balmaceda uprising. Jaime Eyzaguirre, *Fisonomía histórica de Chile* (3d ed., Santiago: Editorial Universitaria, 1973), is a useful and interesting book, worth reading. Ricardo Donoso provides one of the best studies, *Breve historia de Chile* (Buenos Aires: Editorial Universitaria, 1963), and his *Las ideas políticas en Chile* (Mexico City: Fondo de Cultura Económica, 1967) adds much to his reputation as a scholar and is essential for understanding Chilean political history. Perhaps the only Chilean book dedicated to diplomatic history is Mario Barros, *Historia diplomática de Chile: 1541–1938* (Barcelona: Ediciones Ariel, 1970).

Histories of Chile in English usually lack detail, such as Kalman H. Silvert, *Chile Yesterday and Today* (New York: Holt, Rinehart & Winston, 1965), and Jay Kinsbruner, *Chile: A Historical Interpretation* (New York: Harper & Row, 1973). Most histories of Chile consider only the years before or immediately after independence. Brian Loveman's recent *Chile: The Legacy of Hispanic Capitalism* (New York: Oxford University Press, 1979) is the best of contemporary works, excellent in the first half, verging on polemic for the twentieth century.

Thematic studies include Raul Silva Castro, *Prensa y periodismo en Chile, 1812–1956* (Santiago: Ediciones de la Universidad de Chile, 1958), the press in Chilean history; A. Bascuñán Montes, *Recopilación de tratados y convenciones celebrados entre la república de Chile y las potencias extranjeras* (3 vols., Santiago: Imprenta Cervantes, 1893–98), treaties, alliances, conventions; Daniel Martner, *Estudio de política comercial Chilena e historia económica nacional* (2 vols., Santiago: Imprenta Universitaria, 1923), commerce and economics; Rodrigo Fuenzalida Bade, *La armada de Chile: Desde la alborada al sesquicentenario* (2 vols., Valparaiso: Imprenta de la Armada, 1975), an interesting assessment of the navy, focusing on the debt to the British, by a retired naval officer turned historian.

Frederick M. Nunn, *The Military in Chilean History: Essays on Civil-Military Relations, 1810–1973* (Albuquerque: University of New Mexico Press, 1976) is excellent and authoritative. Nunn is one of the few American scholars who shows real understanding of the country—its history, its direction. His *Yesterday's Soldiers: European Military Professionalism in South America, 1890–1940* (Lincoln: University of Nebraska Press, 1983) assesses the European impact on South America's developing military establishments.

Works that analyze the coming-of-age of the United States in the latter nineteenth century include Julius W. Pratt, *Expansionists of 1898: The Acquisition of Hawaii and the Spanish Islands* (Baltimore: Johns Hopkins University Press, 1936); Foster Rhea Dulles, *The Imperial Years* (New York: Crowell, 1956), and *Prelude to World Power: American Diplomatic History, 1860–1900* (New York: Macmillan, 1965); H. Wayne Morgan, *From Hayes to McKinley: National Party Politics, 1877–96* (Syracuse: Syracuse University Press, 1969); and Howard K. Beale, *Theodore Roosevelt and the Rise of America to World Power* (Baltimore: Johns Hopkins University Press, 1956). These books discuss the "new" Manifest Destiny and the growth of the new navy and offer characterizations of national figures. The best work on Theodore Roosevelt and his era is Edmund Morris, *The Rise of Theodore Roosevelt* (New York: Coward, McCann, & Geoghegan, 1979).

More analytical interpretations of American behavior in the late nineteenth century include Walter LaFeber, *The New Empire: An Interpretation of American Expansion, 1860–1898* (Ithaca: Cornell University Press, 1963), which considers the motives of policy: "Spurred by a fantastic industrial revolution, which produced ever larger quantities of surplus goods, depressions, and violence, and warned by a growing radical literature that the system was not functioning properly, the United States prepared to solve its dilemmas with foreign expansion." For a similar view see William Appleman Williams, *The Roots of the Modern American Empire: A Study of the Growth and Shaping of Social Consciousness in a Marketplace Society* (New York: Random House, 1969).

For the relations between economics, politics, and diplomacy, see David M. Pletcher, *The Awkward Years: American Foreign Relations under Garfield and Arthur* (Columbia: University of Missouri Press, 1962), which shows that America's coming of age occurred well before the traditionally accepted "empire years." The Garfield-Arthur administrations were "a preparation and crude testing in response to impulses which, though strong, were still vaguely formed and not clearly understood . . . in their awkwardness and failure they add plausibility to the heroics of 1898. Like an early stumbling rehearsal of a play, this apparently futile diplomacy made possible greater self-confidence and seemingly spontaneous determination a few years later." See also John A. S. Grenville and George Berkeley Young, *Politics, Strategy and American Diplomacy: Studies in Foreign Policy, 1873–1917* (New Haven: Yale University Press, 1966), which includes excellent observations on Harrison-Blaine foreign policy and analysis of the new navy, which the authors contend centered around the activities of Rear Admiral Stephen B. Luce. The newest book to deal with the period, aptly titled, is John M. Dobson's *America's Ascent: The United States Becomes a Great Power, 1880–1914* (DeKalb: Northern Illinois University Press, 1978), which relates that economic expansion combined with political aggrandizement and moral assertiveness in a drive for prestige and power. See also Charles S. Campbell's excellent narrative *The Transformation of American Foreign Relations, 1865–1900* (New York: Harper & Row, 1976).

The possible relation of naval expansion to the *Baltimore* controversy is an intriguing topic. On the evolution of the navy see Harold and Margaret Sprout, *The Rise of American Naval Power: 1776–1918* (Princeton: Princeton University Press, 1939); Donald W. Mitchell, *History of the Modern American Navy from 1883 through Pearl Harbor* (New York: Knopf, 1946); and George T. Davis, *A Navy Second to None: The Development of Modern American Naval Policy* (New York: Harcourt, Brace, 1940), which explains the rejuvenation of the navy by citing the apocryphal Admiral Balch story— that the Chilean navy in 1883 threatened the admiral "that if he did not mind his own business, they would send him and his fleet to the bottom of the ocean." See also Walter R. Herrick, Jr., *The American Naval Revolution* (Baton Rouge: Louisiana State University Press, 1966), which remarks that Tracy strongly influenced policy because of friendship with Harrison.

William D. Puleston, *Mahan: The Life and Work of Alfred Thayer Mahan, USN* (New Haven: Yale University Press, 1939), has been supplanted by Robert Seager II, *Alfred Thayer Mahan: The Man and His Letters* (Annapolis: Naval Institute Press, 1977), and his impressive "Ten Years Before Mahan: The Unofficial Case for the New Navy, 1880–1890," *Mississippi Valley Historical Review* 40 (December, 1953), which contends that Mahan and Tracy were not innovators but codifiers of ideas already current.

Tracy has not elicited as much interest as Mahan, although here one might consult Benjamin Franklin Cooling, *Benjamin Franklin Tracy: Father of the Modern American Navy* (Hamden: Archon Books, 1973), a short work, and John K. Mahon, "Benjamin Franklin Tracy, Secretary of the Navy, 1889–93," *New York Historical Society* 44 (April, 1960). Even more concerned with personalities is Richard S. West, Jr., *Admirals of American Empire: The Combined Story of George Dewey, Alfred Thayer Mahan, Winfield Scott Schley, and William Thomas Sampson* (Indianapolis: Bobbs-Merrill, 1948); Hugh B. Hammett, *Hilary Abner Herbert: A Southerner Returns to the Union* (Philadelphia: American Philosophical Society, 1976); Albert Gleaves, ed., *The Life of an American Sailor: Rear Admiral William Hemsley Emery, from his Letters and Memoirs* (New York: George H. Doran, 1923); Charles Mason Remey, ed., *Life and Letters of Rear Admiral George Collier Remey: United States Navy, 1841–1928* (Washington, D.C.: Charles Mason Remey, 1939); Edwin A. Falk, *Fighting Bob Evans* (New York: Cornwall Press, 1931); Robley D. Evans, *A Sailor's Log: Recollections of Forty Years of Naval Life* (New York: D. Appleton, 1901); Winfield Scott Schley, *Forty-five Years under the Flag* (New York: D. Appleton, 1904). These books use some diaries and correspondence no longer available.

For a view of the first thirty years of U.S.-Chilean relations see Eugenio Pereira Salas, *Los primeros contactos entre Chile y los Estados Unidos, 1778–1809* (Santiago: Editorial Andrés Bello, 1971), a study of a rarely considered period. A sequel is Carlos Mery Squella, *Relaciones diplomáticas entre Chile y los Estados Unidos de America, 1829–1841* (Santiago: Editorial Andrés Bello, 1965). One of the earliest works in English, George W. Crichfield, *American Supremacy: The Rise and Progress of the Latin American Republics and their Relations to the United States under the Monroe Doctrine* (2 vols., New York: Brentano's, 1908), views Latin American history through the prism of dictatorships. A better account appears in Graham H. Stuart and James L. Tigner, *Latin America and the United States* (6th ed., Englewood Cliffs: Prentice-Hall, 1975). William Roderick Sherman, *The Diplomatic and Commercial Relations of the United States and Chile, 1820–1914* (Boston: Gorham Press, 1926), was one of the first books to study United States relations with Chile. See also Henry Clay Evans, Jr., *Chile and Its Relations with the United States* (Durham: Duke University Press, 1927). Frederick B. Pike, *Chile and the United States, 1880–1962: The Emergence of Chile's Social Crisis and the Challenge to United States Diplomacy* (Notre Dame: University of Notre Dame Press, 1963), provides one of the best bibliographies of the Spanish-language secondary literature. Robert N. Burr, *By Reason or Force: Chile and the Balancing of Power in South America, 1830–1905* (Berkeley: University of California Press, 1965), extensively uses Chilean manuscript sources. A recent volume is Arthur P. Whitaker, *The United States and the Southern Cone: Argentina, Chile, and Uruguay* (Cambridge: Harvard University Press, 1976), a fine study, well written. See also Whitaker, *The United States and the Independence of Latin America, 1800–1830* (New York: Norton, 1941).

Useful for Anglo-American relations in this era is the work of Carl Solberg, *Immigration and Nationalism: Argentina and Chile, 1890–1914* (Austin: University of Texas Press, 1970), and J. Fred Rippy, *British Investments in Latin America, 1822–1949: A Case in the Operations of Private Enterprise in Retarded Regions* (Hamden: Archon Books, 1959). Rippy concludes that the return was meager, that the British had no plan for "uplifting the natives," that foreign private capital brought more benefit than injury. The British influence appears in Osgood Hardy, "British Nitrates and the Balmaceda Revolution," *Pacific Historical Review* 17 (May, 1948), although Hardy overrated economics in the Balmaceda revolution. The best book on British economic influence, the nitrate industry, the Balmaceda uprising—indeed this fascinating period of Chilean history—is Harold Blakemore, *British Nitrates and Chilean Politics, 1886–1896, Balmaceda and North* (London: Athlone Press, 1974), well written, astute, provocative, establishing the author as an expert.

Two newer works that treat this same subject, both politically left in their analyses, are Thomas F. O'Brien, *The Nitrate Industry and Chile's Crucial Transition: 1870–1896* (New York: New York University Press, 1982), and Michael Monteón, *Chile in the Nitrate Era: The Evolution of Economic Dependence, 1880–1930* (Madison: University of Wisconsin Press, 1982). Another excellent work on Anglo-American relations toward Latin America and Chile is Edward P. Crapol, *America for Americans: Economic Nationalism and Anglophobia in the Late Nineteenth Century* (Westport: Greenwood Press, 1973), well written, which contends that Anglophobia in late-nineteenth-century United States was based on economic competition and that the U.S. search for markets induced strident anti-British feeling and policy. The latest book to consider Anglo-American relations toward

Latin America is Joseph Smith, *Illusions of Conflict: Anglo-American Diplomacy toward Latin America, 1865–1896* (Pittsburgh: University of Pittsburgh Press, 1979), which attempts to dispel some of the myths about Anglo-American rivalry: the British never developed a plan to exploit Latin America because of Foreign Office prejudice; they sought to protect interests but never openly challenged the Monroe Doctrine; in most cases the British were willing to accept the United States view that in Latin America its fiat was law.

The War of the Pacific, perhaps the beginning of U.S.-Chilean difficulties, is the topic of Gonzalo Bulnes, *Guerra del Pacífico* (3 vols., Valparaiso: Imprenta Universo, 1911–19). See also Pascual Ahumada Moreno, *Guerra del Pacífico* (8 vols., Valparaiso: Imprenta del progreso, 1884–91), for a patriotic Chilean interpretation. Sir William Laird Clowes, *Four Modern Naval Campaigns: Historical, Strategic and Tactical* (London: Unit Library, 1902), surveys seapower and the war, and Peter J. Sehlinger, "Las armas diplomáticas de inversionistas internacionales durante la Guerra del Pacífico," in Walter Sanchez G. and Teresa Pereira L., eds., *Cientocincuenta años de política exterior Chilena* (Santiago: Editorial Universitaria, 1979), discusses the efforts of Chile to neutralize threats of European and U.S. intervention, concluding that foreign attempts to prejudice the outcome of the War of the Pacific prolonged the conflict. On U.S. intervention in the War of the Pacific see Pletcher, Burr, Whitaker, and Smith, already cited. The only English-language monograph devoted to U.S. foreign policy during the war is Herbert Millington, *American Diplomacy and the War of the Pacific* (New York: Columbia University Press, 1948), which concentrates on the failure of diplomacy.

The revolution of 1891 has received much attention and yet remains heatedly discussed. There is no consensus on its origins or results. Still controversial is the personality and role of President José Manuel Balmaceda. The place to begin is Harold Blakemore, "The Chilean Revolution of 1891 and Its Historiography," *Hispanic American Historical Review* 45 (August, 1965). The most recent monograph is Crisóstomo Pizarro, *La revolución de 1891: La modernización* (Valparaiso: Ediciones Universitarias de Valparaíso, 1971), which uses social science techniques. See also Encina, already cited.

Those authors who believe the revolution was a constitutional, political struggle include Pedro Montt, *Exposition of the Illegal Acts of Ex-President Balmaceda which Caused the Civil War in Chile* (Washington, D.C.: Gibson Bros., 1891), and Augusto Matte and Agustín Ross, *Memoria presentada a la excellentísima Junta de Gobierno* (Paris: Imprimerie et Librairie Administratives et Classiques, 1892), by two agents of the Congressionalist junta. Alberto Fagalde, *La prensa extranjera y la dictadura chilena* (Santiago: Imprenta "Santiago," 1891), is anti-Balmaceda and contends the European press accepted the revolution as a political struggle against a despot, José Manuel Balmaceda. The Chilean president's chief defender wrote not long after Balmaceda's suicide: Julio Bañados Espinosa, *Balmaceda: Su gobierno y la revolución de 1891* (2 vols., Paris: Libreria de Garnier Hermanos, 1894). A politician and statesman, some say Balmaceda's alter ego, Bañados claims that the president's violation of constitutional and parliamentary privilege was only the Congressionalists' pretext for insurrection; the revolution was caused by the political ambition of those then rising in political circles, seeking ever more power. Bañados was one of the first to suggest the influence of British capital.

On the possible British connection see Hardy, already cited; William Howard Russell, *A Visit to Chile and Nitrate Fields of Tarapacá* (London: Virtue, 1891); and Maurice H. Hervey, *Dark Days in Chile: An Account of the Revolution of 1891* (London: Edward Arnold, 1891). Blakemore concludes the practical result of British influence was nil in "Los agentes revolucionarios chilenos en Europa, en 1891," *Mapocho* 5 (1966). For a Marxist interpretation of the civil war see Hernán Ramírez Necochea, *Balmaceda y la contrarevolución de 1891* (Santiago: Editorial Universitaria, 1969), and *Historia del imperialismo en Chile* (Havana: Edición Revolucionaria, 1966). For a sociological study arguing that all Chilean civil wars were abortive bourgeois revolutions fought out among rival segments of Chile's dominant class, see Maurice Zeitlin, *The Civil Wars in Chile; or, The Bourgeois Revolutions That Never Were* (Princeton: Princeton University Press, 1984). Balmaceda's refusal to recognize the strength of Congress is the theme of Joaquín Rodríguez Bravo, *Balmaceda y el conflicto entre el congreso y el ejecutivo* (2 vols., Santiago: Imprenta Gutenberg, 1921, Imprenta Cervantes, 1925). For a similar view see Ricardo Salas Edwards, *Balmaceda y el parlamentarismo en Chile* (2d ed., 2 vols., Santiago: Imprenta Universo, 1916); R. Cox Méndez, *Recuerdos de 1891* (Santiago: Editorial Nascimento, 1944); José María Yrarrazaval Larraín, *El presidente Balmaceda* (2 vols., Santiago: Editorial Nascimento, 1940); and Joaquín Villarino, *Balmaceda, el último de los presidentes constitucionales de Chile* (2d ed., Barcelona: Tipografía de E. Domeneck, 1940).

On other aspects of the civil war, see Eugenio Orrego Vicuña, *Un canciller de la revolución: Manuel Maria Aldunate Solar* (Santiago: Imprenta Universitaria, 1926); Eulojio Allendes, *The Revolution of 1891 in Chile* (Valparaiso: Imprenta del Universo de Guillermo Helfmann, 1891); Juan E.

Mackenna, *Carta política dirijida por Juan E. Mackenna* (Valparaiso: Imprenta Mercantil, 1893); and Benjamín Valdés Alfonso, ed., *Una familia bajo la dictadura: Epistolario 1891* (Santiago: Editorial Francisco de Aguirre, 1972). On the new order after the fall of Balmaceda, see Jorge Dupouy Grez, *Relaciones chileno-argentinas durante el gobierno de don Jorge Montt, 1891–1896* (Santiago: Editorial Andrés Bello, 1968).

Books by those who lived during the era of the *Baltimore* controversy are plentiful, such as *The Education of Henry Adams, An Autobiography* (Boston: Houghton Mifflin, 1918); William Allen White, *Masks in a Pageant* (New York: Macmillan, 1928); *Autobiography of Andrew Carnegie* (New York: Houghton Mifflin, 1920); Chauncey M. Depew, *My Memories of Eighty Years* (New York: Scribner's, 1922); Edward Nelson Dingley, *The Life and Times of Nelson Dingley, Jr.* (Kalamazoo: Ihling Bros., 1902); Julia B. Foraker, *I Would Live It Again: Memories of a Vivid Life* (New York: Harper & Bros., 1932); John W. Foster, *Diplomatic Memoirs* (2 vols., Boston: Houghton Mifflin, 1909); Henry Cabot Lodge and Charles F. Redmonds, ed., *Selections from the Correspondence of Theodore Roosevelt and Henry Cabot Lodge, 1884–1918* (2d ed., New York: Scribner's, 1971); Stephen Gwynn, ed., *The Letters and Friendships of Sir Cecil Spring Rice, A Record* (Boston: Houghton Mifflin, 1929); John Hay, *Letters of John Hay and Extracts from His Diary* (2 vols., New York: Gordian Press, 1969); Irwin Hood Hoover, *Forty-two Years in the White House* (Boston: Houghton Mifflin, 1934); W. H. Crook, *Memories of the White House: Personal Recollections* (Boston: Little, Brown, 1911); Harry Thurston Peck, *Twenty Years of the Republic, 1885–1905* (New York: Dodd, Mead, 1906); Thomas H. Sherman, *Twenty Years with James G. Blaine: Reminiscences by His Private Secretary* (New York: Grafton Press, 1928); Henry L. Stoddard, *As I Knew Them: Presidents and Politics from Grant to Coolidge* (New York: Harper & Bros., 1927); John S. Wise, *Recollections of Thirteen Presidents* (New York: Doubleday, Page, 1906); John A. Garraty, *Henry Cabot Lodge: A Biography* (New York: Knopf, 1953).

There is little biographical material on the minister to Chile, Patrick Egan. Some information about his earlier days is in Arthur Bradley Hayes and Sam D. Cox, *History of the City of Lincoln, Nebraska* (Lincoln: Nebraska State Journal Co., 1889); William O'Brien, *Recollections* (New York: Macmillan, 1905); F. Hugh O'Donnell, *A History of the Irish Parliamentary Party* (2 vols., New York: Longmans, Green, 1910). Thomas N. Brown, *Irish-American Nationalism, 1870–1890* (New York: Lippincott, 1966), has a short analysis of Egan's American role in the cause of an independent Ireland. The only special account of Egan's work as minister to Chile is

Osgood Hardy, "Was Patrick Egan a 'Blundering Minister'?" *Hispanic American Historical Review* 8 (1928). See also Blakemore, already cited.

The personality and presidency of Benjamin Harrison have stimulated little historical interest. Arthur Wallace Dunn, *From Harrison to Harding: A Personal Narrative, Covering a Third of a Century, 1888–1921* (2 vols., New York: Putnam's Sons, 1922), one of the earliest accounts, concludes Harrison was a failure. Edward Arthur White, "The Republican Party in National Politics, 1888–1891" (Ph.D. diss., University of Wisconsin, 1941), concentrated on Harrison's nomination and election and the ensuing split in the party. Harry J. Sievers, *Benjamin Harrison: Hoosier President* (3 vols., Indianapolis: Bobbs-Merrill, 1968), is better on Harrison's domestic policy than diplomacy; Sievers concludes that Harrison was a much better man than president. See also Sievers, *Benjamin Harrison, 1833–1901: Chronology-Documents-Bibliographical Aids* (Dobbs Ferry: Oceana Publications, 1969). The election of 1892 is in George Harmon Knoles, *The Presidential Campaign and Election of 1892* (Stanford: Stanford University Press, 1942) and Donald Marquand Dozer, "Benjamin Harrison and the Presidential Campaign of 1892," *American Historical Review* 59 (October, 1948).

James G. Blaine has received limited attention from historians, perhaps because he burned his personal papers just before his death. Harriet Bailey (Stanwood) Blaine, ed., *Letters of Mrs. James G. Blaine* (2 vols., New York: Duffield, 1908), published the few papers that escaped burning. James B. Lockey, "James G. Blaine," vols. 7 and 8 in Samuel Flagg Bemis, ed., *The American Secretaries of State and Their Diplomacy* (New York: Knopf, 1928) covers Blaine's two periods as secretary of state. The first account emphasizes anti-British sentiment, the second suggests he was aggressive but blameless in controversies. Other studies are Edward Stanwood, *James Gillespie Blaine* (Boston: Houghton, Mifflin, 1905); and Charles Edward Russell, *Blaine of Maine: His Life and Times* (New York: Cosmopolitan Book Corp., 1931). The two best sources are Alice Felt Tyler, *The Foreign Policy of James G. Blaine* (Minneapolis: University of Minnesota Press, 1927), and David Saville Muzzey, *James G. Blaine: A Political Idol of Other Days* (New York: Dodd, Mead, 1935). The most recent accounts are Lester D. Langley, "James Gillespie Blaine: The Ideologue as Diplomatist," in Frank J. Merli and Theodore A. Wilson, eds., *Makers of American Diplomacy: From Benjamin Franklin to Henry Kissinger* (New York: Scribner's, 1974), and James F. Vivian, "James G. Blaine: Diplomatic Practitioner or Ideologue?" (paper delivered at the annual convention of the Society for Historians of American Foreign Relations, 1975). Russell H. Bostert, "A

New Approach to the Origins of Blaine's Pan American Policy," *Hispanic American Historical Review* 39 (August, 1959), stresses Blaine's interest in commerce.

The foreign policy of Harrison and Blaine is discussed in Campbell, Dobson, Berkeley and Young, already cited. One of the earliest suggestions that 1898 was not the watershed for American imperialism—that the so-called empire days dawned with Harrison and Blaine—is Alfred T. Volwiler, "Harrison, Blaine, and American Foreign Policy, 1889–1893," *American Philosophical Society Proceedings* 79 (1938). See especially the analysis in Allan Burton Spetter, "Harrison and Blaine: Foreign Policy, 1889–1893," *Indiana Magazine of History* 65 (September, 1969).

Chilean historians have dealt with the *Baltimore* affair so as to keep it alive in the minds of students of Chilean history, and the first monograph was José Miguel Barros Franco, *El caso del "Baltimore": Apuntes para la historia diplomática de Chile* (Santiago: Escuela de Ciencias Jurídicas y Sociales de Santiago, 1950), a dissertation at the University of Chile, based mostly on U.S. sources. Although the United States is presented as unduly aggressive, Barros Franco presents a vacillating Blaine, limited by his ambition to be president; an Egan "stabbing without due deliberation"; and Chilean Foreign Minister Matta, arrogant and unnecessarily aggressive. On the Argentine offer to aid the United States in case of war with Chile, see Barros Franco, "Don Estanislao Zeballos y el incidente del 'Baltimore'," in *Mapocho* 1 (July, 1963). The conflict is reexamined by Patricio Estellé in *La controversia chileno-norteamericana de 1891–1892* (Santiago: Editorial Jurídica de Chile, 1967); influenced by revisionist works in the United States, Estellé sought to explain the *Baltimore* affair by U.S. economic motives. More than eighty years earlier Foreign Minister Matta had attempted the same economic analysis in *Questiones recientes con la legación i el gobierno de los Estados Unidos de Norteamerica* (Santiago: Imprenta Cervantes, 1892).

There are few English-language versions of the *Baltimore* affair. Osgood Hardy considers the impact of U.S. behavior during the the Chilean civil war in "The Itata Incident," *Hispanic American Historical Review* 5 (1922), and the entire U.S.-Chilean conflict in "The United States and Chile: A Study of Diplomatic Relations with Especial Emphasis on the Period of the Chilean Civil War of 1891" (Ph.D. diss., University of California, 1925). See also Harold Lindsell, "The Chilean-American Controversy of 1891–1892" (Ph.D. diss., New York University, 1942). The only recent consideration is Francis X. Holbrook and John Nikol, "The Chilean Crisis of 1891–1892," *American Neptune* 38 (October, 1978), which contends that Tracy was not a "war hound" over the incident.

Primary sources concerning the *Baltimore* affair are not abundant. Three places to begin the search are Richard Dean Burns, ed., *Guide to American Foreign Relations since 1700* (Santa Barbara: ABC-CLIO, 1983); David F. Trask, Michael C. Beyer, and Roger R. Trask, eds., *A Bibliography of United States–Latin American Relations since 1810: A Selected List of Eleven Thousand Published References* (Lincoln: University of Nebraska Press, 1968); and George S. Ulibarri and John P. Harrison, *Guide to Materials on Latin America in the National Archives of the United States* (Washington, D.C.: NARS, 1974). For the publication of speeches, correspondence, addresses, public papers, treaties, and other documents, see Charles I. Bevans, ed., *Treaties and Other International Agreements of the United States of America, 1776–1949* (Washington, D.C.: Government Printing Office, 1971); John Bassett Moore, *A Digest of International Law* (8 vols., Washington, D.C.: Government Printing Office, 1906); James D. Richardson, *A Compilation of the Messages and Papers of the Presidents, 1789–1897* (Washington, D.C.: Government Printing Office, 1898); Benjamin Harrison, *Public Papers and Addresses of Benjamin Harrison, Twenty-third President of the United States, March 4, 1889 to March 4, 1893* (Washington, D.C.: Government Printing Office, 1893); Charles Hedges, ed., *Speeches of Benjamin Harrison, Twenty-third President of the United States* (New York: United States Book Co., 1892); and Albert T. Volwiler, ed., *The Correspondence between Benjamin Harrison and James G. Blaine, 1882–1893* (Philadelphia: American Philosophical Society, 1940). The *Congressional Record* contains what little debate occurred over the *Baltimore* affair, as well as petitions of pacifist groups seeking to prevent war. The Chilean equivalent is the *Boletín de sessiones ordinarias en 1891— Cámara de Senadores* (Santiago: Imprenta Nacional, 1891), located in the annex to the Chilean Library of Congress. The *Diario Oficial de la república de Chile* (Santiago: Imprenta Nacional, 1891–1892) published much of the official correspondence between the two nations.

Essential documents and diplomatic correspondence are in FRUS (Washington, D.C.: Government Printing Office). The Chilean equivalent is *Memoria del ministro de relaciones esteriores, culto i colonización: Presentada al congreso nacional* (Santiago: Imprenta Nacional), located in the library of the Chilean Diplomatic Academy. *H. Exec. Doc.* (Washington, D.C.: Government Printing Office) compilations are the foundation for any study of the *Baltimore* affair, and *H. Exec. Doc. 91* is the most important. The Chilean counterpart is *Estados Unidos i Chile: Notas cambiadas entre la legación de Estados Unidos de Norte-América i el Ministro de Relaciones Esteriores de Chile, a propósito de las cuestiones suscitadas entre ambos paises* (Santiago: Imprenta Ercilla, 1891). Documentation about the

Chilean civil war is in *Cuenta jeneral de las entradas y gastos de la excma. Junta de Gobierno de Chile desde enero a agosto de 1891* (Santiago: Imprenta Nacional, 1894). Correspondence of the British Foreign Office, Chile, 1823–97, provides the British view of the *Baltimore* incident as well as correspondence concerning Anglo-American relations.

The National Archives are an important source for the *Baltimore* affair. The "Medical Journal of the U.S.S. Baltimore," written between April 1, 1891, and February 9, 1892, and the "Log Book of the U.S.S. Baltimore," commencing with Schley's attachment to the Pacific Squadron August 2, 1891, and ending at Mare Island, California, February 9, 1892, are important sources as are the many diplomatic dispatches, consular dispatches, instructions to ministers, notes to and from the Chilean legation in the United States, and records of foreign service posts in Chile. The General Area Files for Chile include notes from Egan to the Chilean government, miscellaneous correspondence of Egan, and notes to Egan from the Chilean government. RG 59 and RG 45 contain most documents relating to the *Baltimore* affair.

Searching for documents in the Chilean archives is not easy, and it is advisable to consult Peter J. Sehlinger, *A Select Guide to Chilean Libraries and Archives* (Bloomington: Indiana University Latin American Studies Program, 1979), for thorough descriptions of sources for research. The Chilean National Archives, the National Library, and the Archive of the Chilean Ministry of Foreign Affairs, in the bombed-out La Moneda Palace, are the principal locations for Chilean documents. One must also search the Library of Congress and its annexes, the libraries of the University of Chile and the Catholic University of Santiago, the Severin Library in Valparaiso, and specialized libraries within the National Library in Santiago.

Index